Peace Education and Human Rights

Mr. Prodip Adhikari

Prof. (Dr.) Jayanta Mete

A.P.H. PUBLISHING CORPORATION
4435–36/7, ANSARI ROAD, DARYA GANJ,
NEW DELHI-110002

Published by
S.B. Nangia
A.P.H. Publishing Corporation
4435–36/7, Ansari Road, Darya Ganj,
New Delhi-110002
Phone: 011–23274050
e-mail: aphbooks@gmail.com

2026

Typeset by
Ideal Publishing Solutions
C-90, J.D. Cambridge School,
West Vinod Nagar, Delhi-110092

Printed at
DIVINE DIGITAL PRINTERS
Ansari road Daryaganj Delhi-110002

CONTENTS

ABOUT THE EDITORS

Mr. Prodip Adhikari (M.A. in History, M.A. in Education, B.Ed., M.Ed., M.Phil.): is a Research Scholar, Department of Education, University of Kalyani. His special areas of interest are Dalits Studies, Women Empowerment, Refugees Studies, Subaltern Studies, Sociological Foundation of Education and Teacher Education. He has attended many state, national and international Seminar, Conference and Symposium and also he participated many state, national and international Workshop at different institutions like JNU (New Delhi), BHU (Varanasi, U.P.), Lucknow University, (Lucknow, U.P.), D.H.S.G.V. (Sagar, M.P.), K.U., (Kalyani, W.B.), J.U. (W.B.). He has some articles to his credit published in national and international Journal and he awarded a National Fellowship by UGC.

Prof. (Dr.) Jayanta Mete is an eminent teacher educator, distinguished author and research guide in the field of Tribal Education, Population Education, History of Education and Environmental Education. He is at present Professor, Department of Education, University of Kalyani, Faculty of Education, University of Kalyani, West Bengal. Dr. Mete obtained M.A in Geography and M.Ed. with flying colours from Visva-Bharati University, Santiniketan, West Bengal,India. He also obtained Ph.D. from the same University. The author supervised 42 Ph.D. scholars and published and presented more than 200 research papers in leading journals and seminars. He authored more than 25 books and edited 40 books on educational issues. He also edits Peer-Reviewed three journals entitled 'Journal of Education and Development', 'Journal of Knowledge', and 'Journal of Educational Thoughts'.

Chapter-1

The Nature of Emotions – Creation and Modification

Dean Van Leuven

Whether our response to an arousal stimulus results in a negative emotion or a positive emotion is determined by our perception of the event.

We have positive, love-based responses, such as joy and happiness. They feel good to us. Our primary emotional experience is the need for love. We feel good when we experience it. When we are experiencing fear or anger, we are out of love and we feel bad.

Fear and anger are feelings not acts. They are not the act that we carry out in what we do or say. They are the creator of the thought that motivates us to act. They are our mental reaction to what we perceive to have happened to us. For example how another has treated us. We feel fear or anger when our belief system tells us that something is not the way we think it should be, or is dangerous to us in some way.

Biological research has shown us that there is no such thing as pure anger untouched by our culture, our conditioning, and our perception of the event. Anger is a signal that something is wrong and that something must be done to change things. Our idea of what is wrong is created from all of our past experience and learning. The physiological symptoms are the same for the love-based emotions as they are for the fear-based emotions. Our mind just interprets them in a different way. The arousal response, both positive and negative, comes from adrenaline. Physiologically our body re-acts exactly the same to fear and anger as it does to love.

If the body produces the same physiological symptoms for love, joy, excitement, anxiety, fear, shame and anger, then we know that the emotional responses to being aroused are acquired ones that we have developed in our own mind.

Once we know that our undesired negative responses are not determined by the event but are only our chosen way of responding to the event, we know that we are not bound to suffer because of them. Changing to a more positive emotional response is always an available option. Since we chose our emotional response in the first place we are capable of choosing a new and more effective one to replace it.

Many are trained how to respond without fear or anger when something goes wrong on the job or in our profession. We do it because that is what we are taught to do. We can also learn to train ourselves to react without negative emotion to the situations that arise in our daily life and in our relationships with other people.

Airplane pilots, firefighters, store clerks, attorneys and others are trained to be problem solvers so that their normal routine is to respond rationally rather than to react emotionally - at least to those things which they are trained to deal with in this way.

For those of us who lack such training, fear and anger often results from our feeling of inadequacy in how to deal with the situation. The answer can be as simple as learning how to solve a problem using rational rather than emotional skills.

WHY WE GET FEARFUL OR ANGRY

Our fear and anger depends mostly on our particular beliefs about the world and how we ought to experience it. Our beliefs about ourselves and other people, about the world and how things should be, and about how life should be lived, come mainly from our experiences growing up. What we learn from those experiences helps us to develop our unique pattern or response to life in the way that we do.

We learn about fear and anger from our parents, our friends and our society. We are usually taught that anger and/or fear are appropriate in certain circumstances. If fact almost every book I have ever read on the subject has suggested that they are the normal way to react – that we express them at certain times - and that such expression is healthy. This is because we live in a fear/anger based society. This is the way our society has learned to think and react.

We are taught that we must protect ourselves from others. We are taught to expect that things be a certain way. We are taught that the world is a dangerous place and that it might hurt us in some way. And we are also taught to be angry when things are not what we want or think they should be.

Our society often teaches us to repress our upset feelings and to be polite. When we do this we are left with an underlying fear or anger that drains our physical, mental, and spiritual energy. Rather than confronting and solving problems with loved ones or colleagues, we ignore the problems and the feelings. But the upset remains under the surface and often is expressed in an indirect way.

Sometimes we use anger because it works, and this strengthens our belief that anger is positive. For example a child will try different techniques – some anger based and some not – and if anger works, he or she will continue to use it. If temper tantrums produce the sought after result, then the child will make sure to have one when he or she wants to change something that is not going the way they want it to at the moment. If temper tantrums don't work the child will eventually realize that and try something else.

Both negative and positive responses are available in any stage of life. Until we find out what works best we keep trying what is available.

Once we grow up we have the capacity to identify what is not working and to experiment with new ideas and actions until we find what works best in any particular situation.

Another reason that anger seems to work is because anger is the active form of fear. It is a much stronger emotion than fear. When you are fearful, being able to shift to anger is a positive and a helpful step. Anger is a step up from fear and can seem helpful, but when you accept anger as a method to resolve a problem you are accepting a very inferior and unsatisfying solution as compared to what is potentially available to you.

The biases of our mind survive because they seem to work for us. They prevent us from losing confidence in ourselves. Our ego seeks only information that agrees with itself. We need to believe in our biases in order to have a basis for our very existence.

It is possible to have a belief system that is open to examination and change. Such openness comes about when we recognize and accept that there always may be a better way of looking at and responding to our world, and to our life.

Fear depends on our perception of an event as somehow dangerous to our existence, or to our well being; or a threat to someone or something that we care about. Fear gets our attention but it tends to immobilize our thinking and our actions. If we haven't already developed a way to respond to a particular situation it causes difficulty because our strong emotional response will get in the way of our minds ability to solve this problem; and to develop the best possible response for the particular situation.

We can learn to look at an event just as something that needs our utmost attention rather than as a negative and dangerous thing that threatens our existence and freezes our thinking process. When we do this we are more effective in dealing with the situation. Our reasoning remains unimpaired and we will find more appropriate responses.

HOW OUR EMOTIONS AND BELIEFS INTERPRET AN EVENT

Our emotional response to a particular event is primarily determined by our preconditioning and by our general way of looking at things – our beliefs. But we can also learn to question our beliefs and change our response.

We have many fear and anger producing beliefs that hinder our progress in life. Such beliefs are the ones that create negative feelings. They make us upset and depressed and don't help us to deal with life as it really is.

The difficulty is that if we see these beliefs as the appropriate way of dealing with things, then we think of our anger as appropriate or justified. Whether we like anger or not, we think that we must have it because we believe it helps us do what we are supposed to do.

Our fear or anger results from our appraisal of a particular situation, which in turn depends on the beliefs we hold, the thought processes we use, the attitudes we practice, and the way we look at things.

We upset *ourselves* by making demands instead of having preferences about how things must be. Once we think things must be a certain way, we tend to use anger-inducing thoughts to increase our anger. Our ego likes to make the situation appear worse than it really is because this justifies our anger.

We look at things the way we do because of the basic beliefs we have developed. These beliefs affect our thoughts, our decisions and our behavior. If we keep our belief system open to review and change we can correct the ones that create problems for us.

IS FEAR OR ANGER HELPFUL?

We develop habit patterns for most of the things we do in life, and they are often difficult to change or break. We break one by putting a new habit pattern in its place. And we do this by practicing the new response over and over, until it becomes a new habit.

We are all born with a strong tendency to be creative and constructive and to solve problems that naturally arise in our daily lives. It is a matter of training ourselves to respond in the way we want to respond.

If we are aware of the beliefs and thought processes that feed our fear or anger, and if we know why we tend to get fearful or angry, then we can change our response in those situations when fear or anger is likely to flare up. We can reprogram ourselves to behave in a different way.

We use anger to show other people they are out of order, but there are other ways to show people that we are unhappy with them. We don't have to use anger as a substitute for our lack of assertiveness. We can learn to be assertive without being angry. We will be much more effective and much happier when we do. We don't have to use anger as a substitute for our lack of assertiveness.

THE THINGS THAT MAKE US FEARFUL OR ANGRY

It is helpful to have a good idea of the things that cause our fear and anger. If we know the causes, then we can learn to either remove them or to change the way we respond to them.

Most of our fear is caused because we see the possibility of something dangerous or something that we cannot control. We have learned that the way to keep ourselves safe is to be fearful. So when we perceive something as threatening in any way we become fearful.

Most of our anger is caused because the outside world does not live up to our expectation or our dreams. We keep insisting that the outside world be a certain way. When it isn't we get angry. For example, you are in a nice restaurant having dinner and small children who are part of the family at the next table are being loud and disruptive, and that upsets you. You have an ideal view of how these children should act. You keep demanding that children act that way even though you have no power to control them. And you get angry when they don't do it your way.

We get angry when others in our culture – or outside of it – don't follow the cultural rules. A major role of anger in our culture is its policing function. For example, you expect people to stay in line and take their turn. Our society demands this behavior because if people don't follow these rules the less aggressive of us will have to wait much longer to purchase our goods and go home. When someone doesn't follow the rules and crowds to the front of the line, others often react by getting angry and shouting at them to get to the back of the line.

Although every culture's rules are subjective, and different segments of our society may have conflicting rules, anger is often employed against those who go against the rules, in order to coerce them into conforming. We have learned to use anger as a method of controlling other people. It seems natural and necessary to use anger simply because this is how we have learned to control other people. And because many of us refuse to accept cultural differences as natural and desirable we live in a very angry world. The government and the media use anger to shape our opinions about other people and other ways of doing things.

Sometimes we get angry because expressing anger is a common and acceptable attribute to our family of origin. One's family has a huge effect on how one reacts to conflict. In some families, fighting is seen as bad. In others, you don't even count for much unless you can stand up and fight for yourself. We not only learn our emotional style from our family, we also acquire the unique set of values our family holds. How our anger gets triggered – and how we express it – are closely tied to the lessons we learned as we were growing up.

We develop a belief system and then get angry when things don't go according to our beliefs. Our ingrained beliefs lead to disappointment, frustration and anger when things don't go the way we think they should.

"Other people" are a major source of our anger. When we don't trust others, we think, "I am going to get them before they get me," and we view everything they do with mistrust, it's as if our brain is out to lunch. We are programmed to mistrust and we automatically respond from our emotions. We don't view the behavior of another person as a new problem to solve. Instead we deal with the situation as one that we already have the answer to. We deal with this new person just as we have already dealt with all of the un-trusted people of our past.

Not being fearful or angry doesn't reduce our ability to feel emotion. In fact it intensifies it. Studies on addiction show that the reason we are addicted to something is that negative emotions mask our ability to fully experience our natural state; which is our positive emotions. We become addicted to something because it allows us to temporarily get past the mask of our negative feelings and feel our pleasure. We feel extremely good during the time the addictive substance suppresses our negative emotions. This is the only way the addicted person knows how to feel good. They want to feel good so much that it doesn't matter that their addiction has serious side effects. When we learn how to experience pleasure naturally the addictive substance is no longer necessary in our life. When we remove our negative emotions so that we can experience pleasure naturally we no longer need our addictions.

WHAT NEGATIVE EMOTIONS DO TO US

Feeling the emotion associated with anger is our first awareness of its presence. But beneath our anger lies a primary emotional pain, such as pride, shame, hurt, frustration, sadness, terror, worry, or fear. Anger is just the way we have chosen to respond to something that has come to our attention that has a negative effect on our state of being.

When we get angry we experience a host of physical changes to our body. Anger interferes with efficient thinking, problem solving, planning, and success in school. When we are angry, our bodies get hot, our muscles tense, our hearts pound, and our thoughts race out of control. When we're in the midst of such physical reactions we need to stop and pay attention to what has triggered the angry reaction and why it has done so. Until we are able to relax and think clearly again, we will not be able to act effectively, or communicate clearly. Instead, we'll be in danger of choosing angry responses that our reflective reasoning would tell us are ineffective or inappropriate.

Anger can actually get to the point where it makes us physically and/or mentally ill. It causes us difficulty with our school work. It can even cause marital instability, conflict, and divorce. It may limit our educational achievement and occupational success. It makes us poor parents. It stands in the way of intimacy. It can cost us lots of money and economic achievements. It can even shorten our life expectancy.

THE COSTS OF NEGATIVE EMOTIONS

Now as you are learning to apply these new skills I challenge you to further develop these skills in order to achieve emotional wisdom in your own life and in our society, so that we all able to live and work together in greater harmony and ever greater personal peace. By this I mean learn to recognize and establish beliefs that produce inner peace for your self that also produce both harmony and well being in our world society.

Because we believe something is going to cure us it does. We refer to this as the placebo effect or wellness thinking. It is such a strong effect that all research on medicines is done without letting the patient know whether he is taking the real medicine or just a sugar pill. The opposite also applies. When we think we are going to get sick we most generally do. If we want to be happy and well it is extremely important to believe that we are. Studies have consistently shown that people with positive mental attitudes live much longer on average than those with a negative mental attitude.

THE CHAIN OF EVENTS IN MAKING A CHOICE

- **How we perceive what the world offers.**

  We react to particular circumstances and events according to our own particular beliefs.

- **How we accept what the world offers.**

  Our beliefs about what happens and what should happen in the world affect how we respond emotionally.

- **How we chose to experience our life.**

  What we choose to do in the world will change not only ourselves but also the world and the way we feel about it.

- **How we respond to what the world offers.**

  How we respond affects everything that happens after that.

- **By the choices we make.**

  The things that happen in our lives come into being as the consequences of our choices.

- **Steps to Developing Emotional Intelligence**

1. Understand how your mind works.
2. Create your goal.

3. Create new beliefs to support your goal.
4. Learn how to recognize and locate problems.
5. Learn how to make changes
6. Do the Work!

- **Checklist for finding a belief that is troubling you**

Ask yourself

1. Exactly what you are upset about
2. What belief you have that is causing this feeling
3. What related or sub-beliefs you have that are supporting this belief.
4. What memories you have that are causing or supporting this belief.
5. Why you believe this belief is true.
6. Is this belief absolutely true?
7. Do you want to change the belief, or keep it?
8. If you decide to keep the belief are you willing to give up being upset?

- **Additional questions to consider if you have difficulty identifying the upsetting belief.**

1. Do I have a belief that I should be upset about this?
2. Do I have a belief that I am "less than" in some way?
3. Do I have a belief that I should have my own way about this?
4. Do I have a belief that others should do it my way?
5. Do I allow myself to do things I don't want to do?
6. Do I have a belief that my existing beliefs are absolutely true?
7. Do I dislike changing beliefs?
8. Do I truly want to get over being upset about what is happening?
9. Do I believe I can find a positive solution if I keep looking?

BIBLIOGRAPHY

1. Amen, Daniel G. MD. *Change Your Brain Change Your Life*: New York, Three Rivers Press, 2000
2. Anodia, Judith. *Waking the Global Heart*: Santa Rosa, CA, Elite Books, 2006
3. Canfield, Jack; Hanson, Mark Victor & Hewitt, Les. *The Power of Focus*: Deerfield Beach, FL, Health Communications, Inc., 2000

4. Chopra, Deepak. *Peace is the Way*: New York, Three Rivers Press, 2005
5. Dreikers, Rudolf, M.D. *Children: the Challenge*: New York, E.P. Dutton 1987
6. Feist, G.J., & Barton, F. Emotional intelligence and academic intelligence in career and life success: Paper presented to the Annual Convention of the American Psychological Society, San Francisco, CA June 1996
7. Foster, Rick & Hicks, Greg. *How we choose to Be Happy*: New York, The Berkley Publishing Group, 1999
8. Goleman, D., *Emotional Intelligence*: New York, Bantam, 1995
9. Goleman, D., *Working With Emotional Intelligence*: New York, Bantam, 1998
10. His Holiness the Dalai Lama. *The Art of Happiness*: New York, Riverhead Books, 1998
11. Jackins, Harvey. *The Human Situation*: Seattle, rational Island Publishers, 1973
12. Jamplosky, Gerald & Cirincione, Diane. *Love Is the Answer*: Berryville, VA, Berryville Graphics, 1990
13. Katie, Byron. *Loving What Is*: New York, Three Rivers Press, 2002
14. Lancer Bob. *Parenting With Love*: Marietta, GA, Parenting Solutions, 1996
15. Maslow, Abraham H. *Motivation and Personality*: NY: Harper, 1954. Second Ed. NY: Harper, 1970. Third Ed. NY: Addison-Wesley, 1987
16. Maslow, Abraham H. *The Farther Reaches of Human Nature*: NY, Viking, 1971. Harmondworth, Eng: Penguin Books, 1973
17. Maslow, Abraham H. *Toward a Psychology of Being*: NY, Van Nostrand, 1962. Second Ed.
18. Mayer, J.D. & Salvony P: *What is Emotional Intelligence?*: In P. Salvony & D. Sluyter (eds.): Emotional development and emotional intelligence educational applications (pp3- 31. New York: Basic Books, 1997
19. McKay, Mathew; Rogers, Peter & McKay, Judith, *When Anger Hurts*: Oakland, CA, New Harbinger Publications, Inc., 1989
20. Middelton-Moz, Jane, Tener, Lisa & Todd, Peaco. *The Ultimate Guide to Transforming Anger*: Deerfield Beach, FL, Health Communications, Inc, 2004
21. Price, John Randolph. *Living A Life Of Joy*: New York, Ballantine Books, 1997
22. Ruwart, Dr. Mary J. *Healing Our World–The Other Piece of the Puzzle*: Kalamazoo, MI, SunStar Press, 1992
23. Sebastian, Dr. Ulla. *Growing Through Joy*: Tallahassee, FL, Findhorn Press, 1999

24. Schulman, P. *Explanatory style and achievement in school and work*, In G. Buchman & H.E.P. Seligman (EDs.) Explanatory style, Hillsdale, NJ Lawrence Erlbaum, 1995
25. Snarey, J. R. & Vaillant, G. E., *How lower and working class youth become middle class adults: the association between ego defense mechanisms and upward social mobility*: child Development, 56(4), 899-910, 1995
26. Solvany, P. Bedell, B., Detweiler, J.B., & Mayer, J. D., *Coping Intelligently*: Emotional Intelligence and the coping process, In C. R. Snyder Ed., Coping: The psychology of what works (pp 141-1640 New York, Oxford University Press, 1999
27. Solvany P. & Grenwal D: *The Science of Emotional Intelligence*: Current Directions in psychological science, 2005 Vol.14-6
28. Tich Nhat Hanh. *Anger*: New York, Riverside Press, 2001
29. Tipping, Colin. *Radical Forgiveness*: Marietta, GA, Global 13 Publication Co, 1997
30. Van Leuven, Dean. *A Life Without Anger*, Camarillo,CA, Devorss & Co.,2003
31. Van Leuven, Dean. *A Peaceful New World*, Eugene, OR, Dean of Peace Publishing, 2006
32. Van Leuven, Dean, *SEWA Life without Anger– Student Manual*, Kathmandu, Nepal, Sunlight Publication, 2007

Chapter-2

Dissemination of Message of Inter-Religious Peace in India Through Social Media

Dr. Gaurav Shah

INTRODUCTION

For most of the 20th century, social scientists thought that religion would have no role to play in modern society and denied the possibility of conflicts due to religion. Processes like urbanization, economic development, modern social institutions, growing rates of literacy and education, pluralism and advancements in science and technology would lead to a decline of religion in politics (Fox, 2004; Healy, 2005). But in 21st century, the 9/11 terror attack; the Iranian revolution; the worldwide rise of religious fundamentalism; and ethno religious conflicts like those in Chechnya, East Timor, Tibet, Sudan, and Sri Lanka ruled out the demise of religion and ascertain that still, religion is an essential element of modern and social phenomena (Fox, 2004). The Inter-Religious conflict has been escalating across the globe in form of many kinds of violence with terrorism being the crudest form among them (Friedman, 2016). India has experienced several communal clashes in form of riots since independence (Rajeshwari, 2004). In the new millennium, post-2002 Godhra riots, two riots namely Assam riots and Muzaffarnagar riots in 2012 and 2013 respectively were mainly in news for a common reason. In these riots fake videos, MMS, Emails etc...were used to spread communal hatred on social media (Shah, 2016; Ahuja, 2013).

In august 2012, India experienced one of the largest urban flash migrations. On August 15 and 16, nearly thirty thousand people constituting fifteen percent of the two lac North East community living in Bangalore fled towards Assam. From Pune only, more than half the city's 20,000 strong North-easterners left (Unnithan& Kiran, 2012). The reason for the exodus was the rumor of revenge attacks by angry Muslims disseminated on social media. Threats were issued to the people of North East (living in Bangalore and other parts of India) through SMS, MMS on mobile phones and social media (Mondal, 2012) that after Eid on August 20, non-Muslims from North-east region will be attacked and would be targeted by "Muslims" in revenge for Bodo militants' attacks on Muslims in Assam (Unnithan& Kiran, 2012; A New Protocol, 2012). This panic, fed by doctored images, some extremely gruesome, had been circulating on the internet and various social media sites like Facebook and Twitter for some days (Ibid). The images were designed to look like Muslims being indiscriminately killed in Myanmar and Assam (Aroon Purie, 2012). Similarly, in UP's Muzaffarnagar, video clip supposedly showing a Muslim mob lynching two boys was used to stir unease and hatred between Muslims and Hindus (Haq, 2013). Later this video was found to be shot in a tribal area of Pakistan two year before the Muzaffarnagar incident (Ahuja, 2013).

RESEARCH QUESTION

Both these incidents show the misuse of social media. The researcher becomes inquisitive that if through doctored videos and emails communal hatred is spread, then there must be some medium that can counter these videos and emails viral on social media.

1. *What could be the tool that can help in alleviating inter-religious conflicts and disseminating the message of peace and harmony between hostile religious communities?*
2. *And further to find out the utility of that particular tool?*

OVERALL ARGUMENT

In his paper 'Religion and Conflict', Reychler believes religious organizations to be the crusader of peace building between hostile religious communities. He says that "Religious organizations are a rich source of peace services. They can function as a powerful warrant for social tolerance, for democratic pluralism, and for constructive conflict-management. They are peace- builders and peace-makers" (Reychler,

1997). Religions contribute to peace-building by "empowering the weak, by influencing the moral-political climate and by developing cooperation and providing humanitarian aid' (Ibid.). But the author of this paper is of the view that religious organizations restrict themselves to their religious principles and conform to the opinions, feelings and ideas of adversary only to the extent the adversary endorses their principles and ethos. As soon as the hostile religious group or community leaves the periphery of ideas of religious organizations the peace building process gets derailed.

Further to answer the research questions, Mohammed Abu-Nimer's[1], model of Religiocentric to Religiorelative: a model for religious transformation and inter-religious peace building was studied. The model in short is a method of inter-faith/inter-religious dialogue that create an atmosphere so that "the believer does not pass a negative judgment on the other religious beliefs or practices, but observes (or recognizes) the different religious and spiritual values, norms, rituals, and behaviors; understands their meaning; and accepts them as they are in their religious and cultural context" (Abu-Nimer, 2001). His idea of organizing training workshops (Ibid.) to process his theory into practice also seems very relevant and useful but it has its limitations. The limitations could be 1-workshops are costly affair to organize.2-dearth of responsible conflict managers who can run the workshop, 3-difficult to find a venue with conducive atmosphere to bring aggrieved religious groups and most importantly 4- these workshops can cover very small number of people, while the people who get affected by religious conflicts in India are huge in number. This made the researcher inquisitive about the kind of interactive platform or tool that could help in building interreligious peace and trust between Hindus, (who constitute the largest religious majority of India) (Population by religious community, 2011) and Muslims (who constitute the largest religious minority in India) (Ibid.; Zakaria, 1988).

The first platform that came to my mind was mass media. Mass media especially Radio and Television have created a kind of 'techno-religious spaces' (Kong, 2001). Through mass communication, an issue can be engendered to a large audience. But the traditional mass communication experience is a one-way, top-down, sender-driven,

1 http://www.american.edu/sis/faculty/abunimer.cfm.

time-specific activity; news seekers are mere consumers who receive only the information provided by news organizations, have little choice over content, and for the most part consume content at a time that is predetermined (Weeks & Lance, 2013). Whether it's print media or electronic media, there is no mechanism for immediate response or feedback, which nullifies the whole purpose of interactivity despite wide reach of mainstream media (Shah, 2016).

India is the world's second largest user of Internet and has second highest yearly growth in usage of the same ("Internet users by the country", 2016). Also, with more than 143 million users of social media("Social media users in India to reach 143 million in April: IAMA", 2015), social media has become not only a source of fast communication but a platform of giving voice to voiceless, thus making individuals, groups, communities and societies at large empowered. Social media has the power to let a small incidence get attention of millions of people worldwide. Therefore the focus turned towards social media which facilitates one-to-one, one-to-many, many-to-one, many-to-many forms of communication (Castells, 2007). Castells define social media to be the reflection of the rise of a new form of socialized communication: mass self-communication- self- generated in content, self-directed in emission, and self-selected in reception by many that communicate with many (Ibid.). But the problem is that most of the people have no access to the new technology and even if it there, maximum doesn't know how to use it....even those that can use their mobile phones and computers finds difficult to express them in their native language on Twitter and Facebook. Lack of literacy is a big hurdle. So how could social media turn out to be a medium that can become the voice that everyone can understand and disseminate? As goes the famous adage by Tess Flanders "Use a Picture; It's worth a thousand Words", moving images or videos can be the solution. A video in native language can be understood by everyone and could be uploaded easily without getting involved in intricacies of typing. The video can be uploaded on WhatsApp, Facebook, Twitter, Youtube, etc... Therefore, to find out the usefulness of online videos in mitigating inter-religious conflicts and building inter-religious peace, some case studies were selected.

METHODS

Statistics show that more than 84% of internet users in India watch online video content ("Percentage on internet users who watch online video content on any device in 2014 by country", 2014). Therefore, only those case studies have been taken that have an online video. The case studies were taken as per convenience. Only those videos were preferred that talks about either Hindus or Muslims or both or connotes Muslims, Hindus or both. Videos containing hate speeches were not taken for the study.

Case Study 1

Kashmiri Muslims In Bandipore Celebrate Shivratri, Want Pandits to return.

An ancient Shiv temple in Bandipore's Sumbal town in Kashmir on the banks of Jhelum hasn't had devotees on Shivratri for years. Not after Kashmiri Pandits fled the town 25 km from Srinagar during the peak of the militancy in the early nineties. But 24th February 2017, Friday morning was different. Kashmiri Muslims living in the town turned up at the temple to celebrate Shivratri, the biggest festival on the calendar of Kashmiri Pandits. A local contractor Imtiaz Ahmad led the prayers after dozens of young men scrubbed the temple floor clean; pouring water on the Shivling, the representation of the Hindu deity Shiva. He also offered fruits and sweets. This video (NDTV, 2017) received 4312 views with lots of comments. This video surely propagates message of inter-religious peace in times of turbulent Kashmir.

Case Study 2

Muzaffarnagar Shot Film/Hindu Muslim Unity

Published on September 13, 2016, it is a fiction story inspired by 2013 Muzaffarnagar riots. A girl from the Hindu Jat community was allegedly harassed in an eve-teasing incident by one Muslim youth in Kawal village of Muzaffarnagar. In retaliation, Hindu relatives of the girl killed the Muslim youth. Then the two brothers were lynched by a Muslim mob when they tried to escape (Bhatt, 2013). In 2013 Muzaffarnagar riots, almost 60 people died ("Govt releases data of riot victims identifying religion", 2014). This fiction video shows that a Muslim youth instigate his community to kill a youth from the Jat Hindu community because the Jat youth was trying to molest a Muslim girl. The Muslim community gets infuriated and kidnaps the Jat youth and decides to kill him. In retaliation, the Hindu Jat community also kidnaps a member of Muslim community and both the communities decide to kill the wrongdoers before the hostile communities. A teacher from the village intervenes and asks both the communities to first find out the real fact and don't pay heed to false rumors. The video (BFF Films, 2016) was watched 224,650 times. Certainly such kind of videos even being fictional helps in curbing the rumors spread on social media and disseminates the message of peace and harmony between hostile religious communities.

Case Study 3

A Hindu & Muslim show harmony, have together been running medical store - Communal Harmony

The city of Sherkot in Bijnor district is known for its rich culture and profound heritage, which is a result of its great history. An example of this can be seen among the owners of 'Ram- Rahim Medical Store' who present a picture of communal harmony in the city. The two friends opened their medical store based on relationship of trust. They hope to inspire others by setting an example of their friendship. Both respect each other's religious rituals and share a unique understanding. And they celebrate all festivals together. Good relations between them with Hindu and Muslim religious background, has played an important role in the growth of their business. They attribute the success of their business to the amicable relations between them. They have running the medical store successfully since 1997. The video (ANI News, 2015) received 9598 views. The video is a living testimony of inter-religious peace and harmony. It gives the message that Hindus and Muslims despite their differences can live together and work together.

Case Study 4

Best Mirchi Murga by Rj Naved... on Hindu Muslim relationships

In this video, the famous radio jockey Naved talks about the bad implications of social media. He shares an incident where two people coming from Hindu and Muslim community upload on Facebook hateful content regarding opposite communities. To teach them lesson, Naved calls them separately introducing himself as member of hostile community. He asks them why they uploaded such content. Surprisingly, none of them was able to answer Naved. Naved recalls them that how people from communities they dislike have helped them in their time of crisis. He urges them to write something constructive and positive instead of malicious content. The video (Lucky Video Parlor, 2014) received a whopping 358,973 views. The video sends a message to the users of social media that they should not get instigated by hate contents.

Case Study 5

Surprising Reactions of Indians when they meet a Pakistani

This four minute and 34 seconds video is a social experiment done by Dhaval a member of Ride for Peace from Mumbai who presented himself as a Pakistani Muslim to cover the response of the local crowd. The video was shot at Connaught Place in New Delhi. In the video, Dhval is shown with a placard stating "I am from Pakistan but I love India as much as you do. Can I get free hugs." Initially, the commuters read the placard and walked away. But after some time it is seen that many boys, girls, women, men, children come and give hug to Dhaval. Many take selfie with Dhaval. The video (Ride for Peace, 2017) received more than 2.5 million views. The video connotes that despite the protagonist of the video being a Muslim and an outsider, receives the warmth and affection from members of varied class, race, religion, nationalities and region.

FINDINGS & CONCLUSION

Case studies 2, 4 and 5 are social experiments done and shown on social media to counter the malicious and hateful religious content uploaded on various social networking sites. The kind of response case study 5 receives (2.5 million views) is a surprise element. The main character of video presents himself as a Muslim from Pakistan. These days India is having acrimonious relations with Pakistan and then also so many people hug the character truly shows that peace is an intrinsic element of Indian society. The kind of response these videos got through the number of views show that social media can also be used for peaceful purposes. Case studies 1 and 3 are glaring examples of peace and harmony between members of two major religious communities of the country.

Founding Father of "Peace Studies", Johan Galtung sees peace as a dynamic process. According to him "*Peace is what we have when creative conflict transformation takes place nonviolently.* Hereby peace is seen as a system characteristic, a context within which certain things can happen in a particular way. The proof of the pudding is in eating; the test of a marriage is when the going gets rough; the test of peace is in the ability to handle conflict" (Galtung, 1996) We see that social media is an interactive and dynamic platform because of the facility of posting uploading images and videos on it. To counter the hate campaigns on social media, videos like mentioned earlier makes social media a platform that induces *creative conflict transformation* to ensure building of peace between religious communities. However, social media comes with some limitations.

- Usage of social media is growing exponentially (14% in 2014) but still the amount of penetration that is percentage of population of India that uses internet is just 19% of the total population. 19% is nothing considering the huge and diverse population of India.
- Social media is still an urban phenomenon and requires skills. Rural or less educated women finds it hard to use internet in contrast to television or radio which doesn't require skill to see or hear respectively, and moreover use of television or radio is very handy compared to laptops or applications in a mobile.
- Internet connectivity and speed is also an issue. In remote villages and towns, the speed which could facilitate smooth running of internet is missing.
- The viewership in earlier mentioned case studies show that when a celebrity (like RJ Naved) is a protagonist in a video, it gets a viewership up to lakhs, whereas videos based on common people gets viewership in thousands. This contradicts the notion that social media is a platform where voices of voiceless are heard.

BIBLIOGRAPY

1. A New Protocol. [Editorial]. (2012). *Economic & Political Weekly*, 47 (37), 8
2. Abu-Nimer, M. (2001). Conflict Resolution, Culture, and Religion: Toward a Training Model of Interreligious Peacebuilding. *Journal of Peace Research*, 38(6), 685-704. Retrieved from http://www.jstor.org/stable/425559

3. Ahuja, R. (2013, September 10). Mujaffarnagar riots: fake video spreads hate on social media. *Hindustantimes*. Retrieved from http://www.hindustantimes.com/india/muzaffarnagar-riots-fake-video-spreads-hate-on-social-media/story-WEOKBAcCOQcRb7X9Wb28qL.html
4. ANI News (Producer) (2015, August 24). A Hindu & Muslim show harmony, have together been ruling medical store- Communal Harmony [Video file].Retrieved from https://www.youtube.com/watch?v=-EguXsqyaKU
5. Ashu Tyagi (Producer). (2016, September 13). Muzaffarnagar Short Film/ Hindu Muslim Unity [Video file]. Retreived from https://www.youtube.com/watch?v=tXkWRYklwKw
6. Bhatt,V.(2013, September 08). What led to the Muzaffarnagar communal riots.*Tehelka*. Retrieved from http://www.tehelka.com/2013/09/what-led-to-the-muzaffarnagar-communal-riots/
7. Castells,M. (2007). Communication, Power and Counter-power in the Network Society. *International Journal of Communication* 1(1), 238-266. Retrieved from http://ijoc.org.
8. Fox, J. (2004). Rise of Religious Nationalism and Conflict: Ethnic Conflict and Revolutionary Wars,1945-2001. *Journal of Peace Research*, 41(6), 715-731. Retrieved from http://www.jstor.org/stable/4149714
9. Friedman, U.(2016, July14). Is Terrorism Getting Worse? *The Atlantic*. Retrieved from https://www.theatlantic.com/international/archive/2016/07/terrorism-isis-global-america/490352/
10. Galtung,J. (1996). *Peace by Peaceful Means*. Oslo: Sage.
11. Haq, Z. (2013, December 03). A dangerous trend: Social Media adds fire to Muzaffarnagar clashes. *Hindustantimes*. Retrieved from http://www.hindustantimes.com/india/a-dangerous-trend-social-media-adds-fire-to-muzaffarnagar-clashes/story-qWmUteMPV1ZkPZkoAlRyDK.html
12. Healey, S. (2005). Religion And Terror: A Post-9/11 Analysis. *International Journal on World Peace*, 22 (3), 3-23. Retrieved from http://www.jstor.org/stable/20753495
13. http://www.american.edu/sis/faculty/abunimer.cfm.
14. Internet users by the country. (2016). Retrieved from http://www.internetlivestats.com/internet-users/
15. Kong,L. (2012). Religion and Technology: Refiguring Place, Space, Identity and Community. *Area,* 33(4), 404-413. Retrieved from http://www.jstor.org/stable/20004181
16. Lucky Video Parlor (Producer) (2014, May 5). Best Mirchi Murga by Rj Naved. .. on Hindu Muslim relationships [Video file]. Retreived from https://www.youtube.com/watch?v=UaSoqBwNJJc

17. Mondal, S. (2012, August 18). Mischief of Social Media in Full Play.*The Hindu. Retrievedfrom* http://www.thehindu.com/todays-paper/tp-national/tp-newdelhi/mischief-of-social-media-in-full- play/article3787446.ece
18. NDTV (Producer).(2017, February 25). Kashmiri Muslims In Bandipore Celebrate Shivratri, Want Pandits To Return [Video file].Retrieved from https://www.youtube.com/watch?v=OPn-vltBts0
19. Percentage on internet users who watch online video content on any device in 2014 by country. (2014). Retrieved from http://www.statista.com/statistics/272835/share-of-internet-users-who-watch-online-videos/.
20. Population by Religious Community. (2011). *CensusIndia*.Retrieved from http://www.censusindia.gov.in/2011census/C-01.html
21. PTI. (2014, March 14). Govt releases data of riot victims identifying religion. *The Indian Express*. Retrieved from http://indianexpress.com/article/india/india-others/govt-releases-data-of-riot-victims-identifying-religion/
22. Purie, A. (2012, September). From the editor-in-chief. *India Today*, 1
23. Rajeshwari, B. (2004). Communal Riots in India: A Chronology (1947-2003). *Institute of Peace and Conflict Studies Research Papers*. Retrieved from http://www.nagarikmancha.org/images/1242-Documents-Communal_Riots_in_India.pdf
24. Reychler, L. (1997). Religion and Conflict. *The International Journal of Peace Studies*, 2(1). Retrieved from http://www.gmu.edu/programs/icar/ijps/vol2_1/cover2_1.htm
25. Ride for Peace India Pakistan (Producer) (2016, June 16). Surprising reactions of Indians when they meet a Pakistani [Video file]. Retreived from https://www.youtube.com/watch?v=HT2dtZ2uCO0
26. Shah, G. (2016). *Ideological Hegemony, Communal Riots & Social Media*. New Delhi, ND: G.B. Books.
27. Social media users in India to reach 143 million in April: IAMA. (2015, June17). Retrieved from http://articles.economictimes.indiatimes.com/2015-06-17/news/63540701_1_social-media-users-urban-india-social-networking-sites (Accessed June 29, 2015).
28. Unnithan, S. & Tare, K. (2012, September).Mumbai on the Brink.*India Today*, 24
29. Weeks, B. & Lance, R. (2013). Predicting Dissemination of News Content in Social Media: A Focus on Reception, Friending, and Partisanship. *Journalism & Mass Communication Quarterly*, 90(2), 212-232.Retrieved from http://jmq.sagepub.com/content/90/2/212.
30. Zakaria, R. (1988). *The Struggle Within Islam The Conflict between Religion and Politics*. New Delhi, ND: Penguin.

Chapter-3

Effect of Yogic Practice on Selected Biochemical Variables Among Obese Middle Age Higher Secondary Boys School

Deb Kumar Das & Dr.S.Selvalakshmi

INTRODUCTION

The present study is an outcome of the effect of yogic practice on selected biochemical variables among obese middle age higher secondary school boys. To facilitate the study 30 obese school boys, from Chennai. The selected subjects were in the age ranged between 14 to 18 years. They were divided into two equal groups' namely experimental group, and control group, on random basis. Before the commencement of the training, purpose of the study and method of yogic practice were explained to the subjects for their cooperation. The researcher reviewed the various scientific literatures pertaining to effect of yogic practice on selected biochemical variables among obese higher secondary school boys. The selected biochemical variables are blood glucose (Fasting) and Triglycerides. The study was formulated as a true random group design consisting of a pre-test and posttest. The subjects (N=30) were randomly assigned to three equal groups of fifteen obese higher secondary school boys. Yogic practice group and control group respectively. Pretest was conducted for all the 30 subjects on selected biochemical variables. The experimental groups participated in respective training for six days per week a period of twelve weeks programme. The control group did not participate in any of the training programme. The post test was conducted on the above said dependent variables after a period of twelve weeks for all the three groups. The differences between initial and final scores were considered as the effect of yogic practice and the obtained data were subjected to statistical treatment using ANCOVA. In all cases the level of significance fixed 0.05 levels.

Obesity means an excess amount of body fat. The prevalence of obesity is commonly assessed by using body mass index (BMI), defined as the weight in kilograms divided by the square of the height in meters (kg/m2). A BMI over 25 kg/m2 is defined as overweight, and a BMI of over 30 kg/m2 as obese. Obesity has reached epidemic proportions globally, with more than 1 billion adults overweight - at least 300 million of them clinically obese - and is a major contributor to the global burden of chronic disease and disability. Often coexisting in developing countries with under-nutrition, obesity is a complex condition, with serious social and psychological dimensions, affecting virtually all ages and socioeconomic groups. Increased consumption of more energy-dense, nutrient poor foods with high levels of sugar and saturated fats, combined with reduced physical activity, have led to obesity rates that have risen three-fold or more since 1980 in some areas of North America, the United Kingdom, Eastern Europe, the Middle East, the Pacific Islands, Australasia and China. The obesity epidemic is not restricted to industrialized societies; this increase is often faster in developing countries than in the developed world. Obesity and overweight pose a major risk for serious diet-related chronic diseases, including type 2 diabetes, cardiovascular disease, hypertension and stroke, and certain forms of cancer. The health consequences range from increased risk of premature death, to serious chronic conditions that reduce the overall quality of life. Of especial concern is the increasing incidence of child obesity. **(www.who.in)**

PURPOSE OF THE STUDY

The purpose of the study was to find out the effect of yogic practice on selected biochemical variables among obese middle age higher secondary school Boys.

HYPOTHESIS

It was hypothesized that would be significant difference between Yogic Practices

(A) and Control Group (B) on blood glucose (Fasting) and Triglycerides among obese middle age higher secondary school boys.

REVIEWS OF RELATED LITERATURE

Subaash.B & Elangovan.R (2014) The present random group experimental study was designed to find out the effect of simplified kundalini yoga and walking on selected biochemical variables among obese school boys. It was hypothesized that there would be significant differences in biochemical variables such as Triglycerides (BMI of 30 to 35) school boys from Kanchipuram aged between 14 to 18 years were selected randomly. The subjects were divided into two experimental groups and a control group of 15 subjects each in a group. Experimental groups underwent simplified kundalini yoga and walking respectively for the period of 12 weeks, six days per week of one hour basically, then slightly increased to 1.5 hours and 1.30 hours. The control group was not exposed to any specific training. The pre-test and post-test was conducted before and after and after the training for all the groups. The Triglycerides (BMI) was measured by weighing machine and meter scale and resting pulse rate was measured by BP monitor machine. The data collected from the subjects were treated statistically through using Analysis of covariance (ANCOVA) to determine the significant difference. The Hypotheses were tested at 0.05 level of confidence. The results and the conclusions of the study showed that simplified kundalini yoga and walking were effective in decreasing significantly as result of Triglycerides (BMI) and resting pulse rate among obese school boys than the control group and simplified kundalini yoga was effective than walking in decreasing Triglycerides (BMI) and resting pulse rate among school boys.

Duraisami (2012), The Purpose of the present study was to analyze the effect of walking and suryanamaskar on Triglycerides of obese men forty five (N=15) obese man were selected at Pondicherry region. Their age ranged from 40 to 55 years. The subjects were randomly divided into three equal groups, group I walking group II suryanamaskar and group III control each consisting of 15 subjects. Two experimental groups were participated in two different training programmers i.e. walking and suryanamaskar for the duration of six weeks for five days in a week for five days in a week in the morning hours between 6.00 am to 7.00 am and control group did not participated in any training except their daily routine works. The data collected before and after the training programme. Analysis of Co-variance (ANCOVA) and scheffe's post hoc test were applied to find out the significance of mean difference among the three groups. The results show that the obtained 'F' Ratio value of Triglycerides 4.116 was significantly higher them the table value 3.23 (P>0.05). There was a statically significant decrease in Triglycerides for both the groups. The findings of the study indicated that the significant reduction on Triglycerides for the walking groups is better than the suryanamaskar groups. But both the groups have shown beneficial effects when compared to the control group.

METHODOLOGY

To achieve the purpose of the Random group experimental study, 30 Higher secondary obese School boys from Chennai aged between 14 to 18 years were selected randomly; the subjects were divided into experimental groups of Yogic practices and a control group of 15 subjects each.

Experimental groups underwent Yogic practices respectively for the period of 12 weeks, six days per week of one hour in the evening. The control group was not exposed to any specific training but they participated in their regular activities.

Yogic practices given to the experimental groups which include Yogic practices, Loosening Exercises, Suryanamaskar, Padahastasana, Parvaatasana, Pachimuttasana, Ardhamatsyendrasana, Bhujanagasana, Shalabasana, Sarvangasana, Halasana, Dhanurasana, Nadishodana, Shavasana, Silence and Peace Meditation.

The selected variables, Blood glucose (Fasting) and Triglycerides was measured by Skin fold caliper.

STATISTICAL TECHNIQUE

The data collected from the subjects were analyzed using Analysis of Covariance to find out the adjusted mean difference among the treatment groups. The Scheffe's post hoc test was used to find out the paired mean significance at 0.05 levels.

RESULT AND DISCUSSION

Results on blood glucose (Fasting)

Table-I: Computation of Analysis of Covariance of Experimental Groups and Control Group on Blood Glucose (Fasting) (Scores in Mg/Dl)

	Exp. Group	Control group	Source of Variance	df	Sum of square	Mean sum of squares	Obtained F ratio
pre test	133.54	134.29	between	2	19.17	9.59	0.45
			Within	28	594.28	21.22	
Post test	128.32	133.46	between	2	222.32	111.16	5.36
			Within	28	580.17	20.72	
Adj. Post Test	128.30	132.83	between	2	155.89	77.94	10.50
			Within	27	200.52	7.43	
Mean Diff.	5.21	0.83					

Signicant at 0.05 level of confidence

Table F-ratio at 0.05 level of confidence with df one and 28(df) =3.34, one and 27(df) =3.34

The obtained F value on pretest scores 0.45 was lesser than the required F value of 3.34 to be significant at 0.05 level. This proved that there was no significant difference between the groups a pretest and posttest and the randomization at the pretest was equal. The post test scores analysis proved that there was significant difference between the groups, as obtained F value 5.36 was greater than the required F value of 3.34. This proved that the differences between the post test means of subjects were significant. Taking into consideration the pre and post test scores among the groups adjusted mean scores were calculated and subjects were significant. Taking into consideration the pre and post test scores among the groups adjusted mean scores were calculated and subjected to statistical treatment. The obtained F value of 10.50 was greater than the required F value of 3.34. This proved that there was significant difference among the means due to twelve weeks of yogic Practices on blood glucose (Fasting).

The ordered adjusted means on blood glucose were presented through bar diagram for better understanding of the results of this study in Figure-1

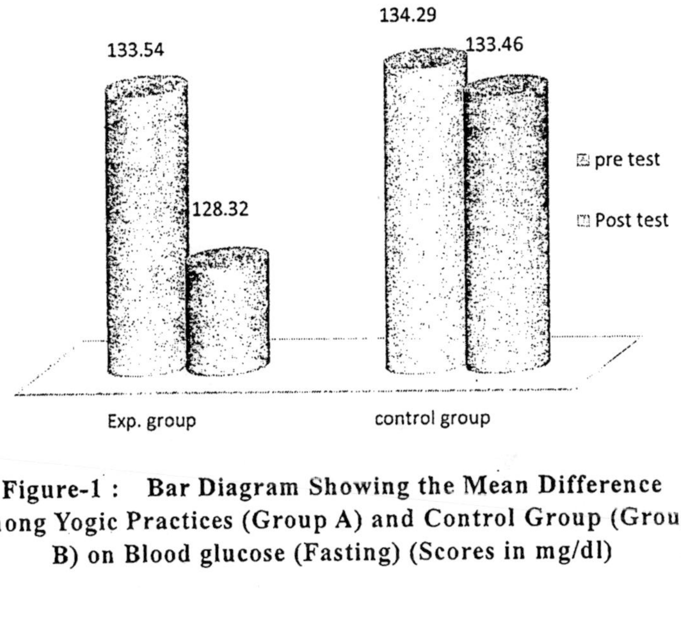

Figure-1 : Bar Diagram Showing the Mean Difference among Yogic Practices (Group A) and Control Group (Group B) on Blood glucose (Fasting) (Scores in mg/dl)

Results on Triglycerides

Table –II : Computation of Analysis of Covariance of Experimental Groups and Control Group on Triglycerides (Scores in Mg/dl)

	Exp. group	Control group	Source of Variance	df	Sum of square	Mean sum of squares	Obtained F ratio
pretest	159.31	174.38	between	2	1706.53	853.27	8.97
			within	28	2664.34	95.15	
Posttest	153.61	173.98	between	2	3113.04	1556.5	19.24
			within	28	2264.74	80.88	

Adj. Post Test	158.93	168.92	between	2	456.17	228.09	6.16
			within	27	999.20	37.01	
Mean Diff.	5.70	0.41					

Signicant at 0.05 level of confidence

Table F-ratio at 0.05 level of confidence with df one and 28(df) =3.34, one and 27(df) =3.34

The obtained F value on pretest scores 8.97 was lesser than the required F value of 3.34 to be significant at 0.05 level. This proved that there was no significant difference between the groups a pretest and posttest and the randomization at the pretest was equal. The post test scores analysis proved that there was significant difference between the groups, as obtained F value 19.24 was greater than the required F value of 3.34. This proved that the differences between the post test means of subjects were significant. Taking into consideration the pre and post test scores among the groups adjusted mean scores were calculated and subjects were significant. Taking into consideration the pre and post test scores among the groups' adjusted mean scores were calculated and subjected to statistical treatment. The obtained F value of 6.16 was greater than the required F value of 3.34. This proved that there was significant difference among the means due to twelve weeks of yogic Practices on Triglycerides.

The ordered adjusted means on Triglycerides were presented through bar diagram for better understanding of the results of this study in Figure-2

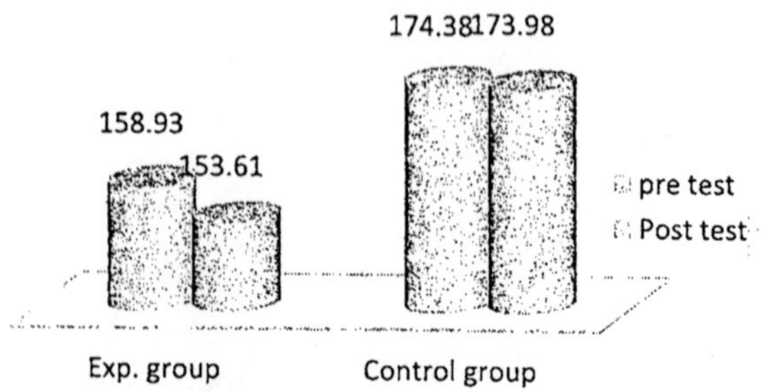

Figure –2 : Bar Diagram Showing the Adjusted Post Test Means of Experimental and Control Groups on Triglycerides (Scores in mg/dl)

CONCLUSIONS

There was significant decrease in the biochemical variables namely blood glucose (Fasting), and Triglycerides reduced significantly due to yogic practice.

BIBLIOGRAPHY

1. Subaash. B &Elangovan.R (2014), Effect of simplified kundalini yoga and walking on selected biochemical variables among obese school boys, ***Journal of physical education sports and allied disciplines.*** Vol.5, No.1&2 July 2014, Pp-53.
2. S. Adhavan, V. Duraisami (2012), effect of walking and suryanamaskar on Triglycerides of obese men, ***"Nournal of physical education sports and allied disciplines"***, vol.3, No.2, P-60.

Chapter-4

Gandhiji's Concept of Education a Silent Revolution Towards Peace

Nakul Mandal

INTRODUCTION

Both Education and Peace are two interrelated concepts. The primary urge of human being is to live in a peaceful society and only true education can provide this. Education means to acquire knowledge concerning the living standard of human society. It develops intellectual as well as mental capacity of man. Education is a lifetime procedure and it opens the windows of knowledge before man and, as a result, individual may aware about their goods and bad. It helps individuals to increase their interest of knowing and make person dutiful and responsible. Education teaches people to investigate truth and reality. Furthermore, education is the backbone of a nation, without which a nation cannot develop her existence. It develops morality and virtue among the nation which are elementary for peace. By educating people, only, peace may come into being. Hence, existence of nation is immensely depends on education and peace. It was Mahatma Gandhi (1869-1948), the great Indian philosopher of peace, whose final aim was to establish a peaceful society and his concept of education is a silent way towards this. Gandhian meaning of education is not only to literate person, but it has a larger meaning. It means an 'all-round development of man' which is necessary for peace. Therefore, the foremost aim of this study is to examine Gandhiji's views on education as a silent revolution towards peace. It will also examine why it is called a silent revolution for peace and how far it is relevance to call such.

OBJECTIVES

1. To understand the relevance of Gandhiji's concept of education in the contemporary Indian situation.
2. To examine the role of education for social, political and economic development of India from Gandhian perspective.
3. To study how Gandhiji's concept of education would unite the common people for peaceful co-existence.
4. How far it is truthful to say that Gandhiji's concept of education is a reliable way towards peace also subject to examine.
5. If it is a way towards peace, then what method would it use for peace making also subject to identify.
6. To explain the factors influencing the success of Gandhiji's concept of education towards peace and how it is implement in the contemporary Indian situation.

METHODOLOGY

The method followed in the study will be chiefly historical and analytical. The study is based on secondary sources of data like Books, Published articles, Research papers, Research reports and relevant websites. It will also pay attention to the contextual and theoretical influences on shaping of Gandhiji's thinking and development of ideas about education and peace and its importance to the contemporary globalised world on the basis of obtainable written material explored.

Mahatma Gandhi was one of the great philosopher-prophet of world peace. He was one of the distinguished humanists forever. His love for humanity has immensely stirred the atmosphere of India as well as of world during the first half of the 20th century. His prime aim was to annihilate all kind of evil power from the world and he wanted to demolish inequality, injustice, untouchability and communal discord from the society. Truth (*Sattya*) and Non-violence (*Ahimsa*) are the two methods through which Gandhiji conducted his experiment for pull down these entire evil doers from society. His basic objectives were to establish a guilty free society in where a friendship among men, liberty of the individual and education for the dignity of the labour of man is necessarily present. Moreover, Gandhiji felt himself as a world citizen. The politics of South Africa and the politics of India was his laboratory and in this laboratory he experiment the ways of truth and non-violence. In addition, when the structure of humanism was threat from different ways by different form of uncivilised tradition; man become crazy with the devastation of human society; morality and virtues are almost wither away from the society; in that a situation Mahatma Gandhi taught us a lesson of humanity and peace. Gandhiji, however, wanted to establish a society in where each man lives his life freely, not to dependent on others. He believes that individual freedom is very much essential for making a good society. And, to him, a good society needs some moral and virtual principle which can arrive only from good education. Through education people develop their thinking power about goods and bad. In addition, education makes a man perfect and it develops morality and virtue among men. The basic objective of education is to identify the reality and truth which are the essentials to achieve affluence and peace. Therefore, before going to any discussion about the topic we should need to analyse separately the meaning and purpose of the both- education and peace.

Meaning of Education

The term 'education' is a very common useful word which means, in general, to enlarge knowledge, skills and attitudes of a person. Though, we are very similar with the word 'education' in our day-to-day life, but the problem is that very few of us only understand its true perception. Definition of education is not remaining same in all time. During the course of time the meaning and objectives of education have been changed. Different people define education in different ways. Some people define it as a perfect knowledge about certain subjects. Some people define it as 'schooling or lifelong learning'. Some say that 'education is nothing, but training of people's mind in a particular direction to bring about desired changes'. (Basic in Education, NCERT, (hereafter BE) 2014, p. 3). Therefore, it is very difficult to define education in a single word. To understand the appropriate meaning of education it is, however, necessary to examine its etymological meaning and some of the views of great thinkers (both Eastern and Western) that illustrate the concept and meaning of education.

The word 'education' comes from three different Latin words: 'educare', 'educere' and 'educatum'. Educare means 'to raise' and 'to bring up'; educere means 'to lead forth' or 'to come out'; and educatum means 'the act of teaching or training'. (BE, p. 3). Therefore, etymologically education means to afford healthful surroundings that would facilitate or bring out and develop the possibilities in an individual. Education seeks to nourish the good qualities and draw out the best in every individual. It seeks to develop the innate or the inner potentialities of humans. (Ibid., p. 3).

'The Palgrave Macnillan Dictionary of Political Thought' define education as "the the process whereby rational beings are instructed, and through which they acquire the beliefs, emotions and values pertaining to a culture. It is the more formal and structured part of socialisation". (R. Scruton, 2007, 200). Dictionary of Education (edited by C.V. Good, 1973), on the other hand, define education as "the aggregate of all the processes by which a person develops abilities, attitudes and other forms of behaviour of practical values in the society in which s/he lives; the social process by which people are subjected to the influence of selected and controlled environment (especially that of the school), so that they may obtain social competence and optimum individual development". (Quoted from BE, p. 3)

Beside the etymological and dictionary meaning of education some great educationists and thinkers are also define it from their own way and it is hereby necessary to discuss such definitions for a better understanding of it. One of the great Indian thinker and social reformer Swami Vivekananda (1863-1902) gave an insightful definition of education. To him, "education is the manifestation of the perfection already in man". The word 'manifestation' implies here that something already exists and is waiting to be expressed. The main focus in learning is to make the hidden ability of a learner manifest. The expression 'already in man' refers to a human being's potential, which is the range of the abilities and talents, known or unknown that he is born with. (My Idea of Education, 2008, p. 17).

Sri Aurobindo Ghosh (1872-1950), one of the great nationalist leaders and philosopher of 19th century India, define education as a lifelong process and, to him "education of a human being should begin at birth and continue throughout his life". (On Education, 1978, p. 9). According to him, education is meant to bring out the best in man, to develop his potentialities to the maximum, to integrate him with himself, his surroundings, his society, his country and humanity to make him the 'complete man', the 'integral man'. In short, Sri Aurobindo says that education should be integral, so that it develops the physical, mental, vital, psychic and spiritual aspects of the human personality. (BE, p. 11). One of the earliest educationists of modern India Rabindranath Tagore (1861-1941) was writes: "the highest education is that which does not merely give us information but makes our life in harmony with all existence". (Ibid., p. 12). Tagore saw education as a vehicle for appreciating the richest aspects of other cultures, while maintaining one's own cultural specificity.

On the other hand the term 'education' is also differently used in West. Western thinkers such as Plato, Aristotle, Rousseau, Froeble, Pestalozzi, and John Dewey and so on define education in their own way. Plato, a Greek philosopher, used it as 'the purification of soul or mind' and, to him, the successful development of education depends on appropriate and healthy environment. (N. Pramanik, 2012, p. 47). According to Aristotle, "Education is the creation of a sound mind in a sound body. It develops man's faculty, especially his mind so that he may be able to enjoy the contemplation of supreme truth, goodness and beauty of which perfect happiness essentially consists of". (Quoted from BE, p. 17). According to John Dewey (1916), "Education is reconstruction or reorganisation of experience which adds to the meaning of experience and which increases the ability to direct the course of subsequent experiences". (Quoted from Ibid., p. 19).

Therefore, definition of education is not an easy matter. Due to change of times the meaning and objectives of education also changed. In ancient time it is has been use as a method to gather knowledge, but in modern time the concept has been differently used. Modern thinkers connect it with the human and social development. It means an 'all-round development of human being'; more particularly we can call the physical, mental, emotional and moral development of individual. Its primary aim is to develop uniqueness and individuality among men either naturally or socially for creating a peaceful society.

Meaning of Peace

The dictionary meaning of the term 'peace' is the 'absence of war'. (R. Scruton, 2007, 515). The basic principle of peace is to avoid violence and it is the peaceful alternative to force. Peace is the ultimate goal of humankind. The basic urge of human organism is to live their life in a peaceful society. For building up of a new and better tomorrow the value of peace is greatly crucial. In today's globalised and interdependent world values of the words like peace, non-violence, tolerance, human right and democracy is much higher than any other object. Peace, however, is a collective approach which can only develop through trust and co-operation with each other. In the preface of his book 'Peace, Love and Liberty' Tom G. Palmer said, "The existence of a peaceful society depends on faith and collaboration. Peace allows people to love. To change enemies into friends. To replace conflict with cooperation. To replace hatred with love and friendship". Peace is related with prosperity, progress and freedom. In fact, to Palmer, 'peace, freedom, prosperity and progress go hand-in-hand'. (T.G. Palmer, Preface, 2014). The principles of peace are applicable in all social circumstances. The cause of peace is concern with the intercourse of governments, and aims merely to prevent war between nations. (The American Peace Society, 1845, p. 2).

Writing and thoughts about peace has been initiated from the ancient times, which have continued in modern times also. Human beings are pleasure seeker; their primary goal is to live a life with happiness and pleasure. In present day situation we are very much interdependent and interconnected with each other. But due to violence and other threat against humanity the present world is more problematic and challenging to us. To prevent this there is a need to assemble a 'culture of peace' amongst all the nations throughout the world. This 'culture of peace', in the words of Cora Weiss (Former President of International Peace Bureau), "must replace the culture of violence if we and our home, planet Earth, are to survive". (L. N. Castro & J. N. Galace, 2010, p. ix). Anwarul K. Chowdhury (Former Under-Secretary-General and High Representative of the UN) writes: "In today's world, more so, a culture of peace should be seen as the essence of a new humanity, a new global civilisation based on inner oneness and outer diversity. The flourishing of a culture of peace will generate the mindset in us that is a prerequisite for the transition from force to reason, from conflict and violence to dialogue and peace. The culture of peace will provide the bedrock of support to a stable, progressing and prospering world for all". (Ibid., p. xiv).

Gandhiji on Education and Peace

On Education: Amongst the various constructive works of Gandhiji to serve the humanity education was the most important one. Gandhiji's concept of education was a result of his socio-political thought and his life philosophy. By education Gandhiji means 'an all-round development of man'. According to Gandhiji education is the development of physical, mental and spiritual power which develops friendly cooperation and integration among men. (Bandyopadhya & Chattopadhya, 2012, p. 142). In 'Harijan' he writes: "By education I mean an all-round drawing out of the best in child and man-body, mind and spirit". (Quoted from India of My Dreams, 1947, p. 156) To him education is not merely to literate person, but it is something more and he holds that, "literacy is not the end of education or even the beginning. It is only of the means whereby man and woman can be educated. Literacy in itself is no education".(Ibid). For Gandhiji, therefore, "child's education should begin by teaching it a useful handicraft and enabling it to produce from the moment it begins its training" and he also hold the view that "the highest development of the mind and the soul is possible under such a system of education". (Ibid.).

Gandhiji's plan of education was very much related with his spiritual philosophy. To him an all round development of human soul is the ultimate goal of humanity. Gandhiji advocates that kind of society in where every individual has the liberty of thought and speech. (S. K. Bhattachraya, 2011, p. 91). And for this he suggests that kind of education by which individuals may become able to think freely and frankly 'Learning by doing' and 'self-development' are the two key principles of Gandhiji's education. Gandhiji had a firm believe that fulfillment of education depends only on after a practical surveillance. Therefore, he writes: "I hold that true education of the intellect can only come through a proper exercise and training of the bodily organs, e.g. hands, feet, eyes, ears, nose, etc. In other words, an intelligent use of the bodily organs in a child provides the best and quickest way of developing his intellect." (India of My Dreams, 1947, p. 155). To him individual may liberate only after his self-development and practical utility (learning by doing) of education will provide necessary pathway for this self-development. According to Gandhiji "unless the development of mind and body goes hand in hand with a corresponding awakening of the soul, the former alone would prove to be a poor lop-sided affair". (Ibid.). Gandhiji was of the view that education should be learning by heart and for this he suggests 'spiritual training'. Spiritual training, he means, is "education of the heart. A proper and all-round development of the mind, therefore, can take place only when it proceeds pari passu with the education of the physical and spiritual faculties of the child. They constitute and indivisible whole". (Ibid.).

Gandhiji advocates free and compulsory education for all because, to him, "it will check the progressive decay of our villages and lay the foundation of a juster social order in which there is no unnatural division between the 'haves' and the 'havenots' and everybody is assured of a living wage and the rights to freedom". (Ibid., p. 157). The primary objective of his 'Basic Education' (*Nai Talim*) was to establish 'Village-Swaraj'. By basic education Gandhiji means "to transform village children into model villagers. It is principally designed for them. The inspiration for it has come from the villages". To him "basic education links the children to all that is best and lasting in India. It develops both the body and the mind, and keeps the child rooted to the soil with a glorious vision of the future in the realization of which he or she begins to take his or her share form the very commencement of his or her career in school". (Ibid., p. 158). The objective of basic education, in Gandhiji's words, 'is the physical, intellectual and moral development of the children through the medium of a handicraft'. (Harijan, 6-4-'40). Gandhiji wanted to organise a silent social revolution by conveying primary education through the medium of village handicrafts and to him, "it will provide a healthy and moral basis of relationship between the city and the village and thus go a long way to eradicating some of the worst evils of the present social insecurity and poisoned relationship between the classes". (India of My Dreams, 1947, p. 157).

Gandhiji vehemently criticise contemporary education system, more particularly the colonial system of education of his time, because, to him, that was not an accurate method for the development of physical, mental and intellectual ability of men. This colonial system of education, to Gandhiji, could only provide certain literary knowledge, none other than anything else. Gandhiji observed that education of his time was politically motivated and controlled by the state. To him the systems of education which the Europeans have useless are the systems of fashion among us. In 'Hind Swaraj' he writes: "It is worth noting that, by receiving English education, we have enslaved the nation. Hypocrisy, tryanny, etc., have increased; English-knowing Indians have not hesitated to cheat and strike terror into the people". (Hind Swaraj, p. 85). In addition, he did not like 'text book' centric education; rather favor practical base education. The method of education, to Gandhiji, will be on mother tongue basis. Because learning by any foreign language there is a difficulty of expression of thought. If a student learn by a foreign language, to Gandhiji, he/she did not express his/her thought properly and there is a probability to forget and to neglect indigenous culture. This is another minus point of foreign language. Considering his theory '*Nai Talim*' (New Education) we find that Gandhiji ardently try to develop an education system which must depends on India's culture and environment. Equal development of body, mind and soul is the fundamental objective of his '*Nai Talim*' and Gandhiji was of the hope that only education by mother tongue can make this possible.

On Peace: Mahatma Gandhi was one of the great philosophers of peace and prosperity. His entire political philosophy was based on non-violence and peace. Non-violence was the guiding principle of Gandhian philosophy. In Gandhiji's own words: "Non-violence is the first article of my faith. It is also the last article of my creed". (Quoted from A. K. Mahapatra (Bengali book), p. 243) He rejects any kind of violence from his life and wanted to develop a non-violent society in where every individual may spend their life in a peaceful way. Concepts of *Sarvodaya* Society, *Ramrajya* and Trusteeship were standing on his thinking of non-violence as well as on peace. Therefore it is no longer wrong to say that peace is the ultimate goal of Gandhian philosophy.

Gandhian concept of Education as a silent revolution towards Peace

Gandhian concept of education was not static; rather dynamic, it is an unending exercise. Activeness and continuity was its main feature. Gandhiji viewed education as a man making process which started from the birth and continue till death of a person. His concept of education is a close pathway to peace. To Gandhiji man is neither a physical existence; nor only a combination of heart and soul; and in addition, intelligence is not the final aim of man. There is a necessity, according to Gandhiji, of exact and righteous combination among body, mind and soul to build up a perfect man and only education may provide this.

Therefore the foremost aim of education, according to Gandhiji, is to create a concert among body, mind and soul. As man's relation with the society is inevitable, more particularly man is a 'social animal', and then an all-round development of man is very much necessary for the development of society. Gandhian concept of *Nai Talim* (Basic Education) had a vision to establish a 'good society' by giving a true education to all. As Kanakmal Gandhi wrote: "His (Gandhiji's) basic national education of 1937 was planned as the basic preparation of Indian children for sharing in a national society which itself aims at basing every aspect of its life, social, economic, political, cultural, on truth and on non-violence - in other words, at a new social order totally different from the existing one".(K. Gandhi, 3.11.1987 in The Story of Nai Talim).

From Gandhian view point true education is the prime route for peace. Gandhiji wanted to develop a skillful national village society in where everyone acts upon their life peacefully. Gandhian concept of *Nai Talim*, however, was the stage of preparation and practice for achieving the goal of peace. It was the appearance of the principle of non-violence in the educational sphere. In Gandhian concept of education there is a call for walk off ahead which is also a characteristic feature of peace. Education for peace means learning to live peace, daily and hourly, wherever one happens to be, learning to tackle and resolve the tensions and conflicts of outlook and interest which are a necessary and valuable part of human experience.(Dr. Ravindra Kumar). Education helps to make one's life purposeful and from the Gandhian perspective education can develop a peaceful mind among individual. Gandhiji suggests an activity based education in where students learn through direct practice and training. The ultimate goal of this type of education is to establish a perfect/good society in where each individual may survive their life peacefully. The principle and practice of *'Nai Talim'* was, therefore, rightly a great means towards peace.

CONCLUSION

From the above discussion we can easily conclude that Gandhiji's concept of education is not only to make people literally; it is not only a concept bound only on knowledge practice; but to a certain extent it is the pathway of 'all-round development of man' and its most important aim was to make a man perfect. The fundamental urge of Gandhiji's concept of education is to relate individuals with their social needs and social service which is a very good essential deal for peace. If we consider the present scenario of our education system what we find that it (education) is not rightly given to our youth. What we learn is not able to develop our thinking power. It is only a career centric education which has no role to develop our physical, mental, spiritual and social potentialities to extend our society towards peace. Present education did not inspire our youth to develop an over-all thinking power; rather it develops a self-centric thinking power and if we look at in our surroundings we find lots of example of this. In this regard Gandhiji's ideas of education certainly have relevance in present day situation. Moreover, moral and virtual development among people is very much necessary in present day situation and Gandhiji's concept of education is may be a good trail of this. Furthermore, education is the backbone of a nation, without which a nation cannot develop her existence. And Gandhiji's concept of education develops morality and virtue among the nation which are elementary for peace. By educating people, only, peace may come into being. Therefore, education and peace are equally related with each other and it has been no longer wrong to say that Gandhiji's concept of education is rightly a silent revolution towards peace.

BIBLIOGRAPHY

1. Bandyopadhya, V. and Chattyopadhya, K. (2014), Bharater Samajtattik Chintadhara (Bengali Version), Levant Books, Kolkata.
2. Bhattacharyya, S. K. (2011), Mahatma Gandhi (Bengali Version), Pragatishil Prakashak, Kolkata.
3. Castro, L. N. & Galace, J. N., (2010), Peace Education: A Pathway to a Culture of Peace, Centre for Peace Education, Miriam College, Philippines.
4. Gandhi, M. K. (1938), Hind Swaraj or Indian Home Rule, Compiled by Mahadev Desai, Navajivan Publishing House, Ahmedabad.
5. Gandhi, M. K. (1947), India of My Dreams, Compiled by R. K. Prabhu, Navajivan Mudranalaya, Ahmedabad.
6. Mother (1978), On Education (Vol.-12), Sri Aurobindo Ashram, Pondicherry.
7. NCERT (2014), Basics in Education (Textbook for B. Ed. Course), Sri Aurobindo Marg, New Delhi.
8. Palmer, T. G. (Ed.) (2014) Peace, Love, & Liberty: War Is Not Inevitable, Jameson Books Inc., Ottawa, Illinois.

9. Pramanik, N. and Roy, Sushil (2012), Pachattya Rastrachintar Ruprekha (Bengali Version), Chhaya Prakashani, Kolkata.
10. Scruton, Roger (2007), The Palgrave Macmillan Dictionary of Political Thought (3rd Edition).
11. The American Peace Society, (1845) The Book of Peace: A Collection of Essays on War and Peace, Vance Publications, Pensacola.
12. Vivekananda, Swami (2008), My Idea of Education, Compiled by Dr. Kiran Walia, Advaita Ashram, Kolkata.
13. Education and Peace: A Gandhian Perapective, by Dr. Ravindra Kumar.
14. Mahatma Gandhi Global Village a Model of Basic Education: To Teach Self-Reliance & Respect for Manual Labour, by Dr. Umakant Chanshetti and Ms. Sangita Shah.
15. The Gandhian Concept of 'Swaraj' in Education, by C. A. Reena Desai.
16. The Story of Nai Talim, by Marjorie Skyes.

Chapter-5

Gandhi's Non-Violence: Peace and Justice in Education

Nasimul Hoque

INTRODUCTION

M. K. Gandhi was not only a social reformer, but he can also be called a source of thinking, who presented his own vision of non-violence and basic values of human life. At the same time he drew on various streams of the philosophies of the East and the west. A mistaken belief persists that violence can end conflict or that war can bring salvation to the world. Gandhi showed the non-violence way, lived and demonstrated its success. In the views of the growing scourge of violence in the world even affecting our day to today life, it is all the more appropriate to do some fresh thinking and reflection on Gandhi's non-violence. The originality and the freshness of Gandhi's mind are illustrated nowhere better than in his principles of non-violence as he molded this ancient concept into a power weapon to resist the evil of exploitation and injustice.

The contribution made by Mahatma Gandhi in the realm of theory and praxis of non-violence in the modern world is seminal. He never claimed any original in this respect and maintained that his principles were 'as old as hills'. However, in an unprecedented way he has revolutionized the concept and working of non-violence. As an activist votary of non-violence he has shown its efficacy in dealing with evils of exploitation and injustice that have plagues humanity in its political, economic and social field.

Various Aspects of Non-violence

Gandhi believes that non-violence is not a cloistered virtue to be practiced by the individual only for his own peace and salvation.

Rather it should be taken as a rule of conduct for the entire humanity. He considered non-violence as the greatest force at the disposal of mankind. It is noted that prior to Gandhi non-violence was taken as a virtue to be practiced mostly at the individual level. But it was Gandhi who revolutionized the concept by taking it to level of common masses. For Gandhi non-violence was not merely a personal virtue, but asocial virtue to be cultivated and practiced by all. In his own words "the religion of non-violence is not meant merely for the rishis and saints. It is meant for the common people as well. Non-violence is the law of our species as violence is the law of the brute"[1].it is event from the above that Gandhi took the concept of non-violence to the cosmic level.

Gandhi believes that as limited beings, we cannot grasp truth in its entirety. The problem arises when people claim that they own the whole truth, and hence they would be justified in imposing it on others, without any restraint. To avoid such an undesirable situation, Gandhian non-violence seeks to ensure dialogue as a basis of mutual trust between conflicting parties. This would help them to understand truth in its relative terms. Gandhi had tremendous faith in the method of dialogues. All his life, he worked through dialogues with everybody including his own self. His philosophy provides space for persons from different strands of life to come together and open up for dialogues for finding alternatives. As he puts it, "I very much like the doctrine of the manyness of reality. It is this doctrine that has taught me to judge a mussalman from his own standpoint and a Christen from his…my anekantavada is the result of the twin doctrines of satya and ahimsa"[2].

In Gandhi's view, moral, social and political truths could not be discovered by sitting and meditating in a cave but through open and free dialogue among the parties with their own understanding of the truth. Gandhi through the process of Satyagraha seeks to change reconcile both the outlook and behaviour of opponents. Thus Gandhi's non-violence is a programme for transformation of relationships and not a mere strategy for peaceful change. It also includes constructive work as an active and transformative force.

Gandhi had a cosmological vision of social relations based on his theory of unity of all life. According to him, all life is interrelated and interdependent. Thus happiness and suffering of any individual affects the rest. He believes that intolerance is also a form of violence and an obstacle in the way of progress. People are mutually dependent on one another, and no one could be sacrificed for the good of the rest. Everyone has to recognize this interdependence and act accordingly.

Gandhi's politics was revolutionary in nature. He presented the vision of an alternative society based on non-violence, mutual respect, harmony, and dialogues. He also shows that we can pursue dialogue in a constructive way if we concentrate on the means rather than ends. According to him, if we take care of the means, the end will take care of itself. He argues that "Ahimsa and truth are so intertwined that it is practically impossible to disentangle and separate them. They are like two sides of a coin, or rather of a smooth unstamped metallic disc. Who can say which the obverse is and which is the reverse? Nevertheless, ahimsa is the means and truth is the end. Means to be means must always be within our reach, and so ahimsa becomes our supreme duty and truth becomes god for us. If we take care of the means, we are bound to reach the end sooner or later"[3].it is important to remember his well known observation on ends and means in *Hind Swaraj*. In his words, "the means may be likened to a seed, the end to a tree; and there is just the same inviolable connection between the means and the end as there is between the seed and the tree"[4].

Non-violence is equivalent to Love

For Gandhi non-violence was "the largest love, the greatest charity" this interpretation of non-violence as love naturally widens the meaning of non-violence. That is why Gandhi said "if I am a follower of ahimsa, I must love my enemy"[5]. One cannot limit Gandhi's non-violenceto mere non-killing as it would be a negative interpretation of his vision. The desire not to harm anyone is important but the intention behind action must be taken into account as well. A robber with a knife stabbing an innocent man is indulging in violence, but a surgeon using a knife on a patient is not committing any act violence. On the contrary it is an act of service and love to save a patient's life. Thus positive concept of non-violence includes promotion of well-being of others. Gandhi firmly believed that "love is a rare herb that makes a friend even of a sworn enemy and this herb grows out of non-violence ...love destroys ill will"[6]. Love is the ethics of caring. It is a powerful force which generates the empathetic understanding of the sufferings of others and extends help to overcome them. It is total and not a fragmented concept.

It brings people together and changes one's behaviour, attitude, and relationships. It enables people to understand each other better and live together peacefully.

Non-violence is a principle of life

For Gandhi, the pursuit of non-violence is a way of life wherein constant self-examination and rigorous discipline are required. It demands the existence of virtues like humility, sincerity and selfless service to others. Non-violence is not just an ideal but something like a scientific instrument that can be, and has to be, applied in life. Non-violence is not like a garment to be put on and off at one's own will. Its seat is in the human heart, and as such it must be an inspiration part of our very being.

Gandhi lived his life experimenting with truth. So whatever came across in his path got connected with him and had to go through the prism of his experience. In the process his ideas and work became inseparable from his life. Hence his words 'my life is my message' still remain relevant. For him non-violence and truth are the guiding principles of life and the fusion of non-violence and Truth is crucial. Violence leads to more violence, falsehood and helplessness; whereas non-violence leads to more non-violence, Truth and strength. Non-violence is the first article of Gandhi's faith and the last article of his creed. The violent person is at war with the world, and feels that the world is at war with him, whereas the no-violent person is at peace with himself and the world. The latter can therefore make difference, as he enjoys freedom and generates the capacity to change.

Gandhi's method of Satyagraha was the exercise of the purest soul-force against injustice and oppression at all levels. It relied on truth, non-violence, value of suffering, faith in human goodness and fearlessness. For Gandhi it was not just a political weapon but a way of life. He kept on sharpening his focus on Satyagraha and innovated various techniques to cope with different situations. It is a method of conversion, based on non-violence and love. For him "Satyagraha is a process of educating public opinion, such that it covers all the elements of society and in the end makes itself irresistible. Violence interrupts the process and prolongs the real revolution of the whole social structure"[7].

Non-violence at the Practical form of life

Gandhi was aware of the fact that complete adherence to Non-violence is almost impossible. The very process of living involves certain amount of violence, no matter how little it may be. What we have to do is to minimize it to the greatest extent possible. In his own words, violence is needed for the protection of things external; non-violence is needed for the protection of the Atman, for the protection of one's honour"[8]. Therefore, he rejected the view that all killing was violence, his approval of killing of the suffering calf, frightening away the monkeys interfering with the crops in the ashram, loss of jobs for the British workers in Lancashire and serving to meat-eaters like Maulana Azad and Louis Fischer, and his approach to Hitler's rule and the suffering of the Jews bring out the complexities of the issue. "In an interview with Louis Fischer discussing the likely peasant movements in independent India, Gandhi did not rule out temporary violence. Thus, while all violence was bad and must be condemned, it was important to distinguish between its different forms and contexts"[9]. For Gandhi, oppression of the weak, attacking the self-respect of the oppressed and willful insult of the powerless are also forms of violence.

Gandhi's basic argument is that non-violence is the most preferable way and violence alternatives are certainly inferior. As Terchek points out, "Gandhi provides us with a critique of violence and offers a sustained theory of non-violence to resolve conflicts. For him, violence denies the integrity of persons and destroys the possibility of individuals, with their different conceptions of the truth, living together freely and peacefully. Gandhian non-violence is a form of power that challenges gamut of injustices and brutalities that inhabit the world and, he believes, is far superior to violence."[10]

Throughout his life, Gandhi propagated the message and the practice of non-violence. His practice of non-violence was a conscious effort of translating his ideas into life. As he rightly points out, "I have been practicing with scientific precision non-violence and its possibilities for an unbroken period of over fifty years. I have applied it in every walk of life, domestic, institutional, economic and political. I know of no single case in which it has failed. Where it has seemed to have failed, I have ascribed it to my imperfections. I claim no perfection for myself. But I do claim to be a passionate seeker after Truth, Which is but another name for God. In the course of that search, the discovery of non-violence came to me. Its spread is my life-mission"[11].according to him life is to be guided not by violence, coercion of fear but voluntary acceptance of duties, co-operation and compassion.

Though Gandhi had acquired unprecedented success, yet towards the end of his life there were unprecedented challenges arising out of partition of the country and communal violence. The brutal violence erupting on the partition of the country was a rude shock to him. He admitted with pain on July 17, 1947 that, "it is true that I had believed that our Satyagraha struggles were based on non-violence. Only lately I realized that it was not true. I admit my mistake"[12]. Nevertheless, he retained till the end of his life the unflinching faith in the efficacy of non-violence.

Gandhi's Non-violence is of vital importance for democracy. According to him, under democracy "the weaker should have the same opportunity as the strongest. That can never happen except through non-violence"[13]. For Gandhi "democracy is the rule of unadulterated non-violence"[14]. Non-violence natured the civil society by encouraging changes required for democratic norms. No democracy can survive without the freedom to express one's views freely without fear or freedom to practice one's faith, or equality in the eyes of the law. Gandhi recognizes the importance of these important principles, and therefore, insists on non-violence. Gandhi's moral and political message is that non-violence cannot just be a personal virtue; it must be a civil virtue. Gandhi encourages us to think as human beings and citizens.

Gandhi's non-violence is of vital importance for Indian democracy. Dipankar Gupta points out that Gandhi's non-violence reaches out to a high intellectual plane, for it presumes that only when one loses a rational argument that violence becomes a tempting option. This is the bedrock of the democratic temperament that Gandhi helped firm up. Without the freedom to practice one's faith, or the unbending equality in the eyes of the law, or the fundamental right to express one's views freely and without fear, no democracy can hope for political longevity. These foundational structures of our polity owe everything to Gandhi and to his insistence on non-violence. Gandhi's non-violence was a public ethics. It was about political conduct. By keeping guns and others blunt instruments out of purview, Gandhi privileged rational debate to win a point. No other Indian leader before or after him has hammered away at this basic political modality with as much unwavering commitment as Gandhi did. Gandhi's non-violence allowed the public discussion of issues that were vexing Indians on a national scale. It is through the medium of Gandhi that Indians could publicly discuss the relationship between communities, the place of women in public life and the interface between faiths. It is not as if a consensus was arrived at on any of these. But the fact that we could now talk about them helped us frame the basic rules of our nation-state. Gandhi helped us think as citizens and that is what democracy is all about.

Gandhi is important today, because there is revolutionary element in him. J.B. Kriplani brings this to surface when he points out that Gandhi set old ideas before people: and he transformed old ideas into revolutionary. Mahatma's non-violence method was much more revolutionary than the bomb, because it was in harmony with the demand of the age. The way of the bomb lacked appeal, so it could not make people free of fear. His non-violent method proved more effective than bomb method [15].

Gandhi's work has inspired and will continue to inspire persons and societies to work for peace and justice. Leaders like Martin Luther King, Nelson Mandela, Dalai Lama and Aung San Suu Kyi proudly acknowledge Gandhi's contribution. Gandhi's vision has helped movements that toppled dictators like Ferdinand Marcos in the Philippines, Augusto Pinochet in Chile and the communist dictatorships in Eastern Europe. Movements for environment, alternative science and technology, eco-feminism, human rights, exploitation, resistance to nuclear programme all have directly or indirectly, knowingly or unknowingly drawn inspiration from Gandhi. In the world torn by strife and lured by violence, Gandhi continues to be a luminous ray of light. The United Nations has accepted that mahatma's legacy of non-violence is of crucial importance to the world and has declared 2nd October (Mahatma's birth day) as the international Day of non-violence in 2008. It is not necessary that non-violence struggles always yield immediate success. The path of this journey is slow and painful. Non-violence is difficult, but not impossible to practice. A comparison of 323 non-violence and violent resistance campaigns from 1900 to 2006 shows that non-violence resistance methods are likely to be more success 53 percent of the time, compared with 26 percent for the violence resistance campaigns [16].

Gandhi had realized early in his political life that violence pauses a formidable challenge. His well-articulated arguments against violence are found in his seminal work *Hind Swaraj*, written on the return Voyaga from London to Cape Town in South Africa (November13 to22, 1909) on board of the Kildonam castle. Non-violence, according to Gandhi, has its source in soul-force and violence in body-force. He uses a number ofterms to describe the qualities of soul-force; love-force, truth-force, compassion-force, suffering-force, and justice-force. The soul is able to exercise these forces natural to it only when the mind is able to exercise control over itself and the passions. Ultimately then, the success of the ethics of non-violence depends on the state of the soul, the mind and the passions in one word, on self-rule[17]. Mark Juergensmeyer elaborates that the guidelines given by Gandhi in response to the terrorism of the Indian activists in London in 1900 may be applied to the current situation. They are: stop a situation of violence in its tracks, address the issues leading to violence, and maintain the moral high ground. What is important is the fact that a non-violent response to terrorism is already an element of political discourse. It is not a new idea, but rather a strand of public thinking that deserves attention and, Gandhi might argue, respect[18].it is time the world realizes that the alternatives to coercion, violence, distrust and chaos is restoration of peace, faith and trust.

CONCLUSION

Gandhi's teachings and practice of non-violence can help people to find their way in the contemporary tangle of violence and hatred. Gandhi's legacy is of paramount importance today, because Gandhi challenges efficiency and legitimacy of violence. His non-violence is a form of power that challenges the injustice and brutalities around us. His struggles were against injustice and oppression prevalent in the society and those of the state. He challenges us to think of what can be done in contemporary times in the areas stretching from personal to political. This task is not that easy. He himself had written, "For infallible guidance, man has to have a perfectly innocent heart incapable of evil. I can lay no such claim. Mine is a struggling, striving, erring, imperfect soul"[19]. This struggling, striving and powerful soul of Gandhi is urging us to strive for higher goals. Gandhi makes us rethink about the entire gamut of the issue of violence around us. His soul searching queries make us uncomfortable, prompting us to question the injustice and inequality prevailing in our society. It is now time to listen to his voice and tune it to our inner voice and start acting.

BIBLIOGRAPHY

1. *Young India*, August 11, 1920.
2. Ibid, January 21, 1926.
3. Latter to Narandas Gandhi, July 31, 1930 in M.K. Gandhi, *The Collective Works of Mahatma Gandhi* (New Delhi: The Publications Division, Ministry of Information and Broadcasting, Government of India, 1971), Vol. XLIV, p.59.
4. Anthony j. Parel, ed., *Hind Swaraj and Other Writings* (Cambridge: Cambridge University Press, 1997), P.81.
5. *The Collective Works of Mahatma Gandhi*, op.cit. Vol. XIII, 1964, P.295.
6. Ibid., Vol.XIV, 1965, p.299.
7. *Harijan*, March 31, 1946.
8. Ibid, September 1, 1940.
9. Bhikhu Parekh, *Colonialism, Tradition and Reform: An Analysis of Gandhi's Political discours*e (New Delhi: Sage Publications, 1999), pp.134-154.
10. Ronald J.Terckek, *Gandhi: Non-violence and Violence*, Journal of power and Ethics, Vol.2, Issue No.3, 2001, pp. 213-242.
11. *The Collective Works of Mahatma Gandhi*, op.cit. Vol. LXXXVIII, 1938, P.356.
12. *Harijan*, May 18, 1940.
13. Ibid, October 13, 1940.
14. Dipankar Gupta, *The Spine That hold Us Up, Hindustan Times*, October 13, 2006.
15. Gopal Krisna Gandhi ed, *Gandhi is Gone. Who will Guide Us Now?* (Ranikhet: Permanent Black, 2007) pp. 91-92.
16. Harijan, November 30, 1939.
17. Anthony J. Parel, ed, *Hind Swaraj and Other Writings*, op,cit., p. lVi.
18. Mark Juergensmeyer, *Gandhism vs Terrorism, Daedalus*, Winter, 2007, pp.38-39.
19. Young India, September 25, 1924.

Chapter-6

Gandhian Hiosophy in Conflict Management and Education for Peace

Dr. Rashmi Rekha Devi

"The man was greater than his deeds; and he is relevant for all times and climes".

The human race is at the crossroads. Advancement in science and technology has undoubtedly and amazingly reduced geographical distances but the distances between hearts have widened. Today's time is troubled with inhumanity, violence and corruption. The financial and economic system has brought the challenges of disparity, injustice, corruption and exploitation. This has lead to great social unrest and disharmony on a global scale. This leads to loss of peace of mind. If individuals are taught how to master their minds and be in a 'balanced state', the 'collective' human mind will also be stable and tranquil. What is required is "Spiritual Revolution/ renaissance". When individuals are at peace, there will be peace and harmony in household, in society, the nation and in the world. It fills people with enthusiasm and inspires them to move forward. Education for Peace is essential to establish world peace in order to create a happy global community. Gandhian philosophy contributes in a constructive and positive way in implementing the curriculum of Education for peace.

The Gandhian thought of peace is worldwide acknowledged. The name of Gandhi is synonyms with peace & non-violence. That is why United Nation announced World Peace Day on 2nd October, the birth date of Mahatma Gandhi. The contribution of Gandhi to the humanity is incomparable.

EDUCATION AND PEACE

Before elaborating on the Gandhian notion of peace education, we need to locate what peace education broadly means. Peace education can be understood as education for facilitating peace. According to Page (2008), "a fundamental concern of peace education is education to prevent the suffering and wastage of warfare within the modern era" (Page, 2008: 2). According to Peace Education Working Group at UNICEF, peace education "refers to the process of promoting the knowledge, skills, attitudes and values .... to prevent conflict and violence."

For Gandhi, peace can be located in "his revolutionary mode of action which he called *satyagraha*, and his challenging goal of *sarvodaya*, meaning the welfare and good of all, a fuller and richer concept of people's democracy than any we have yet known"(Bose, 1981: 159). Peace to Gandhi is primarily located in his idea of *Ahimsa* i.e. non-violence.

QUOTES FROM THE ORIGINAL TEXT

Before turning to Gandhi's analysis of peace education, it is important to focus on original text written by Gandhi and his view points on specific issues related to Conflict management and Peace Education.

THE NEED FOR RELIGION: (RELIGION)

No man can live without religion. *Young India, 23-1-'30* For me moral, ethics and religion are covertible terms. A moral life without reference to religion is like a house built upon sand. And religion divorced from morality is like 'sounding brass' good only for making a noise and breaking heads. Morality includes truth, *ahimsa* and continent. Every virtue that mankind has ever practiced is preferable to and derived from these three fundamental virtues. Non-violence and continence are again derivable from Truth, which for me is God. *Harijan, 3-10-'36*

THE NEED FOR CHARACTER: (CHARACTER)

The end of all knowledge must be building up of character. *Young India, 8-9-'2*

Truth will make you brave and fearless men, able to give a good account of yourselves, wherever you go. Love will make life bearable for you, because love has a special quality of abundance of love in return.
with Gandhiji in Ceylon, p.150

TERRORISM: (VIOLENCE AND ANARCHY)

I honour the anarchist for his love of the country: I honour him for his bravery in being willing to die for his country: but I ask him: 'is killing honourable? Is the dagger of an assassin a fit precursor of an honourable death?' I deny it. There is no warrant for such methods in any scriptures.
Speeches and writings of Mahatma Gandhi

PRAYER: (RELIGION)

Prayer is either petition or in its wider sense is inward communication. In either case the ultimate result is the same. Petition should be for the cleaning and purification of the soul, for freeing it from the layers of ignorance and darkness that envelop it. He therefore who hungers for the awakening of the divine in him must fall back on prayer. Prayer is no mere exercise of words or of the ears, it is no mere repetition of empty formula. It is better in prayer to have a heart without words than words without a heart.
Young India, 23-1-'30

MANUAL LABOUR: (RESPECT FOR MANUAL LABOUR)

You may ask: 'why should we use our hands? and say 'the manual work has got to be done by those who are illiterate. I can only occupy myself with reading literature and political essays. 'I think we have to realize the dignity of labour. If a barber or shoemaker attends a college, he ought not to abandon the profession, of a barber or shoemaker. I consider that a barber's profession is just as good as the profession of medicine.
Speeches and writings of Mahatma Gandhi, pp.388-389, 16-2-'16

A microscopic view of the original text as written by Gandhiji helps us to analyse Gandhian view point on peace education. The idea of *sarvadharma samabhava* i.e. equality of religions as espoused by Gandhi is an effective tool to counter the increasing tensions among different religious groups. *According to Gandhi, "a* curriculum of religious instruction should include a study of the tenets of faiths other than one's own. For this purpose, the students should be trained to cultivate the habit of understanding and appreciating the doctrines of various great religions of the world in a spirit of reverence and broad-minded tolerance. Love and faith can help to reduce the problem of hatred and intolerance in the world."

GANDHIAN PHILOSOPHY AND CHARACTERISTICS OF LOVE

Mahatma Gandhi was a great architect of Peace. Gandhiji said that "Love is reckless in giving away oblivious to what it gets in return... It gives because it must, it is its characteristics. It does not calculate whether there is corresponding gain...Love is its own reward, love has no boundary. It is going out of oneself to the other irrespective of whether the other is friend or foe. It is not mere friendship and good will but a readiness to sacrifice oneself, even for one's enemies. Good will towards a friend is mere 'amity' of mutual affection, where love means friendly feeling even for the enemy. Love thus understood include all, gives all, does not count the cost and expects nothing in return.

Faith

Gandhiji mentioned that faith is beyond reason and it begins where the reason fails. Faith does not contradict reason but transcends it. Faith is based on experience. Faith helps to cultivate inner knowledge, Self knowledge, worldly knowledge, and thus leads to inner purity. Faith is not a thing to grasp, it is state to grow and growth comes from within. The cumulative experience of holy men of all times it the guiding star for humanity. So, teaching Gandhian sphilosophy should be a part of peace education curriculum.

Research work on Gandhian philosophy and education for peace

In some of the recent studies, scholars have tried to contextualize and place the emergence of Gandhian Studies within the framework of education for peace. Field (2006: 231) underlines that "nonviolence education or Gandhian Studies emphasizes positive concepts of peace (rather than peace as absence of strife)." Monisha Bajaj (2010: 47-63) in her study argues that "social and collective action towards peace also appears more frequently in Gandhian studies perhaps because of the focus on structural and cultural forms of violence" (Bajaj, 2010:

54). Similarly, Tint and Prasad (2007: 23-37) have also observed that "there are several programs in Gandhian thought and peace studies, which inform the studies on nonviolence" (2007: 27). Thus, Gandhi emphasized on value education as it is necessary for moral development of individual whereas peace education is vital for human being as a whole.

University of Peace

The **University for Peace (UPEACE)** is an intergovernmental organization with university status, established by treaty in 1980 and having its main campus in Costa Rica. It's stated mission is "to provide humanity with an international institution of higher education for peace with the aim of promoting among all human beings the spirit of understanding, tolerance and peaceful coexistence".

India has been the Master to the rest of the world. Therefore India has the capacity and the caliber to produce peace loving generations through education for peace by giving it a place in education curriculum. Proposal of University of Peace sent by the government of India to UNESCO is a milestone in the way to peace. India, the largest democracy in the world, is a party to the International Agreement Establishing the University for Peace, and is a key factor in global efforts for maintenance of international peace and security, including significant contributions through peacekeeping forces. Banaras Hindu University and the Jawaharlal Nehru University, has taken initiative to partner with Indian educational institutions to establish Joint/Dual master's degree programmes in face-to-face and online formats on contemporary issues of global significance. In India Madhya Pradesh became the first State in the country to set up a Happiness Department, with an aim to.ensure "happiness in the lives of common people". The idea of having such a department has been adopted from Bhutan which has "Happiness Index" to measure happiness of its people. In the same way Education for Peace is not a need of the time but a necessity. Having *Ahimsa* as the nuclei special courses related to peace education should be included in all syllabi and peace education should be imparted at all levels of studies, from primary to higher level.

According to latest research India stands on 122 rank in happiness Index (UNESCO, 21st March. 2017) Our Neighbouring countries Bangladesh, Pakistan and China stand in higher rank than India. Norway stand first as the happiest country in the world. This kind of research shows where we stand in the parameter of Happiness in the map of the world. There is great need of Gandhian Philosophy in promoting peace and happiness in India.

Connect to Gandhian philosophy through activities for creating peace among children

Peace education has become a part of school curriculum. Inclusion of Gandhian philosophy in school activities will help to promote peace in young minds. Apart from teaching Gandhian philosophy as a part of text books, teachers can arrange different activities. These peace promoting ideas and activities cover a flexible range of topics and commitment levels from the practically effortless, to the simply practical, to the powerfully proactive.

1. Ask children to collect references to peace and brotherhood in their religious scriptures.
2. Use of audio visual on the life of great Indian philosophers in the form of film and documentary.
3. Ask them to collect inspirational stories, oral and written about peaceful resolution of a real life conflict.
4. Motivate children to do social services on 2nd October as homage to Gandhiji.
5. Arrange a guest talk by a retired army man who has seen death in the battle to come and tell how there is no glory in War.

CONCLUSION

Gandhi gained first hand experiences in three continents –Europe, Africa and Asia. A man who has seen people and the world very closely, only he can have the insight to solve Conflict and violence. He was a peculiar mixture of the oriental and the occidental, and of the ancient and the modern. His life was a series of experiments with truth. He was making experiments with his own personal life and at the same time, with all aspects of the society-political, economic and social. He worked essentially for the salvation of his country and for the people at large. Gandhian model of conflict resolution has been considerable potential to resolve conflict, where non –violence and Satyagraha play an important role. He believed that peace in the world was possible only through non violence.

BIBLIOGRAPHY

1. Bilgrami, Akeel. (2003). "Gandhi, the Philosopher", *Economic and Political Weekly*, September 27, 4159-4165.
2. Bose, Anima. (1981). "A Gandhian Perspective on Peace", *Journal of Peace Research*, XVIII(2): 159-164.
3. Parekh, Bhikhu. (1997). *Gandhi: A Brief Insight*. Sterling Publication Co. Inc.: New York.
4. Page, James. (2008). *Peace Education: Exploring Ethical and Philosophical Foundations*. Information Age Publishing Inc.: USA
5. Harris, Ian M. and Mary Lee Morrison. (2003). *Peace Education*. McFarland & Company, Inc., Publishers: North Carolina, USA.
6. Peace Education in UNICEF. Susan Fountain. [Online] Available at: http://www.unicef.org/education/files/PeaceEducation.pdf
7. Hague Appeal for Peace [Online] Available at: http://www.haguepeace.org/
8. Gandhi's Views On Education: Buniyadi Shiksha [Basic Education] http://www.gandhi-manibhavan.org/gandhiphilosophy/philosophy_education_%20buniyadishiksha.htm
9. Gandhi, M.K. (1971). *My Views on Education*. Navjivan Trust, Ahmedabad
10. Gandhi, M.K. (1953). *To Students*. Navjivan Trust, Ahmedabad
11. Gandhi, M.K. (1953). *Towards New Education*. Navjivan Trust, Ahmedabad
12. Sinha, Ram Kripal,(2011). *M.K.Gandhi: Sources, Ideas and Action*. Ocean Books Pvt. Ltd.New Delhi.

Chapte-7

Gandhian Views on Peace Education

Ms. Manjeet Kumari

INTRODUCTION

The world has been changed into a global village. Globalization is having a major impact not only on the economic world but also on the whole humanity. Global recession, Global warming, climate change, poverty, conflict and violence are challenges that have dominated in present era. We have built a society, which is violent & explosive. We are living in extremely explosive times where the context of human life is changing every moment. Human values are destroying at a very fast rate resulting in a decline in the quality of life of the people. At present 'Peace & Values Education for Peace building' is required for saving the world. According to Gandhi value education is necessary for moral development as well as social development of individual whereas peace education is vital for humankind as a whole. Peace involves the development of a society in which, except for the absence of direct violence, there is no structural violence or social injustice.

Gandhi ji is more known in the domain of politics and social reform than in the field of education. Yet he is one of the greatest teachers of mankind for all times to come- a prophet of its spiritual regeneration.' We believe that one of the most valuable legacies that he has left to prosperity is his educational teachings crystallized in the basic scheme of education and in his diverse addresses. It is also necessary to understand the theory behind it, the philosophy that inspired it.

Mohan das karam Chand Gandhi, popularly known as Bapu, out of the affection and reverence by the people, Mahatma', on account of his saintly nature and father of the nation' for the regeneration of the country., free from British rule was a great educator, a nation builder, a social worker etc. He took up cases which ultimately touched the life of the common man. He was born on October 2, 1869 at Porbander in Gujrat. His father was a Diwan of a small state. He was married to kasturba at the age of thirteen. His mother was very pious and greatly influenced by her. He got his degree from London. When he came back in India he served the country.

Peace Education

The highest form of aims for any education is inculcating peace and it is an essential value to be cherished by every individual. Parents are the first teacher to their children and peace education is nurtured in the family. The peace is nurtured again at school. Peace education is the process of obtaining the values, the knowledge and growing the attitudes, skills, and behaviors to live in harmony with ones surrounding. Peace is a broad concept with practical and spiritual designations. It can indicate a state of inner calm or end of conflict. "Peace is what you think it is." Peace can be understand as the absence of conflict or violence and conversely as the presence of states of mind and of society such as harmony, accord, security and understanding. Peace education is a planning technique of eliminating the conflicts and violence caused by in justice, inequality and human rights, violations. Peace education is also helpful in reducing the same through appropriate teaching and learning techniques. Therefore peace education is an ultimate goal of education.

Definition of the Peace Education

There is no universally accepted definition for Peace Education. There is good number of definitions available on the basis of different perceptions and approaches. Some of the definitions given by eminent educationists are given below:

- Webster defines peace "as a state of quiet or tranquility, freedom from disturbance or agitation, calm repose". From the above definition it can be said that in the absence of elements such as tolerance, understanding, empathy, cooperation and respect for the difference in others, there cannot be peace.
- Albert Einstein defines the peace "Peace is not merely the absence of war but the presence of justice, of law, of order – in short, of government.

- According to Freire (2006) "Peace education is a mechanism for the transformation from a culture of violence to a culture of peace through a process of "conscientisation".
- According to John Dewey "Peace education is grounded in active citizenship, preparing learners for assiduous participation in a democracy, through problem – posing and problem – solving education, and a commitment to transformative action in our societies."

From these definitions it is understood that the peace education includes itself the higher order human values among the individuals. Further, "Peace education definitions" reveals that it aims at the overall development of the individuals and helps to enhance eternal values in their minds.

According to Gandhiji: - Education

Education as Service to Humanity: Mahatma Gandhi believes that the "True education lies in serving others, oblige them without the least feeling of one-uppishness. The more mature you grow, the more you will realise this. A great deal of religious obligations on us is fulfilled when we nurse the sick". Letter to Ramdas Gandhi (The Making of the Mahatma, p. 97)

Real education has to draw out the best from the boys and girls to be educated. This can never be done by packing ill-assorted and unwanted information into the heads of the students. It becomes a dead weight crushing all originality in them and turning them into mere automata (Harijan December 1, 1993).

By education I mean an all round drawing out of the best in the child and man- body, mind and soul (Harijan, July 31, 1937).

Gandhiji's Philosophy of Peace

"Ahimsa" or non-violence which is law of love is the most fundamental principle of his philosophy of peace. According to Gandhi the universal human value of Ahimsa ought to be nurtured not merely at personal level, but at social, national and international level too if we wish to line in a healthy society. For this aim we should avoid personal, social, national and international conflicts. Non violence is a very effective means to avoid conflict, since it comes from inner realization of the equality of all human beings.

In negative sense it is stage of absent mental intention of injuring, harming, disturbing and agonizing opponent, and as well as positively it is good will towards all human beings. As a peaceful technique to resist injustice, it includes a concrete scheme and leads to self-suffering and sacrifice.

For Gandhi the last step to oppose injustice is "Fasting unto death". Gandhi's approach is ethical, as he believes, that moral degeneration is the root cause of all social evils and problems including conflicts · So he recommends acquisition of moral value such as truthfulness, non-violence or love, self-control, forgiveness, non-enmity or friendliness, compassion, mercy etc. In fact values are the best means discovered by human being to avoid various types of conflict. Undoubtedly conflicts are nothing but the illustration of the violation of moral laws, non performance of duties, negligence of human values, and enjoyment of freedom without caring for responsibility etc.

Hence Gandhi recognize the full worth of moral solution, which is not very costly, and single person can initiate and undertake the task of conflict resolution by attracting worldwide attention. Gandhi, a great political thinker, therefore, he recommended that politics should be a branch of ethics· Moral principles must be followed by politicians, ideologues, social activists as well as ordinary citizen of the world as there is no dividing line between private and public life.

Mahatma Gandhi and Satyagraha

"Satyagraha" was proposed and adopted by Gandhiji as a moral equivalent to war and conflict. As we all know the successful conduct of war involves two things. On the one hand, suppression of the virtues of kindness, friendliness, forgiveness and consideration for the sufferings of fellow human beings, and on the other, encouragement of the feelings of unqualified hatred, anger and hostility towards so called enemies. Thus war leads to total violation of the liberal democratic principles of respect for persons and dignity of the individual. On the contrary, satyagrahi while resisting injustice shows respect for his opponent by making moral appeals to him and expecting him to be responsive. Satyagrahi aims at conversion of the opponent's heart by making him aware of his ill will or in human behavior through self- suffering. Satyagraha aims at winning over opponent by love and gentle persuading and by arousing in him a sense of justice rather than forcing him to surrender out of fear.

The method of Satyagraha is purely moral and humanistic as it involves faith in the inherent goodness and good sense of the opponent coupled with goodwill towards him and readiness to come to an understanding and compromise. In fact Satyagraha aims at settlement of issue or issues with the opponent without causing him even psychological injury but it implies soul - force, courage and determination. A well-conducted Campaign of Satyagraha absolutely untouched by violence in word and deed, made the hypocritical opponent suffer from split personality as his own moral consciousness getting alarmed by the exposure of the immorality of his action. Gandhi believed in the technique of Satyagraha, because he had faith in the goodness of human nature.

Satyagraha as Method of Re solving Conflict

The moral and humanistic grandeur of satyagraha as method of resolving conflict and securing justice has been appreciated by several thinkers, politicians and social workers. Conflict cannot take place if we behave on Gandhian maxim that humanity (rational beings) should always be treated as an end-in-itself. If we wish to keep peace, we ought to follow the UN charter of human rights, according to which dignity of human life must be honoured and maintained without reference to caste, colour, creed etc. We have to redefine the concept of Development and Progress as Human Welfare and well-being by replacing the prevalent misleading concept of development and progress in terms of Economic Development and material progress. If we want peace, we have to replace the humanity negating industrial consumerist culture by idealistic humanism.

Belief in the spiritual constitution of man led Gandhi to affirm equality of all human beings and to declare innate goodness of men. Humanism as the philosophy of Globalism or Global philosophy implies non-discrimination with regard to race, sex language, region, religion, political ideology, social and economic status, international status of the country etc.,since the basic structure and nature of human beings all over' the world is same. We must rationalise our ways of thinking and to think of the world in terms of maps and markets, we should think of it in terms of men, women and children i.e. in terms of mankind.

Non-Violence

Total non-violence consists in not hurting some other one's intellect, speech or action per own thought, utterance or deeds and not to deprive some one of his life. In essence, abstinence in to from violence is non violence. In this context Gandhi clarified in an edition of young India. "To hurt someone, to think of some evil unto someone or to snatch one's life under anger or selfishness, is violence. In contrast, purest non-violence is an epitome in having a tendency and presuming towards spiritual or physical benefit unto everyone without selfishness and with pure thought after cool and clear deliberations. The ultimate yardstick of violence or non-violence is the spirit behind the action".

Non-Violence as the strongest weapon

It is not a weapon of the weak. It has no place for cowardice. It is an active force. Non-violence is impossible without bravery /courage/ fearlessness. Doing at any cost something that one ought to do. The courage of dying without killing having decided upon the rightness of a situation, Gandhi would not like one to be passive spectator to evil. This is the essence of Non-Alignment which is different from neutrality. When freedom is menaced or justice is threatened or where aggression takes place we cannot and shall not be neutral.

Sarva Dharma Sambhav

To avoid conflicts occurred by religious bigotry, Gandhi suggested "Sarva Dharma Sambhav". According to him all religions are equal and true. Man cannot survive without religion so he recommends attitude of respect and tolerance towards all religions. Since the scientific and technological researches aimed at material comforts are ruining human sensitivity and sentiments i.e. human feelings and relations. They should not invent biological, chemical, nuclear, laser and other kinds of sophisticated weapons, which verifies the assumption that science and technology one frequently used as instruments of exploitation, domination and destruction rather than as means in the service of mankind and peace.

Ideological extremism is also a cause of violent confrontation, as it makes the ideologues incapable of dialogue and negotiation while confrontational determination to counter force by force must be replaced by a policy of dialogues and negotiations. Democracy facilitates such policy, so Gandhi suggested the democratic way of governance and life. We can say that Gandhi has been the champion not only of political democracy but also of economic and spiritual democracy as he committed to the vedantic view of Unity-in-diversity and was a supporter of economic equality. Mutual trust and bilateral negotiations, preparedness to discuss the problem collectively with open mindedness, tendency to examine and change (if necessary) our own belief i.e. Flexibility is also required to avoid conflict.

Aims and objectives of Peace Education

Aims and objectives of Peace Education are as follows:-

- To understand the global problems.
- Peace education should have the skills to resolve Conflict and problems in a better way.
- Know and live according by international standards of Human rights, gender and racial equality.
- To appreciate and accept cultural diversity of the society and world.
- Respect the integrity of the earth.
- To encourage the sense of universal brotherhood and values in every individual.
- To develop the sense of responsibility in every individual.
- To educate the individual and develop the ability to recognize and accept the values which exist in the diversity of individuals.
- To strengthen peace, friendship and solidarity between individuals and people.
- To develop the sense of non-violent conflict – resolution among the individuals.
- To teach and encourage the citizens to respect the cultural heritage, protect the environment and social harmony.

CONCLUSION

Mahatma Gandhi can serve as a valuable activator allowing us to rethink our philosophical thinking and positions on violence, nonviolence, and education. Especially insightful are Gandhi's formulations of the multidimensionality of violence, including educational violence, and the violence of the status quo. His peace education offers many ways for dealing with short-term violence, but its greatest strength is its long-term preventative education and socialization. Key to Gandhi's peace education are his ethical and ontological formulations of means-ends relations; the need to uncover root causes and causal determinants and to free oneself from entrapment in escalating cycles of violence; and the dynamic complex relation between relative and absolute truth that includes analysis of situated embodied consciousness, tolerant diversity and inclusiveness, and an approach to unavoidable violence. Peace education is a diverse field that includes the theoretical, research, and practical activities of experts from many disciplines assembled in a number of professional and research associations. For the establishment of culture of peace, it is necessary to accept the principles of uniqueness in diversity and to establish the social norms of respect, dignity, and the rights of every individual.

BIBLIOGRAPHY

1. Allen, Douglas. (2007). "Mahatma Gandhi on Violence and Peace Education", *Philosophy East and West*, July, 57(3): 290-310.
2. Bose, Anima. (1981). "A Gandhian Perspective on Peace", *Journal of Peace Research*, XVIII(2),159-164.
3. Boulding, E. (2000). *Cultures of peace. The hidden side of history*. New York: Syracuse University Press. pp. 89-106.
4. Gandhi, M.K. (1971). *My Views on Education*. Navjivan Trust, Ahmedabad.
5. Groff, Linda & Smoker, Paul (1996). Creating Global/Local Cultures of Peace. In UNESCO (Ed.) *From a Culture of Violence to a Culture of Peace*. 103-127.
6. Hicks, David, Edi, (1988), Education for Peace, New York : Routledge.
7. Page, J.S. (2010). 'Peace Education'. In: E. Baker, B. McGaw, and P. Peterson (eds.) *International Encyclopedia of Education*. Vol 1. 850–854.

Chapter-8

Role of Education in Promotion of Human Rights

Ms. Goldy Gupta

INTRODUCTION

All human beings are born free and equal in dignity and rights. People are different, and so their culture. There is variation in their languages, religions, civilisations, colours, traditions and customs. Despite of all these variations, there is one thing that is common in all; they all are human beings-nothing more, nothing less. However different their culture may be, all cultures adapt some common features like no culture allows violence, terror; human exploitation, torture, brutality etc. These common principles, which are shared by all civilisations, reflect fundamental human rights. In short, human rights are the rights inherent to all human beings, irrespective of their nation, location, sex, national or ethnic origin, caste, colour, religion, race, language, or any other status. All human beings are entitled to human rights equally without any discrimination. These are universal in nature so applicable everywhere and at every time. These are egalitarian too, in the sense of being the same for everyone. These rights are interrelated, guaranteed by law, in the forms of international law, general principles and other sources of international law. Human rights are those rights that pertain to legal rights.

According to UNESCO Publication Human Rights (1996), "Human beings are born equal in dignity and rights. These are moral claims which are inherent in all human individuals by virtue of their humanity alone. These claims are formulated in what we today call human rights. These have been translated into legal rights, established according to the new creating processes of societies, both national and international."

Universal Declaration of Human Rights

International human rights law lays down obligations of Governments to act in certain ways or to refrain from certain acts, in order to promote and protect human rights and fundamental freedoms of individuals of groups. Human rights are commonly understood as basic fundamental rights that a person cannot be denied by any individual or any government simply because he or she is a human being. They are universal and same for everyone. Human rights entail both right and obligation. Human rights developing from the concepts of natural lights became culminate with the thoughts of philosophers like John Locke, Francis Hutcheson and Jean-Jacques and became prominent with American Revolution and French Revolution. Most of the basic ideas and norms of human rights existing now adopted as Universal Declaration of Human Rights by United Nations General Assembly in 1948. Every year 10 December is celebrated as Human Rights Day.

The abbreviated version of the 30 articles of the Universal Declaration of Human Rights provides an overview of the main rights and freedom that every person's birthright. The first two articles are fundamental principles underlying all human rights. Article 3 to 21 consists of civil and political rights. Articles 22 to 27 refer to economic, social and cultural rights. Articles 28 to 30 provide a framework of solidarity safeguarding the universal enjoyment of all human rights .

Article 1	Right to freedom and equality in dignity and rights
Article 2	Freedom from discrimination
Article 3	Right to life, liberty and security of person
Article 4	Right to freedom from slavery and servitude
Article 5	Right to freedom from torture or degrading treatment
Article 6	Right to recognition as a person before the law
Article 7	Right to equal consideration before the law
Article8	Right to remedy through a competent tribunal
Article 9	Right to freedom from arbitrary arrest or exile
Article 10	Right to a fair trial or public hearing
Article 11	Right to be considered innocent until proven guilty
Article 12	Freedom from interference with privacy, including home, family and correspondence
Article 13	Right to freedom of movement and residence in one's own country and to leave and return at will

Article 14	Right to asylum
Article 15	Right to a nationality and freedom to change it
Article 16	Right to marriage and protection of family
Article 17	Right to own property
Article 18	Freedom of belief and religion
Article 19	Freedom of opinion and information
Article 20	Right to peaceful assembly and association
Article 21	Right to participate in government and in free elections and to equal access to public service
Article 22	Right to social security
Article 23	Right to work and fair pay for work
Article 24	Right to rest and leisure
Article 25	Right to adequate standard of living for health and well-being
Article 26	Right to education
Article 27	Right to participate in the cultural life of the community
Article 28	Right to social order assuring human rights
Article 29	Responsibility to community essential to free and full development of the Individual
Article 30	Right for protection of these rights from state or other interference.

The Universal Declaration of Human Rights covers all human rights in 30 clear and concise articles. Article 1 declares that all human beings are born equal in dignity and rights. While, article 2 declares the universal dignity of a life free from discrimination. The first cluster of Articles i.e. 3 to 21, sets forth civil and political rights to which everyone is entitled. The right to life, liberty and personal security in article 3, provides a base for all following political rights and civil liberties, including freedom from slavery, torture and the right to a fair speech and free movements. The second cluster of articles, 22to 27, sets forth the economic, social and cultural rights to which all human beings are entitled. Article 22, in it, clearly indicates that as a member of society, everyone has the right to social security and is therefore entitled to the realisation of the economic, social and cultural rights. The third cluster of articles, 28 to 30, provides a larger protective framework in which all human rights are to be universally enjoyed. Article 30, finally, protects the interpretation of the articles of the declaration from any outside interference contrary to the purposes and principles of the United Nations.

Characteristics of Human Rights

- **Universal:** Human rights are universal in nature. It means that these are right of all people at all times and in all situations. They are said to belong to all humans in every society.
- **Individual:** The concept of human rights is derived from the acceptance of men as free and equal in dignity and rights. Where the worth of individual is not recognised, there is no place of rights.
- **Inalienable:** Human rights are also supposed to be inalienable; because they flow from and protect human existence, they cannot be taken away without endangering the value of that existence.
- **Paramount:** It means that none can be deprived of human rights without a grave affront to justice. Human rights represent certain freedom which are sacred and which should never be invaded.
- **Practical:** It means the Human Rights are the claims which are not physically impossible to be realised. Moreover, these can be extended to the majority and should not be restricted to a minority.

These are enforceable in nature, otherwise, these never can reach to the all people. National commission on Human Rights have been set up to ensure their implementation.

Need and importance of Human RightsSource of Inspiration

The declaration of Human Rights serves as a great source of inspiration to the people especially who are oppressed and remained under colonial regimes.

Recognition of elements of Dignity and Equality

Many states and societies take several measures towards the fulfilment of this ideal.

Basic Need for Human Life

Human rights are basic need of an individual. It is necessary for the overall development of an individual. In the absence of it, a human being loses his identity as a human being in the true sense.

Inclusion in the Constitution

States include Human rights in their constitutions, keeping in view the significance of it.

Helpful in Human Welfare

The implementation of the human rights would result in happy, prosperous, healthy and contented life for many people.

Role of Education in promotion and protection of Human Rights

Education, itself, a tool for creating the real idea of human rights and making every people to know its importance in their daily life. It is also a tool for eliminating the violations of human rights. An educated civilization can only know its rights and hence have the knowledge to protect it. According to Kofi Annan, the former Secretary General of United Nations, "Without education, we cannot see beyond ourselves and our narrow surroundings to the reality of global interdependence. Without education, we cannot realize how people of other races and religions share the same dreams, the same hopes. Without education, we cannot recognize the universality of human aims and aspirations". UN mandates that education shall be directed to the strengthening of respect for human rights & fundamental freedom. It is important to make each and every people literate just not in order to make them educated and capable of earning but also recognize and aware about their rights towards themselves and each other. An educated person only can stand for its right.

The global task of promoting & protecting all human rights & fundamental freedoms so as to secure full & universal enjoyment of these rights cannot be fulfilled without mass awareness and sensitivity to human rights issues. The grand agenda of global peace & prosperity is possible only with people understanding & imbibing the human rights values. Peoples' participation is a must in resolving human rights conflicts. This matured participation can be a possibility only with human rights education. (Jayakumar, 2007). The General Assembly has defined Human Right Education as 'a life-long process by which people at all levels of development & in all strata of society learn respect for the dignity of others & the means & methods of ensuring that respect in all societies.

Human rights education is an education about the rights of human beings: rights of inherent, rights are indivisible, rights are inalienable, and rights are universal (Netragaonkar, 2011).

Human Right Education is about empowering the individual to both recognize human rights abuses and to commit to their prevention. Thus, a core part of Human Right Education is the strengthening of respect for human rights. It is now a global responsibility of every person and the government to promote education and hence promote human rights. Article 51A(1) of Indian Constitution 1950, imposes a duty on all citizens to develop scientific temper, humanism and the spirit of inquiry & reform. The effective discharge of this duty will require Human Right Education to give people enhanced awareness & greater openness. Right to Education has also been incorporated. The Constitution mandates the state to direct its policy towards securing that children are given opportunities and facilities to develop in a healthy manner and in conditions of freedom & dignity and that childhood and youth are protected against exploitation and against moral & material abandonment.

Human Right Education of the children as well as the other people is indispensable to the full realization of the responsibility under this constitutional directive. Indian state has an obligation to foster respect for international law and treaty obligations as laid down in Article 51 of the Constitution. Human Right Education is inescapable and a legal obligation in India. Human Rights is not treated as a separate subject in the curricula. NCERT has felt that all contemporary concerns & issues cannot be included in the curriculum as separate subjects of study. It has called upon incorporation of certain emerging concerns including human rights in the course content.

University Grants Commission appointed Sikri Committee in 1980 for reporting on the different ways and means for promoting Human Right Education in India. The committee suggested inculcation of values without marks weightage in schools. At college levels it was felt that all disciplines should be including human rights topics at least which are directly relevant to their disciplines. But, it is disappointing to observe that the NCF 2005 has failed in identifying the content of the Human Right Education in schools.

RTE 2009: A Human rights-based approach of education assures every child a quality education that respects and promotes her or his right to dignity and optimum development. The right to education is marked priority on the agenda of the international community since right to education is not only a human right in itself but also is essential for the exercise of all other human rights. A number of human rights treaties accepted and did development and social transformation. The right to education flows directly from the right to life. The right to life and the dignity of an individual cannot be assured unless it is accompanied by the right to education. Victims of injustice and violations of human rights will have no faith in justice and values. Right to education and Human Right Education will fall through. The government and the society should be prepared to foot the bill if concrete results are desired (Mahapatra, 2012).

Suggestion

- Human rights concepts of religious freedom and religious tolerance can be inculcated while teaching topics in history subject.
- Human rights concern about self determination can be introduced to students while teaching them colonialism and imperialism.
- While teaching about Sati and Widow re-marriage, suppression of women and the need for reverse discrimination can be taught.
- Democracy equality can enhance human values in a person. Rule of law and social justice gives immense opportunities to discuss and understand human rights and human duties.
- Languages offer many gateways for Human Right Education. Stories, poems, paragraphs can be carefully selected. Themes on French Revolution, Nazism can be used to discuss the evolution of human rights. Dramatic clubs and literary activities can be utilized effectively. Students can be motivated to write poetry, drama and essays on human rights. Poster making competition, elocution or contests, debates etc. can also be held on similar themes.
- The school should celebrate the World Human Rights Day which can go a long way to create awareness among students, parents and the neighbourhood in the community.
- Initiatives should be taken to enrich the school library and personal collection with books and materials on human rights.

CONCLUSION

All of the suggestions suggest that the time is ripe for Human Right Education to come to the forefront of international consciousness, and to fulfil its intended role as a preventive tool. Human rights education is an important tool to bring the peace and harmony in society. Human rights education should be included at all levels and reframed time to time as inculcation of deep respect for human rights and freedoms are the supreme goals of education. Without equity, liberty, and justice, dignity it is impossible to promote and cultivate the peace, tolerance, and harmony in the society. Education should be granted to one and all across the country and world. Human Rights are the foundation stones of human values, disciplines and dignity. It should be enhanced, protected and promoted to every nook and corner with the help of education.

BIBLIOGRAPHY

1. Chand, Jagdish. (2007). Education for Human Rights. Delhi: Anshah Publishing House.
2. General Assembly Resolution 49/184 of 23 Dec,1994 proclaiming UN Decade for HRE (1995-2005)
3. Human Rights in India. Retrieved on April 28, 2017 from http://en.wikipedia. Org/wiki/human rights- in Indian.
4. Jayakumar, S. (2007). Human Rights Education-Role of Teachers. Western Regional Seminar, H.J. College of Education, Khar. Retrieved from http://www.vpmthane.org/law1/Princ-Articles/Human_Rights_Education.pdf
5. Jayantibhai V. Patel (2010). Human rights Education: Inclusion in the curriculum of teacher education. *Edutracks*. 9 (7).
6. Mahapatra, N. (2012). Role of Education in Promotion and Protection of Human Rights. Odisha Review, 26-30. Retrieved from odisha.gov.in/e-magazine/Orissareview/2012/sep/engpdf/27-31.pdf
7. Naseea C. (2008). Human Rights Education "Conceptual and Pedagogical Aspects". New Delhi: Kanishk Publishers.
8. Netragaonkar, Y.D. (2011). Role of Teacher Educators in Promotion and Protection of Human Rights Education. Researchgate. Retrieved on May 27, 2017 from https://www.researchgate.net/publication/286354227_Role_of_Teacher_Educators_in_Promotion_and_Protection_of_Human_Rights_Education
9. The Universal Declaration of Human Rights. Retrieved on May 22, 2017 from http;//www.un.org/en/documents/udhr/index.shtml.

Chapter-9

Role of Peace Education in the Current Context

Dr. Devika R.

"If we are to teach real peace in the world we shall have to begin with children".

-Mahatma Gandhi

"All education is for peace".

-Maria Montessori

INTRODUCTION

We live in a very beautiful planet, fully blessed with its rich bio-diversity and strongly supported by Science and Technology which is in its zenith. Man has almost conquered everything under his feet, yet insecurity, conflicts, wars, and so many life threatening issues is on the rise. Peace breaking issues prevails with in each state, inter-state, between the different nations, international levels, various communities, races, religion, gender and so on. International organizations such as UNESCO have made 'the prevention of conflict and peace building as among the top priorities to curb the problems that leads to disturbance of tranquility. According to UNESCO (2009), the peace education is the process of promoting the knowledge, skills, attitudes and values needed to bring about behavioural change that will enable children, youth and adults to prevent conflict and violence, both overt and structural; to resolve conflict peacefully; and to create the conditions conducive to peace, whether at an interpersonal, inter-group, national, or international level . The skills for peaceful relations, training and research in sustainable development, the human rights education, good governance, Holocaust remembrance are yet other priorities to build peace in the whole world.

Education is a key tool in combating poverty, in promoting peace, social justice, human rights, democracy, cultural diversity and environmental awareness. Education for peace implies an active concept of peace through values, life skills and knowledge in a spirit of equality, respect, empathy, understanding and mutual appreciation among individuals, groups and nations.

Peace Education should be integrated with the school curriculum and higher education courses as there is a serious threat to a harmonious living around us. With the first underlying assumption for peace education, which will be later mentioned in this chapter, a strong awareness towards the problems around us should be made to the students. Once the right awareness is brought before the students, ways to handle those by teaching students by orienting and training them in life skills should be conveyed through the school curriculum. Such courses should also cover human rights, democracy, international understanding, tolerance, non-violence and multiculturalism along with the life skills.

What can be the various reasons for such uproar and non-violence that prevails in our society? Why man behaves as if he is not human, what is happening to his/her humane nature? Why man doesn't care for his fellow beings? Man seems to slip down everything from themselves tolerance, love, emotional balance, values and so on. It's high time to act for building up peace and tranquility in the whole world. Education seems to be the only way out for this. UNESCO believes that education is a human right for all throughout life to attain peace and that access to it must be matched by quality. The Organization is the only United Nations agency with a mandate to cover all aspects of education. The right education with the professional touch to it can do a lot in promoting peace building and development.

What is peace education?

Peace education is the process of acquiring the values, the knowledge and developing the attitudes, skills, and behaviours to live in harmony with oneself, with others, and with the natural environment. A student in a peace education class learns the various ways by which problems can be solved caused by violence and conflicts. Peace education tries to alarm the students about the growing conflicts around us and tries to inculcate in them the ill effects of violence. A consciousness about peace is developed in a peace education class, which can provide the basis for a just and sustainable future.

Peace education is a method to alter beliefs, attitudes and behaviours of people from negative to positive attitudes so that conflict is resolved and violence is prevented according to Jenkins (2008). Oslo Institute of International Peace and Research (PRIO) writes that peace education is promotion of knowledge, skills, attitudes and values to bring about positive behavioural changes in order to enable children, adult and youth to avoid conflict and violence and to develop sense of care, love and respect for each other on earth as global citizens. Kester (2007) elaborates that the content of peace education includes knowledge about peace movement, peacemakers, direct and indirect violence, peace as an active process, nurturing culture of peace, human rights and responsibilities, worldviews and ideologies, nonviolent communication, community and dialogue. The method of peace is collaborative, cooperative, participatory and active. The structure of the teaching learning process in peace education includes storytelling, case studies, role plays, empathy activities, negotiations, discussions, mediation practice, journaling, reflection circles and alternative future exercises. The survival and progress of peaceful society depends on peaceful, positive and educated minds according to GcGlynn (2004). Ahmed and Khan (2014) examined and ascertained the role of peace education in restoring the confidence among the communities of certain affected areas of Pakistan. Staehr(1974) has defined peace education as the initiation of learning processes aiming at the actualization and rational resolution of conflicts regarding man as subject of action. Mushakoji (1974) has defined peace education is that which deals with peaceless situations. These include struggles for power and resources, ethnic conflicts in local communities, child abuse, and wars. According to Reardon(1982), peace education is the learning intended to prepare the learners to contribute toward the achievement of peace.

Assumptions of Peace Education

The peace education is based on the following assumptions:

Assumption1: Conflict is an inherent part of human condition

Conflict is natural and is a normal part of everyday life. Right from the time humans' evolved, some million years ago, conflicts or indifferences in numerous forms too emerged, which resulted in many revolutions and change in the environment upon which they thrive. Democracy and peacefulness prevail only when a democratic society successfully combat those conflicts with its ability to manage disagreement and dissent among people.

Assumption2: Violent conflict can be prevented.

All conflicts need not becomes problematic until and unless it escalates to violence. But such violent conflicts can be prevented. With a proper training to our students to make use of 'life skills' to tackle such situations, develop respect and empathy towards our fellow beings, and open to the ideas others; to listen with care and attentiveness; to act responsibly when faced with conflict, a young generation with a mindset to construct peace can be generated. Conflict need not cross the line to violence.

Assumption3: There are many ways to be a peace builder.

Peace building is based on knowledge, skills, and attitudes that can be learned. Everyone can be a peace builder with the right concern about our fellow beings and one's humane nature. Many roles are involved in it and the youth can be the greatest contributors for peace making. As they can take a critical attitude towards society so as to generate a culture of tolerance based on dialogue and social inclusion. Thus the youth can be looked upon as a significant contributor towards peace making.

Thus the alliance for a safe world can be dealt by incorporating peace building skills among the people throughout the world. Life Skills Based Education for Violence Prevention and Peace Building promotes the development of knowledge, skills, attitudes and values among the people that in turn will bring about behavioral change that will enable children, youth and adults in preventing conflict and violence. Changes in the overt and structural level need to be made to resolve conflict peacefully; and to create the conditions conducive for maintaining peace around the world.

Approaches to Peace Education

How can the peace education embedded with the school curriculum? A formal orientation to peace education should begin from the school curriculum itself. Several opportunities for peace education is latent in the curriculum, maximum opportunities should be infused within the school and teaching learning activities.

Peace education should focus on the following combination of skills can help in preventing violence and to build up peace.

- Communication: active listening, self-expression, paraphrasing, reframing
- Conflict resolution skills(problem solving, critical thinking, decision making)
- Coping with stress
- Coping with emotions
- Assertiveness
- Ability to cooperate
- Affirmation
- Critical thinking skill
- Interpersonal relationship
- Peace building skills
- Honesty
- Compassion
- Ability to generate alternate solutions in students
- Constructive conflict resolution

The following attitudes should be developed in the students as part of peace education:

- Positive self-respect and a strong self-concept
- Tolerance and acceptance of others
- Gender equity and empathy
- Reconciliation
- Social responsibility
- Sense of justice and equality
- Joy in living

The various approaches to peace education can be classified as with-in school and outside school.

1. With-in school approach

The initiative for peace education should start from the school environment. Peace education is most effective when the skills of peace and conflict resolution are learned actively and are modelled by the school environment in which they are taught (Baldo and Furniss, 1998).

- ***Curriculum development***

To inculcate in children a positive attitude for peace education, a number of universities in our country have developed peace education in to their curricula, usually consisting of activities around themes such as communication, cooperation, and problem solving. The peace education courses offered includes an introductory chapter consisting of meaning and definition of peace education, aims and goals of peace education, principles, life skill education, and offering training in peace developments skills. A lot of student centred learning activity should be included in the curriculum rather than including the contents that require rote learning. Activities that provide opportunities to empathise with oneself and others, to understand the connections between need and feelings, to help children understand tolerance and differences in others with respect to religion, caste, opinions, perceptions, beliefs, and personal values should be included. Sufficient time should be provided with in the classrooms to conduct these activities and to make discussion in a free open environment. The activities that are planned within the curriculum should evoke in students empathy, a fellow feeling for one other and ultimately the students should be encouraged to come up with alternate solutions to maintain harmony.

- ***Pre-service teacher education***

The teacher education institutions have started taking initiatives for the peace education courses in our country. Teacher educators across various states are trained in various peace education skills in handling student aggression, and to promote honesty, compassion and harmony, under the training for peace education to promote life skills among students. The peace education is now a part of the teacher-training programme of the National Council of Educational Research and Training (NCERT), which formulates school curricula and teacher training programmes in India. The Maharashtra State Council of Education Research and Training (MSCERT) have provided training for 40 participants from the three states viz. Maharashtra, Gujarat and Madhya Pradesh. Experts from various fields guided the participants how to handle violent students, react to their queries, help them counter social evils and respect others.

- **In-service education**

The in-service teacher education has been carried out in many countries across the globe. As is the case with pre-service teacher education, in-service teacher education may focus on participatory teaching and learning methods, as well as content areas such as children's rights or conflict resolution skills.

2. Outside school

The peace education programmes should not be confined to activities that take place within school. Workshops, training programmes, and activities for out-of school youth can be planned along with other initiatives that focus on the media, publications for youth, and community-based arts programmes can be developed for the purpose of peace education. Camps for youth can be conducted which provides opportunities for students from different backgrounds and differences to assemble at one place for recreational and community service activities.

Sports and recreation programmes that focus on building teamwork, cooperation, sportsmanship, and decision-making skills can also be made part of peace education programmes.

Parents can also be made part of peace education programmes by conducting workshops for them.

Students can be encouraged to watch videos and programs that encourage peace and the beauty of living in harmony. Magazines that focus on themes of peace can be subscribed in the educational institutions.

Puppetry is yet another media for discussing sensitive issues. Puppets draw viewers into the drama without causing them to feel threatened by the actions in the drama.

Arrangement of contests and exhibitions by the school authorities can build awareness of peace and conflict issues in students.

The new technologies such as internet provide children and youth around the world with the opportunity to discuss issues of common concern. Images, videos and animations of the global issued that lead to wars and its ill effects on the humans are available in the internet. Viewing these images and videos can very much touch our mind and a proper thought on it can help one to find alternative ways to solve an issue or a problem.

Rationale for peace education

Education is quintessential for building lasting peace and works best as an instrument in resolving conflicts. The attitudes of the individuals can be transformed effectively through education as it equips the people with significant awareness about the growing concerns, non-violence, and equips them with knowledge and skills to effectively handle and grapple with various challenges of life. Education trains the people to develop adequate tolerance, respect for the mankind and enables the people to resolve problems of life. It is a source of peace and progress, because it promotes harmony and tranquility. Thus the role of education in peace building and development is an unquestionable fact. The ultimate results of successful and effective education are peace and progress. Well planned education combined with effective training is the key sources to peace development. Teachers can be role models and peace builders for students. There is a limit to the role of textbooks and moral education classes on imparting peace among children. The best way to handle is by the right teacher-student interaction and to help students' become good human beings and make each one of them in such a way that they can contribute towards the betterment of society. Education can equip individuals to live in harmony and to work for sustainable peace and development of their societies. Integration of peace education in the classroom curriculum and school activities is the best way to achieve this goal.

The access to quality education is a right that should be sustained even in the most difficult circumstances. Education can offer knowledge and skills that provides protection, where as in the longer term, it provides opportunity for the development of values and attitudes that prevent conflict and build peace. Education has the potential to build the capacities of children, parents, teachers and community members to prevent, reduce and cope with conflict and to promote equality and peace. Education has crucial linkages to a society's social, economic and political spheres. Education is central to identity formation, can promote cohesive societies and contribute to state-building. On the other hand, education can undermine all of these processes. Inequitable provision of services or biased curriculum and teaching methods can reinforce existing exclusion and stereotypes. Thus, education needs to be delivered effectively and equitably to ensure that it is a driver of peace rather than war.

The key to a 'One world' irrespective of the huge diversity in culture, races, religion, caste and creed, beliefs, customs can only be achieved by bringing human beings closely together is through 'Education'. The civil society suffers a lot much because of situations of violent conflicts and war in many parts of the world. It is in this context, we need to realize the crucial role of education in contributing to build a culture of peace and condemning instances in which education is undermined in order to attack democracy and tolerance.

The educational action for promoting the concept of peace concerns the content of education and training, educational resources and material, school and university life, initial and ongoing training for teachers, research, and ongoing training for young people and adults. The peace education mainly deals with life skills, value education among children during classroom interaction. A culture of peace must take root in the classroom from an early age.

It must continue to be reflected in the curricula at secondary and tertiary levels. However, the skills for peace and non-violence can only be learned and perfected through practice. Active listening, dialogue, mediation, and cooperative learning are delicate skills to develop. This is education in the widest sense. It is a dynamic, long term process: a life-time experience. It means providing both children and adults with an understanding of and respect for universal values and rights. It requires participation at all levels - family, school, places of work, news rooms, play grounds, and the community as well as the nation. Thus Peace educators should address the problems that lead to disharmony around the globe in a classroom. Questions must be raised in the classroom regarding violence and the ill effects it created. Students must be trained to keep an open eye on the issues that could lead to disruption of peace. They should be trained to ask, why violence occurs. Is there any other alternative to solve the problem rather than conflicts and violence? How to we reach other ways to solve the problems peacefully? Children too often learn in the textbooks of history about the violent means of wagging wars to glorify the supremacy of kings and kingdoms. This might create a tendency not to question such violent acts and attacks.

CONCLUSION

Education is the only force that can unite humans together for a peaceful harmonious living. The issues and problems that lead to violence are on the rise in all parts of the globe. The people all around the globe lack tolerance and empathy. Love for oneself and love to one particular groups and communities, religion, caste is growing in number. Education is the best way to curb this violence and should be implemented at all levels of education.

BIBLIOGRAPHY

1. Ahmed, I., & Khan, F. (2014). Role of Peace Education in Restoration of Community confidence in the Wake of Terrorism Wave. *Research Journal of Recent Sciences, 3(2)*, 81-86.
2. Baldo, M., and Furniss, E., 1998. 'Integrating life skills into the primary curriculum'.New York, UNICEF.
3. Jenkins, T. (2008). International Institute on peace Education: Twenty-six Years Modelling on Critical Participatory Peace Pedagogy. *Journal of Peace Education and Social Justice*, 2 *(2)*, 144-150.
4. Kester, K. (2007). Peace Education: Experience and Storytelling as Living Education. *Peace and Conflict Review*,*2(2)* pp.23-34.
5. GcGlynn, [2004]: *Addressing Ethnic Conflict through Peace Education.* International Perspectives. New York: Palgrave Macmillan.
6. Mushakoji, K. (1974). "Peace Research and Education in a Global Perspective." In hristolph Wulf, ed. Handbook on Peace Education(pp. 300-314). Germany: Frankfurt/Main: International Peace Research
7. Reardon, B. (1988). Comprehensive Peace Education: Educating for Global Responsibility.
8. New York: Teachers College Press.
9. Staehr, V. G. (1974). Education for Peace and Social Justice. In Christolph Wulf, ed. Handbook on Peace Education (pp. 295-311). Germany: Frankfurt/Main: International Peace Research Association.
10. https://www.unicef.org/education/files/PeaceEducation.pdf

Chapter-10

Sahaj Yoga: Realizing the Inner Wealth

Dr. Mithila Urmila Bagai

INTRODUCTION OF SAHAJA YOGA

Sahaja Yoga is different from other yogas because it begins with Self-Realization instead of this being the unobtainable dream of a distant goal[1].

On 5th May, 1970 in the small city of Gujarat, Nargol, Shri Mataji Nirmala Devi *Ji* experienced pure transformation and True awareness and took upon the noble task of providing en masse self-realization free of charge. This led to the birth of Sahaja Yoga.

Yoga is usually associated with *asanas* (exercises) or breathing techniques to gain fitness and well being. But the unique feature of Sahaja Yoga is that it does not force the seeker to attain a thoughtless state. Sahaja Yoga is effortless. It allows the thoughts to pass and wait for them to get dissolved to achieve a calm and peaceful mind.

The fundamental aim of Sahaja Yoga is to help people get their self-realization that in turn takes care of physical and mental well-being.

Shri Mataji explains self- realization in her own words:

"Global unity of mankind can be achieved through this awakening that can occur within each human being, so that transformation takes place within us. By this process a person becomes moral, united, integrated and balanced. One actually gets the experience of the feeling of the all-pervading divine power as cool breeze. "Know thyself" is the main theme of all the scriptures - it becomes evident and one reaches the absolute understanding of oneself.

Thus one becomes peaceful and joyous in life. One becomes collective as a drop falling into the ocean of compassion. This method works for the multitudes and not individually. Of course one cannot pay for the experience of Divine Love. Moreover, it is the last breakthrough of our evolution. This is the actualization of such transformation, which is taking place now, worldwide, and has been proved and experienced by hundreds of thousands in over 85 countries."[2]

Sahaja is a Sanskrit term where *saha* means 'with' and *ja* means 'born'. Every human being is born with the female, living Kundalini *Shakti* residing at the sacrum bone at the bottom of the spine that has got suppressed due to the mental diversion to lust, greed, material possessions and negative emotions like jealousy, ego, inferiority or superiority complex. The regular practice of meditation in Sahaja Yoga aids in spontaneous awakening of Kundalini Shakti and connecting it with the all pervading power. This renders a state of immense joy and thoughtless awareness. Shri Mataji says that this is the last stage of human evolution where a society becomes collectively conscious of True knowledge and connects with oneself and the cosmic power.

Earlier the sages devoted many years in meditation to evoke the inherent Kundalini powers and unite it with the super consciousness. But with the help of Sahaja Yoga, Shri Mataji has activated the *guru tatva* (guru chakra) in every seeker and made them their own gurus (masters) to attain the last stage of evolution of humankind that is the unity within oneself. The seeker of truth does not require the assistance of any individual to achieve *yoga* (pronounced as *yog* meaning unity). This, Shri Mataji says, will reduce conflicts and bring ever-lasting peace imperative for the survival and sustenance of humankind.

Shri Mataji Nirmala Devi *ji* explains the subtle system present in every human body and how the activation of each center of energy due to regular meditation and foot soaking techniques will unwrap the hidden and powerful energies that will not only keep the mind cool and calm but also aids in prevention and treatment of various formidable diseases like cancer and tuberculosis. The coolness of the mind is no abstract statement made here. A Sahaja Yogi/Yogini, after self realization, can actually feel cool breeze at the top of the head or on the palms. Initially, hotness might be felt on head or palms because as the Kundalini rises it clears all the centres of e ergy from negativity. But once the undalini · blossoms out of the fontanelle bone at the top of the head, it inte rates our subtle system and unites with the all pervading power of i ine ove which is the life giver.

Shri Mataji emphasizes that it is e tremely important to have a co ection with the Nature as it flour˙shes life and socie . S i Mataji says, "All work is done by Na re. ou cannot even sprout a seed into a flower. Na re does all th living ork. Man only does the dead ork.' A blooming bond with Nature flushes out all toxins and evils from enviro nent and uman bo y. eace can on y be achieved within society if ındividua s are inte ally peaceful. actions and conflicts within a h man mind ampli into rivalries and war in society. So it is vital to resolve and dissolve tensions within a human mind first througl meditation. egel in his theo of dialectics explains thesis, anti thesis and synthesis occurs when the socie is in transition. he contempora conflicts reflect the turb lent transition in socie in order to find the be er way of living.

Since the countries are free from colonial yoke, it is significant that people get freedom from the feelings and a achments that have enslaved them rom within and causing rampant con icts.

uring a conversation with Mahatma Gandhi Shri Mataji once en uired the reason behind his strict schedule of wa ing up at am and fastiı g. Gandhi said for the countr to attain a gigantic tas of national freedom, it ˙s important to be disciplined. n this Shri Mata˙i, fondly called Nepali in her childhood by Gandhi for l er nepali facial features suggested Bapu if you want to discipline people, why not give them discipline froı within." And this self discipline can be achieved through inner transformation. On this, Gandhi s ˙d it is impo ant to have political independence and then aim for inner freedom.

And when ndia enjoyed the much awaited tryst with destıny, Mahatma Gandhi met Shri Mataji and asked her to start her mission of freeing people from the ignorance fanaticism and paı ial nowledge and enslavement froı material possessions. he time has come for the ıealization of inner potential of human eings. But it was only when Shri Mata˙i sincerely ful lled her responsibilities of being a duti l wife to an eminent bureaucrat Sir . . S ivastava, three times Secret General to nited Nations Maritime Organisation and personal secretary of India's second Prime Minister Lal Bahadur Shastri and got her two daughters married, that She at the age of 47, embarked on en masse self realization.

Shri Mataji said that self-realization is the birth right as Kundalini is present in every individual.

A BRIEF LIFE SKETCH OF SHRI MATAJI NIRMALA DEVI *JI*:

Born on 21st March, 1923 in Chhindwara, an Indian district in Madhya Pradesh, Nirmala Shrivastava known by the honorific title Shri Mataji Nirmala Devi *ji* was a royal descendant of the illustrious Shalivahana dynasty of India. Shalivahana means 7 vehicles which is also symbolic of seven *chakras* in a human body. Nirmala means immaculate. Carrying forward the legacy of her ancestors that had an uncompromising adherence to morality, Shri Mataji since her childhood reflected exceptional qualities in morality and spirituality. Her father was an eminent lawyer and scholar. He was well versed in 14 languages and also translated Quran in Hindi. Whereas her mother was the first woman in India to receive an honors degree in mathematics. Hailing from a robust science background, She studied medicine at the Christian Medical College in Ludhiana and the Balakram Medical College in Lahore. Her grandmother, Sakhubai Salve was a fierce lady unnerved by the unpredictable upheavals in life. Despite being pregnant with Shri Mataji's father Prasad Rao Salve, she escaped from the cruelties of her in-laws after the demise of her husband.

Shri Mataji participated actively in India's freedom movement. From the age of seven, She spent most of her time in Gandhiji's ashram. Gandhiji used to take advice from Shri Mataji as he believed that the children sometimes give better suggestions than the older ones. And it was Gandhiji who, on 29th January 1949 a day before his assassination, holding Shri Mataji's daughter Kalpana in his arms persuaded her to commence the mission of bringing inner transformation and en masse self realization.

As a college student in Christian Medical College, Shri Mataji participated actively in Quit India and was even arrested and tortured by Britishers but that did not dent Her spirit to fight for freedom. Her entire family was an epitome of courage, self-sacrifice and compassion during freedom struggle movement. Never the one to bow down to injustice, her family converted to Christianity after experiencing the cruelties meted out to widow women in Hinduism. Shri Mataji's family sternly instructed every member not to shed a tear in case of an arrest. She was 8 years old when Her parents were arrested and She single handedly took care of her siblings though on a frugal living.

Shri Mataji has contributed immensely in social service by establishing NGOs, home for destitute women and children, several international schools, a health and research centre, and an international academy promoting classical music and fine arts. She believed that all human beings are united by the common bond of Kundalini *Shakti* that is prevalent in everyone. That's why during partition when a Muslim refugee knocked the door of Shri Mataji to seek protection for his life, she readily gave in and also courageously shooed away the rioters who were baying for the refugee's blood.

In 1970, when Shri Mataji's husband Sir C.P. Shrivastava was posted in London as the Secretary General of United Nations International Maritime Organization, She started by giving self-realization to a few people in U.K and then later on toured entire United Kingdom. The inner transformation experienced through Sahaja Yoga gave immense contentment to seekers. And there on, Shri Mataji travelled 13000 kms across six continents that is almost equal to travelling the globe three times. Sahaja Yoga became the grass root spiritual movement. Today it is present in 95 countries. Her exceptional spiritual and motherly qualities have healed people with diseases irrespective of nationality or their religion and gave them peace and calmness. In 1996, Shri Mataji was nominated for the Nobel Peace Prize. From 1989-94, United Nations Sahaja Yoga Organization invited Shri Mataji for four consecutive years to speak on ways to achieve world peace. In 1995, She was the guest speaker at the fourth World Conference on Women in Beijing. In 1997, Claes Nobel described Sahaja Yoga as "a source of hope for humanity"[3]

HOW SAHAJA YOGA BRINGS INNER PEACE?

Shri Mataji Nirmala Devi *Ji* explains how an individual can gain integration of mind, body and soul through Sahaja Yoga. A human body has seven centers of energy called *chakras* and three channels called *nadis*. This subtle system inside every human body looks after an individual's physical, intellectual, emotional and spiritual well-being. Each of these seven *chakras* is rich with immense qualities.

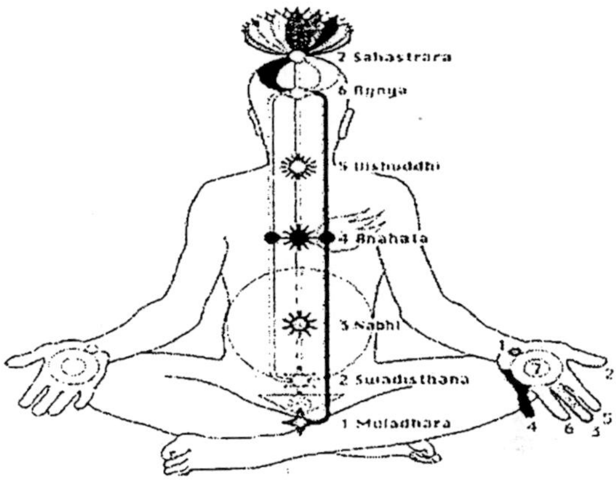

Figure 1: The Subtle System

The above figure shows seven *chakras* and three channels. Each chakra has its own magnificent qualities.

- **Mooladhara *Chakra*:** This is the first *chakra* that is below the sacrum bone. Sacrum bone is also known as sacred bone as the powerful Kundalini *Shakti* resides in it. Kundalini *Shakti* is the power of the soul. This chakra exhibits pure, child like joy and innocence. A child is governed by inner wisdom and the modern lifestyle values of flamboyance, arrogance, jealousy, possession does not affect. It is like a natural flow of river unimpeded by any prejudices, prior judgments or societal conditionings. Similarly, the activation of this *chakra* brings a charming simplicity, purity and joy in one's life. It enhances dignity and balance and stimulates an individual to the direction and purpose in life. This alluring quality is ever present in every human being but is waiting to be manifested as pure joy when the Kundalini rises.
- **Swadishthan *Chakra*:** This second *chakra* excites creativity, pure attention and pure knowledge in an individual. Meditating on this chakra, helps in connecting us to our inner world and enables us to accomplish inner peace and calmness. As the individual establishes inner peace, they start cherishing the beauty and joy around them. Vices like frustration, jealousy, ego diminishes. An active Swadishthan *chakra* helps in gaining pure knowledge of Reality that is experienced on palms through vibrations. In Sahaja

Yoga, while sitting in meditation, vibrations are felt on our fingers and palms that indicate subtle blockages. The regular meditation helps in the clearance of this Swadishthan chakra that keeps the liver, kidney and lower abdomen healthy. This *chakra* gets adversely affected due to over thinking of past or future events leading to diseases like diabetes and blood cancer.

- **Nabhi *Chakra*:** The third *Chakra* is the Nabhi *Chakra*. Regular meditation activates this *chakra* that gives us a sense of generosity, complete satisfaction and contentment. A Sahaja yogini/yogi attains peace and gets relieved from tensions and stress. Clearing of blockages from stress then facilitates the rise of our spirituality, morality and righteousness and renders complete balance at all levels in life. This *chakra* takes care of the liver that is the organ of our attention and concentration.
- **The Void:** In spiritual traditions, this area is known as 'ocean of illusions'. It is termed as illusions as it comprises of feelings of greed, attachments, possessions and ill feelings towards other that is not Real. These are temporary disturbances. As the Kundalini crosses this center, an individual gains the principle of mastery. We become our own gurus. We realize the true knowledge of Reality. Our life no longer gets governed by material possessions, laziness, and evil habits like smoking or drinking. We become our own deciding factor. Shri Mataji says, "In Sahaja Yoga you become your own guru, your own spiritual guide since you can feel on your fingertips all your subtle problems and have the power to cure them using your own Kundalini."
- **The Heart *Chakra* or Anahat *Chakra*:** Our Spirit resides in this fourth *chakra* that is uncorrupted by any desires or false ego. It is pure. After self-realization, our attention becomes one with our Spirit. All our doubts, worries, and fears diminish and we gain new confidence in life. This *chakra* looks after the health of our heart and lungs and any imbalance in it can cause asthma or lung diseases.
- **Vishuddhi *Chakra*:** The fifth *Chakra* is the *chakra* of diplomacy and of pure relationships with others. Nourishing this *chakra* with regular meditation brings compassion and kindness in voice. Tendencies that destroy a relationship like of domination, a feeling

of inferiority or superiority complex diminishes. Balance in this *chakra* builds benevolent and graceful relations. It enables oneness and gives us the connection with the Whole universe.

- **Agnya *Chakra*:** The sixth *chakra* is the *chakra* of forgiveness. Forgiveness is a powerful feeling as it relieves the forgiver with any burden or bondage. The individual no longer attaches herself to false or vacuous thoughts and concentrates solely on achieving Oneness with its Spirit and universe. It let go of anger, hatred and resentment and discovers the joy of generosity and humility. It is very important to forgive and release this *chakra* from any ego or hatred as the Kundalini reaches its final destination by crossing this center. Roving eyes, self-centeredness or watching impure things disturbs the chakra. Watching the sky, nature or earth can cleanse it.
- **The Sahasrara *Chakra*:** Blossoming of the Kundalini happens at the seventh *chakra*, the Sahasrara where it meets with the Supreme consciousness and the individual experiences pure bliss and thoughtlessness. For few minutes, the yogini/yogi gets insulated from any sort of worries, fears or tensions. Not even an iota of thought enters. The mind is in complete vacuum state. It is the feeling of accomplishment of Universe within oneself. It gives us the absolute perception of Reality.

This process of self-realization where Kundalini *Shakti* passes through all the *chakras*, resuscitating their respective qualities and finally integrating them at the Sahasrara level, brings harmony, joy and balance in the subtle system and keeps away from myriad problems in life. In addition with these *chakras*, there are three channels of energy that too gets cleared during the ascension of Kundalini *Shakti*.

Having too many blockages in the left channel causes overthinking of past emotions, desires and affectivity. Clearing this channel removes the superego that is the storehouse of all our memories, habits and conditionings.

Right channel deals with actions and planning and our physical and mental activity. Removing blockages from this channel removes our ego. Ego leads to obsession with oneself and the idea of 'I' and the feeling of superiority over others.

Clearing of the third channel that is the central channel allows for the unhindered passage of Kundalini, integrating us with the super consciousness.

When the subtle system of the human body gets connected with the all-pervading power, a beautiful sense of peace and joy is established. This inner peace then translates into peace with the others. An intrinsically peaceful person does not conflict unnecessarily over the possessions of immaterial materials. And the contribution of every individual's peace aids in building a peaceful society and the heralding of harmony and fraternity. Better sense of understanding and respect towards each other reduces dichotomy in society and the polarization of 'They' and 'Us'. The methods of meditation helps in dealing with conflict, post conflict trauma, and devising ways to resolve and reduce conflict.

POLITICAL ASPECTS IN SPIRITUAL REALM

Shri Mataji Nirmala Devi *ji* articulated her ideas on various significant political aspects that can aid in building a peaceful society.

- **On Freedom:** She staunchly endorsed the idea of freedom by participating actively in Indian National movement. Shri Mataji believed coercion is not the way of life. An individual first need to have civil rights to cherish self-realization. She believed in spiritual freedom as well. Kundalini *Shakti* can only transcend the seven *chakras* when the individual freely seeks for it.
- **On Religion:** Shri Mataji likened the growth of religions to a one large tree that is singular but has many flowers. In ignorance people pluck those flowers and fight with each other forgetting that these flowers have come from the same tree[4]. She emphasized that people irrespective of religion and culture are united by a common bond of Kundalini *Shakti*. Shri Mataji explains that there are two forms of consciousness- one is the, immediate consciousness that hold our long held beliefs at the superficial level and second is the collective consciousness that is achieved through regular meditation when the Kundalini *Shakti* rises creating a calm and still mind. Thus, collective consciousness acts as an integrating force.
- **On Health and Medicines:** Shri Mataji detested superficiality. She emphasized that medicines treat the diseases that happens

in part of a body but meditation first does not allow diseases to occur and second it treats the organism as a whole and not as a part. Shri Mataji has been a medicine student for long years but have to abandon it during freedom struggle. She discovered that every human body is governed by a subtle human system and nerve plexuses (Refer Fig.1). Any imbalance in the *chakras* and subtle system leads to physical and mental diseases. Meditation through Sahaja Yoga aids in integration of *chakras* and Kundalini thereby preventing any imbalance or diseases in a human body. Dr Ramesh Manocha, an Australian General Practitioner and Research-Fellow in the Natural Therapies Unit of Royal Hospital for Women in Sydney reported that Sahaja Yoga meditation helps in treatment and prevention of disorders of hypertension, menopause related disorders, and stress related symptoms and asthma. Shri Mataji said that human subtle system is like an inverted tree with its roots up in brain and branches in body. The roots have to be watered regularly through meditation so that the beneficial effects reach the *chakras* or branches in a human body.

- **On Education:** Shri Mataji believed that students need not require only intellectual and emotional growth but also spiritual well being. For this, She created educational system with Sahaja Yoga at its core. The main objective of education is to improve focus and gain confidence and self-understanding. Shri Mataji highlighted that education is a collective process to be shared equally by parents and teachers. And the study of natural environment is a pre-requisite as it inculcates a sense of respect towards Mother Earth. Shri Mataji's schools are across the globe where children are extremely confident and extremely humble[5].
- **On Family:** Shri Mataji has said that husband and wife are the two important pivots in a wheel. They should respect and love each other. A wife should be nourishing, generous and loving like Mother Earth. She should be a peacemaker in times of family conflict and a source of family's strength. While a husband must take care of the family and ensure that needs of every member is met. Balance and peace should exist between different siblings. So peace in the family translates to peace in society.

- **On Consumerism:** Shri Mataji traveled for nearly 40 years to teach the world that spirituality and nature are deeply intertwined. She and Her siblings were taught to seek forgiveness from Mother Earth as we touch her with our feet everyday. She was deeply concerned with the overgrowth of plastics and the dangers of nuclear energy. She warned against the over exploitation of energy consumption and suggested car-pooling to reduce pollution in atmosphere. Shri Mataji was also a staunch supporter of hand made goods rather than machine-made as it reduces our dependence on industries and machines. An artisan through its creativity creates goods that are in balance with environment.
- **On Women:** Shri Mataji lamented that society has not given enough opportunities to a woman to manifest her greatness. She urges woman to maintain their qualities of generosity, humility and forgiveness and not to adopt evil masculine attitude of aggression and violence as the society will doom. The society is in dire need of the balanced women so as to have a peaceful environment.

CONCLUSION

Albert Einstein once said, "The most beautiful thing we can experience is the mystical. It is the source of all True art and science." Confucius suggested that for the world to be put in order, the hearts must first be set right. Hegel in his book 'New Cosmology' said that to understand cosmology a whole should be studied not the part.

The discipline of political science has unfortunately deprived itself of including a yogic approach to life in understanding social, political, economic and personal problems of society. Only a part has been researched and analyzed whereas the whole has been completely marginalized.

Shri Mataji Nirmala Devi *ji* started Sahaja Yoga as a grass roots movement traveling across the globe and giving self-realization. With rising conflicts in society, time has come for every individual to seek inner transformation and realize their True potential.

As Shri Mataji says,

"So we have to respect all the people, all the human beings, whatever nation they come from, whatever country they belong to, whatever color they have, because they all have their Kundalini."

BIBILIOGRAPHY

1 Sahajayoga.org. *About Sahaja Yoga*. Retrieved from www.sahajayoga.org: http://www.sahajayoga.org/whatissy/how_sy_different.asp

2 *Sahaja Yoga Meditation*. (2017, July 23). Retrieved from sahajayoga.org: http://www.sahajayoga.org/whatissy/default.asp

3 Sahaja Yoga. *Taking it to the World*. Retrieved August 1, 2017, from www.sahajayoga.org: http://shrimataji.org/site/life/public-life.html

4 Sahaja Yoga. *The Essence of Integration*. Retrieved August 1, 2017, from shrimataji.org: http://shrimataji.org/site/work/cultural-integration.html (n.d.).

5 Shri Mataji Nirmala Devi Ji. *An Enlightened Education*. Retrieved August 1, 2017, from shrimataji.org: http://shrimataji.org/site/work/enlightened-education.html

Chapter-11

The Relevance of Peace Education and Role of Teacher in 21st Century

Dr.Subhash Sarkar & Mr. Debasish Debbarma

INTRODUCTION

Peace is a global phenomenon, this is the term which is used in global context, in every region of the universe the need of the hour is peace, that's why it is considered as global phenomenon. Today in 21st century we the people in the universe witnessed different violence, conflict and horrible situations in the name of politics, religion and so on. The conflict in the present situations arise in regard to ethnic identity, caste, community, economy and so on; the economic conflict arises due to wider gap between poor and rich, which is also a constraint in behind of making an egalitarian society. These are not confined to one country; these harmful situations have captured in every corner of the universe. We could see terrorism at the intra and inter country level and due to these every year millions of the people were victimized and many were killed in the affected countries, not only this the conflict situations in regard to policy, diplomacy and so on in between different countries at times lead to the violence and degrades the prosperity, harmony, universalization and international integration. The so called educated persons have forgotten their obligations towards bringing peace, which is prime requisite to keep the harmony, prosperity in society. We can refer to many events apart from world wars which had broken the international cooperation and understanding such kind of issues to be dealt with due importance. In context of this, peace can be alternative of violence and can uphold the prosperity, harmony in the country as well as globally.

Needless to mention today people are becoming selfish, demanding, self centered, greedy of power and in order to fulfill their selfish demands they choose violence as a weapon. This has made the peoples to live in miserable and difficult situations of life. It is very rare to see people are worrying about society and its environment, although, there were some personalities who had worked tremendously to bring the peace in society; as a result they succeed in this field. It is worthy to mention here the great personalities like Swami Vivekananda, AurobindoGhosh and many more spiritual leaders had emphasize on peace and people too believe on it and remember them for their contribution to society and selfless efforts but forgot the commitment to keep their ideals which is to uphold the peace in society.

In order to reflect peace in present society, education can play a prime role, as only education is the platform to reach to the peoples, it is education which is considered as miniature of society and the students who are the future of society actively take part on it. It is believe education plays pivotal role for building peace as only with it peace can be promoted. People learn their role and obligations towards society through education, at the same time the student's gathers new knowledge and behaviors. This enables them to live peacefully with others in society and this has been endorsed by many peace educators, such as, David Hicks, Ian Harris and Betty Reardon endorsed that education has the power to transform the society (Ardizzone, 2002). The importance of peace can be disseminated to masses of society through education. In this context, there should be pedagogy, which to be learnt by the teachers for easier promotion of peace in society through students. In fact pedagogy is the process ofimplementation of peace education, which is to be dealt by a teacher. Now a day's peace education is being taught in schools through over the traditional and co-scholastic curriculum, which plays significant role to promote the peace to students as well as society. Needless to mention school can play pivotal role to spread the messages of peace to entire society.

Defining Peace and Peace Education

"Peace is not merely the absence of war but the presence of justice, of law, of order-in short of government."–Albert Einstein

Etymologically, the English word 'peace' evolve from the French concept which stands for 'agreement' which means agreeing to stop a conflict or war. Even in more easy way we can define Peace as a situation where the absence of dispute, conflict, struggle and violence. Whatever an individual thinks or does whether it is right or wrong is ultimately to obtain peace and happiness; hence, it is clear it cannot be attained outside from world. More comprehensively we can understand it as the absence of hostility that enables to build the international relationships, bringing the harmony in socio-economic aspect and building democratic political culture which can serve for the interests of human being. In fact, this work towards the absence of fights between and within the nations which is globally accepted conception. Peace is the integral part of social justice and securing society therefore, peace takes special place in present society and there is need to hold discussion in regard to this subject as justice and security has been burning issue in society, which we have seen many time in danger situation and many time due to failure of justice and security the world under went to face many critical situations. In order to uphold peace globally justice should be provided to every individual. However, it appears in different means to every individual and according to their preferences.

The concept of peace education was well clarified by UNICEF in 1999 and defined asthe process of promoting the knowledge, skills, attitudes and values needed to change behaviorthat facilitate children, youth and adults to prevent conflict and violence. In order to sustain the peace in present society; the people must perceive it in good manner. Peace education is being imparted at educational institutions in the form of information, attitudes, values, skills which is for resolution of conflicts without violence along with building and maintaining prosperous relationships (Johnson and Johnson, 2003, 2005, and 2006). The first educator who first realized the need of peace education was Montessori accordingly, it reflected on her book "Education for a New World", she had written 'Preventing conflicts is the work of politics; establishing peace is the work of education'. Thus, there is no doubt to teach about peace through education, in fact these are the two parts of the same coin. The meaning of peace stands similar as value which occurs since birth to till death. In order to enjoy a peaceful life which is also ultimate goal of education, one individual must be nurtured at home by parents and again to be nurtured at school. Peace education had begun to teach about the peace to peoples, which teach people about humanity. In fact, it is the appearance of integral culture of body, mind, intellect and spirit, these elements constitutes every man and woman irrespective of caste, creed, language and other differentiation. Peace is greatly needed to every human being till the end of life, without peace one cannot imagine about life. Peace education is the composition of the skills, attitudes, values that enable one individual to contribute to peace and maintaining it.This means peace education is taught to deal with conflicts without occurrence of violence, to think it creatively, learning to deal with cultural differences in useful manner.

Essentialities and Necessities of Peace Education

Nowadays conflict, violence, contradiction, dispute, terrorism etc. becomes the trend in society. People are not conscious towards society that causes for suffering of miserable life in the working place, market, school or whatever else at all. We have witnessed in educational institutionsin the name of different movements and unrest; violence has become a very common practice. Originally, we are living in the technology era where violence is inseparable part of society in the forms of terrorism, war, crime, injustice and exploitation. This makes upset the whole society, people are expected to see some changes in the society instead the extent of violence and conflict are increasing in society at large.

Today people at large live in miserable conditions and seeking to overcome such situations for survival. It can be said that the prevailing constant violence has not only impact in our environment and society similarly; it has an immense impact on children and their innocent minds. This leads tohorrible need of nurturing the mind, heart and thoughts of children that sustain peace and its related values. Despite having materialistic views of current education system today our education system has emphasized on the humanistic thoughts of great educators like Rousseau, Henry Thoreau, Tolstoy and Maria Montessori; they wanted to keep education alive, reviving to the need of developing the humanistic side of education. Education must play key role to develop thehuman personality for making conscious people in the mission of mankind and the present conditions of social life. Today education has many challenges task that is capable of saving people from the present dilemma and helping them to develop human in spiritually and mentally. For teaching peace at school level, we must develop a curriculum which can create such an environment where the students can take active part in learning and do practice such values in respect of real sense of their life. The NCF describes, at the primary stage, children become conscious of both themselves and their immediate environment and begin to form the concept of right and wrong. Accordingly, at the next stage, they are able to develop reasoning abilities by themselves and alsolearn to raise question, discuss and holds healthy conversation with elders on the basis of ethical dilemmas. Hence It is through this complex process such as, dialogue, sensitization to issues, learning skills for resolution and imitating good role models, children are able to create their value systems, and proactively choose peace over violence, thus, peace education is nothing except a teaching of skills and values that teach an individual torespect for all humans and strive for a change in attitudes.

Dimensions of Peace Education

It is believed peace education is a training process for developing and changing their positive attitude towards other, and if peace education plays this role then it has several dimensions which can be detailed as below:

- **Education for International Understanding:** The present 21st century is witnessed with the great achievements in terms of discovery at the same time associated with conflict and violence. The 21st century has discovered seven issues which to be addressed these are the prevailing conflict between local and global, universal and individual, tradition and modernity, long term and short term, spiritual and material, competition and concern for equal opportunity, explosion of knowledge and limitation of human being. Measures to be given on these problems and these are possible only with peace education.
- **Education for Democracy:** The field of the peace education has reached to democracy education also, today's political scenario are associated with conflict, violence and so on. Therefore, peace education has to play crucial role to sustain the democratic environment by ensuring peace. Peace education endeavor to promote a conflict-positive direction in the society by training the students that enables them to perceive conflict as a platform of creativity and growth. Such skills enable them to think critically

and promote the values of freedom of speech. Thus, it is clear peace education can encourage people to be a responsible citizen for building democratic society.

- **Education for Promotion of Human Rights:** In the present society of 21st century we are witnessed of violating human rights in the name of politics, terrorism, social movements and so on. Therefore to reduce, control and eliminate the violence peace education is highly needed. Peace education has expanded its root to human rights; moreover, the circumstances relating to peace are ultimately integral part of peace. Hence, Peace education began to emphasize on the human rights. Usually focus has been made on policies that ought humanity in order to move more closely to a peaceful society. The aim is to make true the vision of peace among the participants of human race, accordingly people to be experienced the functions of personal freedom and also to be protected legally from violence, coercion and humiliation.
- **Education for Environmental Responsibility:** With the growth of population of world, the extent of pressure has increased in terms of producing food, energy, water, natural resources, land population and this has been increasing at alarming rate. Environmental degradation is being considered as technological as well as psychological problem. In this regard peace education has extended the hand to play the role for conservation of environment and it is possible throughout its curriculum as the learners from urban to rural, poor to rich participating in educational settings. Hence, peace education must play precious role to promote environmentalism through recycling, composting, and waste of disposal.

Approaches of Peace Education

Generally we do believe education must provide the opportunity to nurture the values within and outside of schools for achieving peace. But, there is no specific strategy to achieve these objectives. Many researchers are of the view that peace education has to be taught at schools as a separate subject while, others are of the view that it can be taught by combining with other traditional subjects. However, while approaching towards peace education the local circumstances must be given priority. It is to be noted here that there is no universal approach for peace education but few approaches are listed below which can be incorporated in schools for promoting values:

- **Developing Peace Oriented School Environment:**The process of peace education is effective when the skills, values, conflict resolution skills are taught and modeled by the school environment. It is believed that emphasis could be given to improve the school environment and which has been done by many countries as only there is one goal to create peaceful environment. Further, this can keep the consistency between the messages of curriculum and its educational setting. Generally children's rights are neither upheld nor denied at the schools and in this regard for bringing peaceful environment instructions to be given at the discipline methods, organizing classroom and school day and so on. From the perspective of peace education the role of teacher or administrator is crucial for that due training must be given to teachers for examining the issues relating to school environment. Many countries has incorporated this approach in their curriculum, for instance, Liberia has adopted peer mediation programme that enable youth leaders to play the role of conflict managers.
- **Developing Peace OrientedCurriculum According to Time:**Many countries began to develop curricula by incorporating peace education, by keeping different activities in curricula that are based on certain themes, such as, communication, cooperation, tolerance and empathy and so on. While, developing curriculum keeping on mind to build a good conception of empathy to oneself and others, one must learn to distinguish between need and feeling. A series of instructions to be given to the students at the school by engaging many students at the same situation in different activities that enable the child to understand feeling of cooperation, tolerance, empathy and so on. Therefore, it is suppose to build and promote the peace in the present society of 21st century.
- **Promoting Peace Education in Teacher EducationProgramme:** Peace education has taken place in the field of teacher education also; many countries are strived to update the quality of pre-service and in-service teacher educationprogramme. Teacher education Institutions began to adopt many skills such skills provide the opportunity to have group discussions it includes cooperating group

work, interactive and participatory teaching methods and so on. To boost the quality of teacher education programmes these kinds of teaching methods must be included in curriculum that enable the teachers to respect the child irrespective of caste, creed, sex etc. and can express their values of cooperation, appreciation of others view. For promoting peace through education such kind of activities can be employed throughout the curriculum. The need of peace education inteacher education was realized by Sri Lanka where they integrated peace education into each of traditional subject, this is an important feature of teacher education programme that is running in a national teacher training college.

- **Prospect for Peace Education:**The opportunity for peace education is limited, hence the need of peace education in the context of education to be broaden. The imparted matters for peace education such as,creative skills, attitude and values can promote the peace in society. Therefore, meeting the demand of peace education in present society requisite steps must be taken so that the messages of peace can be disseminate to masses of society.

Peace Education for Resolving Conflicts and Violence

In the present era of 21st century the people of society are being witnessed with different kind of unrest in school or social context, war, terrorism, killing innocents and so on, in reality these all are the outcome of violence. The present society failed to secure the peace, although these cannot be removed totally but it can be reduced. In this regard, peace education can play a key role to resolve these conflicts, violence and sustaining peace. The prime role of peace education is to bring the peace in the world.Now a day the word conflict becomes the part of life but the society does not consider its nature as good. In fact, it looks like conflict is increasing in today's modern life. One thing is clear from the concept of conflict that it will change the situation. Usually, conflict arises among the people due to differences in needs, values, goals, competition and so on. Peace education provides the skill and knowledge to its students to deal with the conflict situations non-violently. Moreover, a fact is clear thatstudents learn to respect others and change their attitudes towards non violence situations. The peace educators of the view that education is a strategy to resolve the conflicts and violence as only throughout its curriculum student get the scope to learn about peace strategy, peacemaking and peace building for a non-violent society.

Peace education is to find out the problems of violence and conflict which are exist in present society, accordingly provide the measures on such problems. It is to be mentioned here UNESCO have taken several strategies as a global effort for building and promoting the peace throughout the world. However, if we want to create a peaceful society we must revive the traditional curriculum of schools. Needless to mention peace education builds love, friendship and global understanding that proceed to sustain peaceful global society. Teaching an individualabout the skills, values relating to peace enable an individual to understand the reason of conflicts and make familiar to manage, reduce the conflict, violence for a peaceful society.Thus, adoption of conflict and violence resolving programme in peace education enables students towards global understanding and making a good relation in between the academic field and real world.

Teacher and Peace Education

In the present technology and digitization erathe role of the teacher is challenging. There was a time when the teacher was only a source of information but now a day the role of teacher become very complex, teachers are not only confined by teaching, they need to have the knowledge of pedagogy, research and so on. Teacher plays key role in the process of implementation of peace education curriculum, in order toimplement the peace education in schools the teacher must possess certain qualities, such as, a teacher must pledge to his students for active participation in teaching learning processes of schools, encourage learner to communicate freely with others, build basic idea about human rights and tolerate with cultural and linguistic differences. While imparting peace education at schools the teacher must show the act of non-violence in term of actions, tolerance, and solidarity in the certain activities of the school and outside social context. Keeping on mind the students to engage in several activities such as cooperative learning and participatory learning teacher must use instructional methodology, so that peace education can more foster peace in schools. To make the students ideal persons and free from the attitude of discrimination teacher can practice gender equality and illustrate some practices for discrimination free in personal and professional dealings. To bring the feeling of global understanding among the students practice also can made of skills of care, tolerance, conflict and violence resolution and empathy in dealing with their fellows, parents and other stake holder of society. Teacher can play a prime role for implementation of peace education curriculum as they are well familiar with the use of participatory and interactive as well as cooperative group work and collaborative work, such kind of practices enable the teachers to be the masters of skills of implementing peace education that also help the students to build the knowledge and skills of peace education. Thus, the teachers to be committed to promote peace by ensuring the inclusion of peace education and conflict resolution programmes in traditional courses for making the aware the upcoming generation and better world.

Teacher in imparting peace education

Apart from the above mentioned role of teacher in promoting peace, there are many ways that canemploy to promote the peace in present society these are thecurriculum and co-curricular or co-scholastic, these activities are the first priority given area for creating peace and being considered as one of the most effective way to build and promote the peace in present society. The context of approaches towards promoting peace in present society is as follows:

- **Through Traditional Curriculum:** Today in the present challenging era of digitization, the most of the effective way to build peace is through traditional curriculum, as it is the only way where the students who are the next generation of society take part in. Peace education takes place in two fold way, one fold is to teach the people about the emerging dangers of violence and another one is to enable them and develop their capacity to prevent violence that enable them to sustain the peaceful society. At the some institutions peace education is being taught as separate subject instead it must be integral part of school curriculum. Peace education must be included as integral part of general education for ensuring peaceful society. While, framing the school curriculum it must include the substance of equality, social justice, dignity, resolving the violence and conflicts, human rights, democracy, spread of universal values of love and global issues throughout the curriculum. The peace education curriculum along with global issues and international understanding must focus on the local needs for developing the attitude to think globally and act locally.

- **Through Co-curricular or Co-scholastic Activities:**It is one of the most effective, universal and recently used activities for implementing peace in society. In modern education curriculum co-scholastic activities occupies special place that enable the students towards peace. At the schools a number of co-scholastic activities can be organized on the basis of various themes for peace.

The co-scholastic activities that can be used for building and promoting the peace are as follows:

- ***Games and Sports:***Games and sports are one of the most important co-scholastic activities for promoting the peace in present society of 21st century. Every student must attend in sports and games, which facilitateall-round development of a student, these activities will develop the feeling of global understanding and international brotherhood.
- ***Celebration of special days:***The environment of peace can be created by celebrating the special days, such as, human right day, world women day, bethibacahaoandolon ma-betisanmelon and so on. Such kind of activities will help to sustain the peace in present day.
- ***Debate:***This is one of the important medium through which peace can be promoted; it is such an area where students can conduct research on different issues of peace. It is debate where an individual can hold healthy discussion on controversial issues in a safe environment. For taking up peace issues schools should organize debate competition.
- ***Literary activities:***The literary activities in schools, such as, poem writing, essay writing, writing articles on peace related issues can promote peace to a great extent, therefore students must be given opportunity in schools to participate in literal activities. Further, this can help in spreading the message of peace to masses of society.
- ***Music:***Music can play key role in imparting the peace education to students. Schools should take the inventivenessthat students arebeing taught to make the music a part of their day to day life. Playing patriotic songs can develop the feeling of nationalism among the student minds. Besides, it can develop the feeling of belongingness, group feeling, feeling of being connected with rest of the world.

- ***Seminar and conference:***It is an exceptional way of expressing and communicating feeling that one individual may not able to do with other ways. Schools should be striving to organize the seminar and conferences relating to peace education. This is such kind of activity where the teachers as well as students resolve any particular issue or problem in a calm environment.

MAINTAINING PEACE IN PRESENT DAY SOCIETY

In the light of prevailing conflicts and violence of present society, we would like drop some suggestions for maintaining and promoting peace in present society.

- To make aware the people about the need of peace in society there is need to organize awareness programmes and it can be done through education, community groups and public organizations.
- In order to cultivate the messages of peace to people media can be involved to this process so that along with teachers media can play significant role towards peace building in present society.
- Teacher must inculcate the values of non-violence among the younger generation and taught them to respect every religion so that peace can be maintained in present society.
- Academicians can play key role for maintaining peace in society that is possible through peace education, for increasing the peace education they can seek for funding agencies or corporate sponsors to fund for introducing or developing the programme.
- Academicians should be endeavor to make the partnership with any reputed peace building institutions, NGOs, religious organizations, development organizations and training institutions for jointly taking action against violence, conflicts and creating peaceful environment in society.
- Teacher should take initiative to organize cultural programmes in society this helps them to explore their culture and brings unity to fight against terrorism.
- The need of peace education programme apart from the educational institutions it must be introduced to policy planners and political leaders. It will enhance the field of peace education and its acceptability among people.

Concluding Remarks

At the end we can conclude by remarking several points which are associated with peace education that the present 21st century has brought tremendous comforts benefits for the people but meet the some emerging trends like crime, war, violence, terrorism and so on. Considering such problems it becomes essential to integrate attitude, values relating to peace into the traditional curriculum for possessing teaching and learning in schools and it will be more effective when it is linked with general subjects. Peace education is such education which teaches love, fairness, trust, and co-operation towards building peaceful society. Peace can be promoted when it is imparted through co-scholastic activities; these are one of the universally accepted medium to create peaceful society. Thus, peace education can be considered as a challenge of the status that enables an individual to respect others, in fact it is needed for a struggle for the liberation of people. Moreover, there are some challenges in regard to implementation of peace education as a least of people are ready to adopt it but society at large must accept it's necessity in current generation and strive for proper implementation of peace education for promoting, building and creating peaceful society.

BIBLIOGRAPY

1. Aggarwal, J.C. (2005). *Education for Values, Environment and Human Rights.* Delhi: Shipra Publications.
2. Anand, S. (2014). The Contemporary Issues and Significance of Peace Education in India. *Impact Journals*, 2(10), 47-54.
3. Ardizzone, L. (2002). Towards International Understanding: The transformative Role of Peace Education. *Current Issues in Comparative Education*, 4(2), 16-25.
4. Arulsamy, S. (2013). Peace and Value Education. New Delhi: Neelkamal Publication Pvt. Ltd.
5. Behra, S.K. (2013). Role of Teacher in Peace Education. Samwaad, 2(1), 16-24.
6. Chakraborty, M. (1997). Value Education: Changing Perspectives. New Delhi: Kanishka Publishers Distributors.
7. Charles, K., &Selvi, A. (2012). Peace and Value Education. New Delhi: Neelkamal Publications Pvt. Ltd.
8. Dangwal, K.L., &Srivastava, S. (2015). Fostering Peace through ICT. *International Journal of Research and Analytical Reviews*, 2(2), pp. 64(73).

9. Doley, P. (2016). Peace Education: It's Necessity in the context of Assam and North-East India. *International Journal of Humanities & Social Science Studies*, 2(4), 189-195.
10. Ezema, P.N., Ezema, C.I.L. (2012). Teacher Education As A Sustainable Strategy For Building A Culture Of Peace And Implementing The Millennium Development Goals In Rural Nigeria. *An International Journal by Global Educators for All Initiative*, 1(1), 1-4.
11. Palanithurai, G. (2017). Need of the Hour is value Education not in Thought but in Action. *University news*, 55(11), 17-20.
12. Sharma, D. (2015). Peace Education: Making the World More peaceful. *University News*, 53(21), 3-6.
13. Sharma, Y.K., &Katoch, K.S. (2007). Education for Values, Environment and Human Rights. New Delhi: Deep and Deep Publication Pvt. Ltd.
14. Singh, K. (2015). Concerns of School in Nurturing Peace Education. TechnoLEARN, 5(1-2), 9-13.
15. Tint, B.S., & Prasad, G.K. (2007). Peace Education in India: Academics, Politics, and Peace. *The Canadian Journal of Peace and Conflict Studies*, 39(1-2), 23-27

Chapter-12

Unrest Amongst Youths vis-à-vis Peace Education: Role of Family Society and School

Dr. Sunita Agarwalla

INTRODUCTION

Indiscipline and agitation by the youths has become a common phenomenon in almost all the countries across the globe. Unrest in the higher education institutions has become a matter of great concern for all the people who are associated with the field of education. It is observed that students resort to different types of violence and vandalism at the smallest issue. Be it about the admission of someone in an institution, be it late declaration of results, any social issue and so on. They go for strikes and sit on dharnas till their demands are fulfilled by the concerned authority. They don't even bother to think whether the demands are legitimate or not. They just get irritated over an issue and sometimes even resort to violence like breaking of glass, pelting stones at the authorities, causing large damage to public property etc.

Almost every day in the newspapers and television we read and hear news of unrest amongst the youths studying in college and universities. The acts of indiscipline may be as simple as disobeying a teacher or even grave as defying the authority and creating law and order problems like assaulting someone, burning public transport, looting shops, manhandling their teachers etc.

We know that youth have a lot of energy, which when not channelised properly can lead to unrest amongst them. Apart from this, they also have their own frustration and value conflicts with their parents, teachers and elders of the society. So, whenever they get a chance to release their frustration, they resort to unrest. "Unrest" simply means "disturbed condition." So "youth unrest" can be said to be a state of collective dissatisfaction and discontentment amongst the youths.

Unrest amongst youths can be viewed from three perspectives –

1. Firstly, when there is unrest amongst the students regarding some issue.
2. Secondly, when some type of agitation or unrest takes place due to youths.
3. Thirdly, there is some social unrest in the country and it has its effect on the youth. For example: the recent "India against Corruption" movement by Anna Hazare, where lakhs of youths participated under the banner of 'youth against corruption'.

CAUSES OF UNREST AMONGST YOUTHS

Unrest amongst youths is caused due to various reasons as –

(*i*) **Undue pressure from parents:** It is observed that most of the parents have high expectations from their children. They pressurize their children to achieve high marks and criticize them, if they cannot do that. This causes frustration in the youths leading to unrest.

(*ii*) **Lack of role model:** Today youths have nobody to look up, whom they can consider as role model. They look upto the political leaders and film stars as role models, who themselves do not have any value in life. This creates a craze for money, power and glamour in them.

(*iii*) **Influence of media:** At present we find that the media-both print and visual do not follow any ethics while telecasting the programmes. Large scale violence and vulgarism shown in the television, create violence in the minds of the youths.

(*iv*) **Peer pressure:** Sometimes youths resort to unrest under peer pressure also.

(*v*) **Family:** Youths who come from broken homes, who are socially isolated and are unattached to their family, also resort to unrest just to satisfy their emotional needs.

(*vi*) **Insurgency:** Places where insurgency and terrorism prevails, create a feeling of negligence and insecurity in the minds of the youths. They resort to violent behavior at the smallest provocation.

(*vii*)**Migration:** Migrant students feel themselves isolated from the larger community. Such students join agitation as a refuge.

(*viii*) **Academic backwardness:** Students who are academically weak in studies also resort to violence and unrest.

(*ix*) **Lack of guidance and counseling:** Our schools and colleges do not provide any facility for guidance and counseling to the students. As they do not get proper guidance, they resort to unrest.

(*x*) **Corruption:** Large scale corruption in the society is also another cause of youth unrest. Youths face problem of finding suitable jobs after passing out. They also see that the undesirable students get jobs by paying bribes. This causes frustration in them leading to unrest.

(*xi*) **Generation Gap:** Generation gap between the elders and youths also leads to unrest. The elders fail to accept the rapid changes taking place in the world and hesitate to fulfill even the legitimate demands of the youths.

(*xii*)**Impact of globalization:** Due to globalization, the hopes and aspirations have gone up. Our education system and society fail to fulfill these, which leads to unrest amongst them.

Peace Education

Peace can be said to be a state of mind when we are not feeling any restlessness or are free from any stress. It also may be said to be a cool and quite state of mind when we do not feel insecured due to nay external threat. If a country is said to be in a state of peace, then it means that there are no internal disturbances of any kind or external threat of war.

Another term associated with peace is 'Peace of Mind'. It may be said to be a state when we are having positive thoughts and a feeling of happiness.

When we talk of 'Education for Peace" it may be educating the children about the importance of peace and ways to maintain it. It may also be said to be education about peace where the children may be taught about the till effects of war, exploitation, disparity and violence. They are made to understand that non-violence is need if we want a stable society.

Education for Peace

Education for peace may be said to be a subject which can help us to study about the nature and needs of the society. It also aims at making people aware of their rights or well as of others. It is basically teaching the people values like tolerance, humanity, respect for each other's opinion etc. which can help in creating a society free form exploitation, disparity, violence and injustice. It also makes people aware of human rights.

According to S.P Chaube Education for peace may be understood in the following four ways:

1. It is an anti-war education.
2. It is an education establishing liberation.
3. It is a kind of learning process for enabling one to assimilate lessons in tolerance and creativity.
4. It is a life style for establishing a peaceful international society.

UNESCO's concern on peace:

The commitment of the United Nations to peace education is also reflected in the instruments on the rights of the child. The 1959 Declaration of the Rights of the Child might be summarized as emphasizing the right that children have to protection and education. The seventh principle expressly states that a child has the right to an education that will develop a sense of moral and social responsibility. As a corollary of this, one could argue that a child has the right to peace education. In the same vein, the 1989 Convention on the Rights of the Child Article 29.1 (d) indicates that the education of the child shall be directed to "the preparation of the child for responsible life in a free society, in the spirit of understanding, peace, tolerance, equality of the sexes, and friendship among all peoples, ethnic, national and religious groups and person of indigenous origin." Given the importance of peace and peace education for children, it is not surprising that peace education figures prominently in promotional literature from the United Nations' Children's' Fund (UNICEF), although UNICEF's emphasis on peace education mostly concerns post-conflict situations. In 1996, UNICEF adopted peace education as part of its anti-war agenda.

One of the general observations one might make regarding UN international instruments dealing with peace education is that they have become gradually more assertive in terms of rights and expectations. This is evident with the 2002 document A World Fit for Children, which was adopted unanimously by the UN General Assembly. In Article5, "A world fit for children" is described as one of sustainable development "founded upon principles of democracy, equality, non-discrimination, peace and social justice and the universality, indivisibility, interdependence and interrelatedness of all human rights, including the right to development" (UNGA, 2002b). Much of the document focuses upon the right of children to protection from harm and violence. However, an important section deals with the challenge of providing quality education. Within Article 40, the signatories to this document indicate that they will implement a range of strategies and actions, including, at point 40.7, strategies and actions which will" ensure that education programmes and materials reflect fully the promotion and protection of human rights and the values of peace, tolerance and gender equality, using every opportunity presented by the International Decade for a Culture of Peace and Non-Violence for the Children of the World, 2001-2010" (UNGA, 2002b). Clearly this is a forthright commitment to peace education.

ROLE OF SCHOOL

The school must take the following steps to impart peace education to the young children:

1. Days of international and national importance as earth day, world environment day, republic day, Independence Day etc. must be celebrated in the school. They must be taught about the importance of the same.
2. Students must be encouraged to take part in activities of Red Cross, Scouting and Girls Guide, NSS, NCC etc.
3. Students must be encouraged to do community work. They must be made to participate in community festivals and help it in times of need like flood, earthquake etc.
4. Schools must celebrate the birthdays of the great personalities of the world.
5. Seminars and debates must be organized amongst the students on issues those will promote international peace.

6. The educational institutions must invite experts and people of international fame working for establishing peace to deliver talks for the students.
7. Films which help in promotion of peace must be shown. It must be kept in mind that education for peace cannot be taught as a separate subject. The ideals must be put in the contents of each and every subject, so that it is repeated by the teachers of different subjects over and again.
8. The curriculum of the educational institutions must cover a lot of subjects, so that the students can opt for subjects of their own choice. The Kothari Commission in this regard remarks, "For solving the students' problems the programmes of education should be made more adequate and the existing ills in the same should be carefully eliminated."
9. Provisions should be made to provide vocational guidance and vocational education to the students.
10. The head of the institution must be able to provide academic leadership to the students.
11. The teachers must be committed to their profession.
12. Education must be related to real life experiences. There must be no gap between what is taught in the schools/ colleges or universities and the real life of the students.
13. Arrangements must be made for the education of the backward and gifted children.
14. The relationship between the teachers and the students must be very cordial and that of mutual love and respect. Teachers must be friends, philosopher and guide of their students in the true sense.
15. The infrastructural facilities must be improved. The Kothari Commission also in this regard remarks, "The standard of services offered to the students in hostels, libraries and on the campus should be improved in any programme of education, its worthwhileness should be assessed the context of the future life of the students."
16. The authorities must keep a track, so that the political parties do not interfere in the working of the institution and are not able to instigate the students to resort to indiscipline.

ROLE OF FAMILY

The family has a great role in instilling peace in the minds of the children from a very small age. The following measures can be taken by them in this regard:

1. Children must be given love and a sense of security by their parents. The environment of the home should be such that the children learn values. Parents must be careful about their behaviour in front of the children.
2. If the children exhibit any signs of indiscipline, the parents must seek the help of a counselor.
3. Parents must not compare the children either siblings, friends or relatives. This may develop inferiority complex in the minds of the youths and to boost confidence they resort to unrest.
4. Parents must not criticize their children for their failures. This lowers down their self confidence and they join groups to show off.
5. Parents must not pressurize the children to take up courses and subjects which they are not interested it. It is also seen that parents often try to fulfill their own dreams through the children, putting undue pressure on them to achieve the same. Such pressure causes unrest in the youths.
6. Parents must instill self confidence in the children, by praising every small act of success of theirs. Children, who have high self confidence, will never resort to unrest.

CONCLUSION

From the above discussion it can be concluded that youth unrest is undeed a great problem in the present world. But the youths cannot be blamed for that. It is lack of proper understanding, guidance on the part of the parents, teachers and elders that force the youths to resort to such unrest. It is also a trend in the world today, to resort to unrest to get one's demands fulfilled. The youths experience large scale violence going on in the society.

The answer to this is peace education, which can be formally provided in the schools from an early period of life and informally by the parents and society, by themselves practicing peace. The behaviour of the elders also have a great influence on the youths. It is a collective responsibility of all concerned to provide proper guidance to today's youths, so that they work towards bringing peace in the world.

BIBLIOGRAPHY

1. Agarwalla Dr. Sunita: Emerging Issues and Education, " Bookland, 2012
2. Ahuja Ram: Social Problems in India, Rawat Publications, 2012
3. Taj Dr. Haseen : National Concerns and Education, Neelkamal Publications, 2012.
4. Sarma Mukunda : Problems of Youth, EBH Publishers, 2010.

Chapter-13

Women's Participation in Peace — How Does It Matter?

Dr Nabanita Deka

INTRODUCTION

There is no peace without development, and no development without peace – and neither peace, nor sustainable development without the active participation of women in both processes. Women have always played key roles in armed conflict, be it as nurses, careers, combatants or workers. Women also contribute to peace in a multitude of ways. Yet these contributions often go unrecognized and remain undervalued because they take place often outside official, high-level forums, or because they do not fit with activities traditionally associated with peace building and conflict prevention. As a result, their skills, insights and energy are overlooked; and a misleading image of women as mere victims of conflict, and passive beneficiaries of interventions, prevails. From the dinner table to the boardroom table, women's participation in decision-making processes is increasing in societies around the globe. Yet twenty years after the historic United Nations Fourth World Conference on Women in Beijing, in which 189 countries called for "full and equal participation of women in political, civil, economic, social and cultural life," women's participation at another table—the peace table—lags behind.

WHY SUCH TOPIC HAS BECOME SO URGENT?

To many people, peace is an inverse, or even a mere corollary of conflict, but such a vague notion does not lead to a clear understanding or definitions of what it is that people are trying to promote or achieve in peace building. Most approaches to peace building have either ignored or marginalised issues of gender and women. Women consistently remain a minority of participants in peace building initiatives receiving less attention (usually just as mere beneficiaries or victims of conflict) than men in policies; and gender analysis rarely informs peace building strategies. This is in spite of the fact that there have been many United Nations and European Commission resolutions including Resolution 1325 which for close to a decade have criticised such marginalisation and neglect and promoted women's involvement in peace and security. Such resolutions were not drawn out of thin air, but built on at least two decades of practical experience in and evaluation of gender and women-focused policies in the area of development. The resolutions and the various conventions call for gender issues and women's need to be given much more serious attention in all policies relating to conflict and peace. While women and peace is a topical issue and has been for a very long time, it continues to demand from the world a more genuine attention and clarity of purpose if we are to fully enjoy positive peace for all. Women are peace seekers in the world.

LET'S SEE ITS HISTORICAL PRESPECTIVE

The participation of women is critical to the success of any peace building process – if half the population is excluded or faces discrimination, peace will be impossible to achieve. Women peace builders bring different perspectives and priorities to men, and their role in re-establishing the social fabric in the aftermath of conflict is vital. The role of women in peace building is recognised in many international agreements and resolutions, and the 2011 Nobel Peace Prize, awarded to Ellen Johnson Sirleaf, Leymah Gbowee and Tawakkol Karman, was public recognition for the impact of women peace builders. But whilst women peace builders have made vital contributions to peace processes in diverse places such as Northern Ireland, Guatemala and Liberia, the reality remains that women are denied meaningful participation in many peace processes. They continue to be largely absent from official peace negotiations. Women's general political participation is an issue; women are often not included in peace talks because they are missing from key decision making posts, particularly those relating to peace and security. Formal peace talks are often essentially elitist processes that prioritize the participation of combatants above a more inclusive and cross sectoral representation of society. Women's participation is hindered by men's and women's perceptions about women's place in society and in public life. Women are often restricted in their ability to participate in peace talks because of their limited economic freedom or competing demands on their time (e.g. childcare), Lack of experience of formal political engagement and advocacy. It is important to note here that what is needed to support women's participation in peace processes varies from one context to the next. Women are adept at bridging ethnic, religious, political, and cultural divides. Social science research indicates that women generally are more collaborative than men and thus more inclined toward consensus and compromise. Women often use their role as mothers to cut across international borders and internal divides. Every effort to bridge divides, even if initially unsuccessful, teaches lessons and establishes connections to be built on later. A few experiences spring up as I reflect on the contributions that women have made in peace processes. At the peace talks that led to the Good Friday Agreement in Northern Ireland, male negotiators walked out of sessions and left, leaving a small number of women, like Monica McWilliams and other members of the Northern Ireland Women's Coalition, at the table. These women focused on mutual concerns and shared vision, enabling the dialogue to continue and trust to be rekindled. In the Middle East during the violence of the first Intifada, Israeli and Palestinian women like Naomi Chazan and Sumaya Farhat-Naser created Jerusalem Link, an umbrella group of women's centres on both sides of the conflict, to convey to the public a joint vision for a just peace. In a time when both communities forbade cross-community meetings, Jerusalem Link activities were permitted because "it's just a group of women talking." A range of factors that have been identified in practice include women needing support for further education, organizational and advocacy skills, as well as addressing structural barriers such as resistance to women's participation, the burden of unpaid care, and lack of access to resources. To determine what support is appropriate, solid gender analysis of the context at hand should be undertaken.

WOMEN AS MEDIATOR FOR PEACE IN EVERY FRONT

Women have played and continue to play moderating roles within families. They mediate for peace between family members. Our mothers have played this role for years and yet we have constantly failed to acknowledge (as we should) their absolute central role in preventing the escalation of family and community conflict. The world over, groups of women often demonstrate a stronger commitment to prevention or ending of violence and maintenance of long-term peace and hence constitute a highly motivated and able group of stakeholders for peace building who nonetheless are often sidelined or even ignored. Women are highly invested in preventing, stopping, and recovering from conflict. Women are motivated to protect their children and ensure security for their families. They watch as their sons and husbands are taken as combatants or prisoners of war; many do not return, leaving women to care for the remaining children and elders. When rape is used as a tactic of war to humiliate the enemy and terrorize the population, they become targets themselves. Despite or because of the harsh experiences of so many who survive violent conflict, women generally refuse to give up the pursuit of peace. It appears that communities or states that have ignored or have not appropriately recognised the positive contribution that their women make in their society remain developmentally behind or become dysfunctional. This is no coincidence. There are many examples today where conflict continues to hurt the innocent especially women and children and where human rights are put aside due to 'immediate concerns' and also, unbelievably, through fundamental institutional 'acceptance and silence' or manufactured consent not to rock the boat. History has demonstrated that women, in both an individual and group capacity, are extremely effective as peace-builders. This is not to say that men are not also peacemakers, nor that women are never violent, but rather that the achievements of women in this capacity are often overlooked and merit further attention. However, the inequalities between men and women that still prevail in our societies limit the impact of women in creating a culture of peace to much less than their true potential.

SOCIETAL WIEW REGARDING THIS ISSUE

The implications of gender on peace education are many and diverse. First, society must recognize the potential of women as peace-builders, and actively promote their inclusion in peace-making processes. Second, violence against women, which is one of the most common forms of violence worldwide, must be eliminated, with awareness education about the issue as the first step towards this goal. Finally, societal consciousness of gender inequalities and discrimination against women in all spheres must be raised so that these issues can be recognized and addressed. The differences in the socialization of boys versus girls and gender equality in education are especially relevant topics under this category. A key aspect of UNESCO's campaign to foster a worldwide culture of peace is to "ensure equality between women and men," thus affirming that gender is an important consideration with regards to peace education (UNESCO, 2000).The differences between society's treatment of men and its treatment of women are often so customary that they have become ingrained in the collective mindset as perfectly normal and correct. However, if we stop and reexamine these behaviors, it becomes evident that many of the differences in society's attitudes towards men versus women are neither positive nor conducive to building a culture of peace. Consider something as basic as the toys girls and boys commonly play with: for girls it might be pretty dolls, while for boys it might be miniature soldiers. This divide begs the question: "To what extent are girls and boys in our society being socialized equally or differently when it comes to learning how to care, empathize with others and engage in or endure violent behavior?" Issues of war and peace have become highly genderized, so much so that associating warfare with men has become a rarely-questioned norm. All over the world there are more men than women in the military. This fact probably has a pre-socializing effect on boys. In countries with compulsory military service, this service is normally compulsory for boys only. This socialization may explain why women are more likely than men to support conscientious objectors, to be against war toys and against war. Since the 1970s the United Nations and other international women's conferences have adopted Equality, Development and Peace as an organizing theme and framework for women's activities in development. Women would not only benefit from peaceful structures, as opposed to violent structures which oppress them, but they also have a role to play in building peaceful relationships and structures, and cultivating values, attitudes, relationships and structures which UNESCO has referred to as a "Culture of Peace". Culture of peace is consistent with the women's movement theme that equality, development and peace are inextricably linked. There can be no lasting peace without development and no sustainable development without full equality between men and women. Mahatma Gandhi viewed women as the incarnation of ahimsa and added that due to a different socialization process, women have tended to grow up more peaceful than men and more capable of solving conflicts in a nonviolent manner. Peace often starts in the minds of women, Mahatma Gandhi added (Gandhi 1992).

LET'S CHANGE THE SOCIETAL RECEPTION RIGHT FROM THE GRASSROOT LEVEL

"She playfully showed with a smile and a wink, and a Teddy Bear hug - it could be the beginning of a honey-laden decade in a brave new world - by wisely trading guns for Teddy Bears". Yeah that's true. Women can change the world. But for this beginning should be made at home. Women's peace maker's role starts at home. Women are the major educators of the children at home, and continue to be so as they grow up. The quotation above shows that it is possible and necessary for mothers to change the very toys and concepts that boys grow up with (that is unfortunately, often the gun), and exchange them for the toys that bear the concept of love, like for instance, the hugging of a Teddy Bear, as we see above. Any effort to promote peace and to protect women and girls against aggression, which does not involve the early Peace Culture training and peace education of boys, will necessarily be short-lived. This includes the violent toys boys are attracted to and play with, under the general ambience that a toy gun makes them manly and "macho." Children's Television and Media programs are inundated with violent content, reinforced by stereotypic sex-role behavior. All this has to be drastically changed, and peace culture toys should replace violent toys in schools and homes, and on the market. How can we achieve such a tremendous change? Only through a colossal new Peace Culture System discussed in the following that would build a harmonious ambience where boys would want to hug teddy bears, instead of brandishing guns. Then the market too would change and produce teddy bears instead of guns. Education worldwide today is mostly run by women teachers, and this can provide an important channel for the revolution needed in the creation and establishment of a powerful and Peace Culture System in schools. Even in the few schools where peace education is taught, around the world, the curriculum in peace studies does not give due attention to the possible contribution of peace literature and the arts. The subject of peace studies and peace literature in general, has received relatively little attention in education, and not enough serious research has been conducted on the role that women, literature and the arts can play in promoting peace culture. In order to play an effective role in peace building structures, especially when their participation and perspectives have not been brought into discussions and decisions from the beginning; women and women's organizations are in need of political, technical and financial support and follow-through in order to do so. Women are community leaders, with formal and informal authority. Women are often at the centre of non-governmental organizations (NGOs), popular protests, electoral referendums, and other citizen-empowering movements whose influence has grown with the global spread of democracy. Because women frequently outnumber men after conflict, they often drive the on-the-ground implementation of any peace agreement; they therefore have a responsibility to be an integral part of the peace process.

LET'S GIVE WOMEN BETTER REPRESENTATION IN THE PEACE PROCESS

The common association of women, and the female gender with peace, suggests that policies to work with women ought to be fundamental to peace building. Both men and women have the potential for peacemaking and the responsibility to build and keep peace. The women, however, seem more creative and effective in waging peace. It is the women's emotional strength to transcend pain and suffering, and their predisposition to peace that provide them with greater potentials for peacemaking. It is therefore often the case that ideas about some of women's distinctive qualities (whether these are thought to be biologically or socially determined) become identified with the way forward in peace building, and strategies therefore focus on ways to enhance, support and extend the work that women are thought to be well-equipped to undertake. There is a general tendency for the leaders of institutions and political organisations to be the only participants at peace settlements, with very little grassroots participation. Women in general are thus marginalised, as they are always poorly represented at leadership level. Outside parties have had some limited success in enabling women to participate in peace talks. For instance, the Life and Peace Institute was successful in ensuring that women's peace groups gained access to some of the Somalia peace and reconciliation talks (even though they only gained observer status). Merely being invited to attend talks, peace conferences, or other peace forum, is insufficient, however, as very few women have the education, training or confidence to participate fully, even if they are in attendance. As one peace activist expressed it, there are too much technicalities that women have to learn. In terms of the technical capability to discuss and articulate the issues, women are much less prepared because they have not had the luxury of all the education, exposure and study that men have had when they go out and take long years to discuss. Women need to be encouraged, trained, and listened to when they speak in order to develop the self confidence and self belief. In order to play an effective role in peace building structures, especially when their participation and perspectives have not been brought into discussions and decisions from the beginning; women and women's organizations are in need of political, technical and financial support and follow-through in order to do so. Women are community leaders, with formal and informal authority. Women are often at the centre of non-governmental organizations (NGOs), popular protests, electoral referendums, and other citizen-empowering movements whose influence has grown with the global spread of democracy. Because women frequently outnumber men after conflict, they often drive the on-the-ground implementation of any peace agreement; they therefore have a responsibility to be an integral part of the peace process. Some women's organisations have developed the capacity to work openly to protect and extend human rights (especially in many Latin American countries). Other women's organisations have extended the work they took on during conflict to ensure that the social fabric did not collapse, through various forms of community organisation and welfare provision (especially where groups were established in 17 camps of refugees or displaced people during conflict, (such as in El Salvador, Guatemala, Rwanda and Burundi). Others more directly focus on the need to talk about, and take action on, strengthening peace in the name of women (such as in Israel/the Occupied Territories, former Yugoslavia, and the Federation of African Women's Peace Networks and Femmes-Africa-Solidarité in Africa). Finally there are those women's organisations which explicitly attempt to challenge women's oppression and gender inequality in post-conflict situations (such as those which facilitate women's participation in war-crimes tribunals and truth processes). Many of these organisations also attempt to build bridges between groups of women with very different experiences of conflict, who might otherwise be separated by their ethnic, regional or political identities. In order to play an effective role in peace building structures, especially when their participation and perspectives have not been brought into discussions and decisions from the beginning; women and women's organizations are in need of political, technical and financial support and follow-through in order to do so. Women are community leaders, with formal and informal authority. Women are often at the centre of non-governmental organizations (NGOs), popular protests, electoral referendums, and other citizen-empowering movements whose influence has grown with the global spread of democracy. Because women frequently outnumber men after conflict, they often drive the on-the-ground implementation of any peace agreement; they therefore have a responsibility to be an integral part of the peace process. Some women's organisations have developed the capacity to work openly to protect and extend human rights (especially in many Latin American countries). Other women's organisations have extended the work they took on during conflict to ensure that the social fabric did not collapse, through various forms of community organisation and welfare provision (especially where groups were established in 17 camps of refugees or displaced people during conflict, (such as in El Salvador, Guatemala, Rwanda and Burundi). Others more directly focus on the need to talk about, and take action on, strengthening peace in the name of women (such as in Israel/the Occupied Territories, former Yugoslavia, and the Federation of African Women's Peace Networks and Femmes-Africa-Solidarité in Africa). Finally there are those women's organisations which explicitly attempt to challenge women's oppression and gender inequality in post-conflict situations (such as those which facilitate women's participation in war-crimes tribunals and truth processes). Many of these organisations also attempt to build bridges between groups of women with very different experiences of conflict, who might otherwise be separated by their ethnic, regional or political identities.

CONCLUSION

Women make up 50 per cent of the population, how can you possibly attempt to create and maintain international peace and security when you're excluding 50 per cent of the population?" That women make a difference when they are in decision- and policymaking positions is no longer in dispute. When women participate in peace negotiations and in the crafting of a peace agreement, they keep the future of their societies, their communities, in mind. They think of how their children and grandchildren will be able to live in their own homeland in a peaceful and secure environment, how they will benefit from the structure of peace envisaged in the agreement. They have the broader and longer-term interest of society in mind whereas, historically in post-conflict situations, men are interested in ensuring that the peace process will give them the authority and power that they are seeking. A lasting peace cannot be achieved without the participation of women and the inclusion of gender perspectives and participation in peace processes. Informal peace initiatives of grassroots women's groups and networks, organized across party and ethnic lines, have carried out reconciliation efforts and have been increasingly recognized by the Security Council. Let me conclude by stressing again that sustainable peace is inseparable from gender equality. In coming years, women must play a most significant and substantive role in making the transition from the culture of violence to the culture of peace. We should not forget that when women are marginalized, there is little chance for an open and participatory society.

REFERENCES

1. Brock-Utne, B. (2009). A Gender Perspective on Peace Education and the Work for Peace. *International Review of Education,* 55(2-3), May, p. 205-220.
2. Tripp, A. M. (2012) 'Women's Political Empowerment in Statebuilding and Peacebuilding: A Baseline Study. November 2012. London: UK Department for International Development.
3. Thistlethwaite, S. B. (2011, October 11). Nobel peace prize 2011: Peace is women's work. The Washington Post. Retrieved from http://www.washingtonpost.com/2011/10/11/peace-is-women-work
4. Tickner, J. A. (1999). Why women can't run the world: International politics according to
5. Francis Fukuyama. International Studies Review, 1(3), 3-11. doi: http://dx.doi.org/10.1111/1521-9488.00162
6. Thompson, M. (2006). Women, gender, and conflict: Making the connections. *Development in Practice, 16*, 342-353. doi: http://dx.doi.org/10.1080/09614520600694976

7. UN Women (2012) Sourcebook on Women, Peace and Security.New York: UN Women.
8. UN Women (2011) Progress of the World's Women: In Pursuit of Justice, New York: UN Women.
9. United Nations (2002). Women, peace and security. Study submitted by the Secretary General pursuant to Security Council Resolution 1325. Retrieved from
10. http://www.un.org/womenwatch/daw/public/eWFS.pdf

Chapter-14

Aspects and Arrangements of Education at the Age of "Struggle for Empire" (C 650-1300 Ad)

Srabani Chatterjee

INTRODUCTION

India has played very crucial role in the sphere of education through centuries. Pupil from different countries came to this country for study. That's how India promotes peace and aesthetic philosophy to the world over time. In this paper I want to put emphasis on facts and philosophical thoughts related to education of a particular period of time. I choose such title for my paper i.e. "the age of 'struggle for empire'" instead of using early medieval period I choose this term because using the concept of periodization in Indian history is all together an debatable issue. Moreover I personally dislike this kind of uniliner scheme of dating. So I choose the name for the timeperiod of my paper from the name of the book "The Struggle for Empire", which is the 5th edition of the "The History and Culture of the Indian People" series published by Bharatiya Vidya Bhavan. Another intension of me is to offer homage to those great scholars who wrote and edited the series. Now come to the point. The scheme and scope of education in ancient & early medieval India is verily discussed topic. Which I mean to emphasize is that how religion played a vital role behind all these factors. Not only philosophy or essence of religion but also mechanism and institutions played a crucial role. The religio-economic institutions like Brahmadeya settlements were the chief centres of study in the said period. So, emphasizing on them I want to show other factors like regionalism of language and script, growing verbosity in literature and their mutual relationship as well. Likewise the factors and philosophy related to education could be understood.

Education not only has very vital role to play in our life but also in our national life. That's why every nation promotes as much effort as can be for the upliftment of education for future generation through ages. In ancient India arrangements were made for basic and higher education from the very beginning of civilization. But the arrangements and aspects of learning are different through ages. The period which I choose for my study in this article roughly falls within C.650-1200 A.D. This time period is precisely the period after the fall of Imperial Guptas and marked by political disintegration and struggle for empire building or unification. Generally this period is termed as early medieval period in Indian history. But there is much controversy regarding the proposed periodisation and I'm also not very convinced about using the name for "The Struggle For Empire", which is the 5th edition of the "The History and Culture of the Indian People" series published by Bharatiya Vidya Bhavan. Another intension of me is to offer homage to those great scholars who wrote and edited the book which precisely contains socio- economic- political history within the time frame of 650- 1200 A.D. which is the time period of our paper as well. And what is unique regarding education is the arrangement of educational institution specially the use of religious institution as education centres. The concept is not all together new, Buddhist Viharas worked as universities in earlier period. What is new is role played by Brahmadeya settlements in nurture and nourishment of education throughout the nation. Brahmadeyas are essentially the lands donated to Brahmana beneficiaries which are a striking socio- economic feature of Post- Gupta age. These Brahmadeya settlements played very crucial role in spreading Vedic culture throughout the country and provide and promote education in regional levels. That's how it thrust regionalism and sectarianism in education.

Many well versed scholars like Max Muller, Winternitz and U. N. Ghosal had important contribution in revealing the past of ancient Indian education system. I used their works for my study. Besides these secondary sources, there are loads of land grants documents precisely the copper plate inscription which can be found throughout the subcontinent. Especially the inscriptions from South India are very helpful in the study. They not only corroborate the other sources but also give some new information. Likewise I use both primary and secondary sources as method of my study during preparing this article.

Let us see how all the factors and arrangements worked together and what the outcomes are. In the post-Gupta centuries, India saw the concentration of the centres of education in religious establishments, such as the Viharas, mathas and temples just as the church was the principal organizer of education in Europe in the medieval times. Colleges also existed in some royal capitals such as Dhar, Ajmer, Anhillapura and of very famous Nalada, Vikramshila and Taxila etc. The fame of Mithila in North Bihar and Nadia in Bengal as centers of brahmanical learning increased in these centuries. Kashi (Varanasi) with its Shaiva monasteries was also a flourishing seat of brahmanical learning. Khemendra tells us that students from such distant regions as Gauda (Bengal) travelled to Kashmir for study in the Mathas. The evidence of Hemchandra reveals the existence of Vidya- Mathas in Gujrat in the twelfth century. Numerous agrahars in the south were developing as educational centres. Amongst notable universities, one can mention Nalanda, Vikramshila and Odantapuri (all in Bihar), Valabhi (Gujrat), Jagadadala and Sompuri (in Bengal) and Kanchipuram in Tamil Nadu.

The concept of temple libraries was evolved from eighth century. The real beginnings in his sphere were laid by the Jains. The long lists of their preceptors – bhattrakas and shripujyas, and the place of honour given to them are symptomatic of this development. Their espousal of the cause of Shatradana (gift of religious texts/manuscripts) explains the great bhandaras (store house) such as Patan, Khambhat, Jaisalmer etc. which became integral parts of Jain establishments in Gujrat, Rajasthan and Karnataka in particular. The trend was picked up by brahmanical mathas as well and we get a phenomenal proliferation of the manuscript tradition almost all over India.

That tantra and mantra became a favourite subject of study may be inferred from the fact that a full-fledged department of Tantra was run in the University of Vikramshila. The Tibetan traveler Taranatha, who came to India in the 17th century, is very eloquent about tantric curriculum at Nalanda, Odantapuri and other prominent universities of Bihar and Bengal. The growth and popularity of occult sciences also constitute a significant feature of the post-eighth of centuries. The list of subjects pursued by people in the thirteenth century has been given in Rajashekhara's Prabandhakosha. It includes many occult sciences in the long list of more than 70 subjects.

Chief factors which are the most notable phenomena in the sphere of learning in this particular time may be recounted:

1. Regionalism of languages,
2. Emergence of regional scripts and
3. Growing verbosity in literature.

The post-Gupta centuries are epoch-making in the history of language and literaturè. Although the large- scale dispersal of Sanskrit knowing brahmanas was resulting in the spread of that language in distant areas due to the land-grant phenomenon. The scope of Sanskrit was gradually getting confined. It was being used by the ruling class at the higher administrative levels. In the Naishandhiyacharita, we find the dignitaries present in the svayamvara of Damyanti having the fear of not being understood and, as such, taking recourse to Sanskrit.

According to Al-beruni, vernacular literature which was used by the common people was neglected by the upper and educated class. However, a development of undeniable significance is the differentiation of Apabhramsha into proto- Hindi, proto- Bengali, proto- Rajasthani, proto- Gujrati, proto- Marathi, proto- Maithili, etc. The Apabhramsha, which formed a link in our period between the Old- classical languages such as Sanskrit and Prakrit on the one hand and modern vernaculars on the other, originated much before our period. The Kuvalayamala, an eighth century work, enumerates as many as 18 Apabhramshas spoken in various regions of India, which turned into modern Indian languages later. In the list of Rajasshekhara, Prakrit, Paishachika, Apabhramsha and Deshabhasa are mentioned along with Sanskrit as subjects to be studied by a prince. Vernaculars such as Avahatha, Magadhi, Shakari, Abhiri, Chandali, Savali, Draviti, etc. formed part of curriculam mentioned in the Varna Ratnakara. The pace of linguistic variations quickened in the country in the post-Gupta centuries mainly on account of lack of inter-regional communication and mobility. The migrating brahmanas enriched the vocabulary of regional languages. They also helped to develop and systematize local dialects into languages through the introduction of writing.

The emergence of regional scripts runs parallel to the growth of regional languages. As there are numerous languages, so also there are quite a large number of scripts used to express these languages. From Maurya to Gupta times the script changed mainly as a result of the passage of time and anyone knowing the Brahmi script of the Gupta period could read inscriptions from any part of the country. This was not possible after the seventh century. From this period the regional variations become so pronounced that one has to be well-versed in several scripts to be able to read. Obviously, the regional script was produced by regional insulation and the availability of the locally educated scripts to meet the needs of local education and administration. Manuscripts, inscriptions and other written material use Devanagari, Assamese, Bengali, Oriya, Tamil, Telegu, Kannada and Sharada (in Kashmir) scripts. That the proliferation of scripts went beyond linguistic confines is clear from the case of Tamil. A study of various inscriptions leads one to an inescapable conclusion that though the Cheras, the Cholas and the Pandyas adopted Tamil as their language, each seems to have adopted a different script, perhaps to indicate their regional identity. The Cheras used a cursive variety of Tamil Brahmi called 'VATTELUTTU' (rounded script). The Pandyas seem to have popularized the 'KOLELUTTU' (script of straight lines) and the Cholas combined the two. This is not all. For philosophic and religious discourses, in the three kingdoms put together, the scholars gave rise to the Tamil Grantha script. Hundreds of manuscripts in this script are said to have reached as far north as Tibet, where Buddhist monasteries became great repositories.

While editing a medieval Sanskrit text called Subhashita-Ratnakosha, D.D. Kosambi brought to light many neglected poets but characterized it as a decadent poetry or writing of a decadent age. Sometimes we understand such phenomena in absolute or total sense. It is not necessary that economic, political, social and cultural decline run simultaneously. Also, the yardstick of "decadence" cannot be worked out in absolute terms. The erotic sculptures of Khajuraho, Bhubaneswar, Konarka and Belur may appear to some to be products of a perverted mind but the same art pieces are taken by others to be manifestation of vital cultural ethos of people.

The post-eighth centuries saw prolific literary outputs in realms of philosophy, logic, legal texts, devotional poetry of the Alvars and the Shaiva Agamas, Kavyas, narratives, lyrics, historical biographies, scientific writings, shilpashastras, etc. Nonetheless, in keeping with the growing paraphernalia and personal vanity of the new landed classes, the language of most of these literary compositions became extremely verbose and ornate. This ornate style marked by pompous adjectives, adverbs and similes became the hallmark of literature as well as inscriptions. Although the prose style of Bana, which is known for highly complex and elaborate sentence constructions, was not exactly initiated, it did continue to serve as a model for the post- seventh century writings.

In the realm of poetry too, dvayashraya or Shelsha Kavyas were being produced consciously. These works contain verses conveying two different senses when read in different directions. The Ramacharita of Sandhyakara Nandi presents both the story of Rama and the life of king Ramapala of Bengal. The marriages of Shiva and Parvati and Krishna and Rukmini are described in a twelfth century work (Parvati Rukminiya) produced in the Chalukya court. Hemachandra is credited with the composition of Saptasanbhana having seven alternative interpretations. The tendency of working out the intricate pattern of double, triple or even more meanings reflects the artificiality of life.

Most striking feature of education system prevailed in this age is the crucial role of religion played in behalf of education. What I meant to say is education in ancient India always leans to religion but the forms and factors implemented are somewhat unique. As the earlier times records are completely silent about the methods of primary education. As for the mass, education successfully provided by the public recitation of the epics, puranas and other religious work. In the sphere of higher education we all know that the Smriti texts described the scheme of higher education elaborately for the three upper classes. Students have to stay at the house of his teacher after the sacred thread ceremony and have to live a humble life there. Period of study for each class is mentioned. Among the daily duties of the student, daily begging for food occupies an important place. Another noteworthy point is that Smriti-chandrika, Vigyaneswar and Aparaarka beating a pupil for correction is admitable. The beating should be done with rope or a split bamboo, and not with the hand, and it should be applied not to the head but to the lower part of the body. Violation of this rule by the teacher is an offence punishable by the king. The scheme for technical education cannot be find out easily due to lack of source material. However Italian traveler Marco Polo gave vivid description of the very practical method of training tradesman's apprentices in the Pandya region. At the age of thirteen the parents dismiss their boys from home with small pocket money for earning their livelihood. During the season for pearl fishing they purchase small number of pearls from beach and sell them to the merchants in their homes. They were likewise trained to be keen traders.

While discussing the factors we already have pointed out that the large scale dispersal of Sanskrit knowing brahmanas due to receiving land grants shows the spread and development of language in distant areas. But this is not about all. It has some other important parts to play as well. B. D. Chattopadhyay has argued for land grants as part of larger social and cultural process by the expansion of state society through the process of local state formation, the transformation of tribes into peasants and caste formation and cult formation and interaction. This period saw the popularity of temple- based sectarian religion. Different inscriptions from different parts of India, to be frank maximum from south India shows that brahmana settlements or bramhadeyas were keenly attached to the temple management and related works. It is clear that the brahmadeyas played vital role in the spread of temple-oriented sectarian religion. These brahmadeya settlements have through royal patronage. The proliferation of land grants to brahmanas not only saw an enormous output in the sphere of Sanskrit literature but also spread of education as well. Besides the monastic university of Nalanda, Vikramshila, Sompura, Jagaddala, these brahmana villages and temple institutions worked in spreading education even in the remotest corner of the country. Here patronage through land grants has played an important role in promoting education. Because this type of wealth based on control of land, and the emergence of clusters of settlements inhabited by the brahmanas provided a section of brahmana intelligentsia with the security and wealth necessary for sustained intellectual activity.

We have in fact dozens of epigraphic evidences to show how the temples gradually became the centres for education, not only religion based but secular also and how royal and individual personalities were at their utmost ready to provide all kinds of financial, structural and medical help. In the regions of Madhyadesa a Saiva temple with a matha and a hall of study was founded by the Queen mother Alhanadevi, according to an inscription of A.D. 1155. A brahmana in the time of Vikramaditya VI appointed a body of 104 villages – mahajanas as trustees for his gift of certain lands. Under the terms of the trust a certain portion of land with a house- site was assigned as maintenance (bhatavrritti) to a teacher for teaching the grammatical work called Nyasa and Mimamsa work of Prabhakara, while another portion with a house- site was made over to a teacher in Mathematics, Astronomy, Prosody and Grammar for his personal requirements as well as for teaching his pupils feeding them once a day, and supplying them with cloth once a year. In the Kakatiya kingdom a famous Saiva teacher allotted out of two villages assigned to him by Queen Rudeamadevi certain lands for maintenance of a Saiva temple along with a college, a feeding house for Saiva mendicants, and so forth. The college maintained a staff of three teachers of Rigveda, Yajureda, and Samveda respectively, and five teachers of logic, literature and the agamas. Allotment of land was made likewise to a physician for attending upon the resident- teachers, students, and attendants. However the largest numbers of records of endowments for learning that have came down to us for this period are those of the imperial Cholas especially from the reign period of Rajaraja I and Rajendra Chola.

CONCLUSION

So as we can see regionalism of languages, emergence of regional script and growing verbosity in literature are the chief factors of learning in the said period. And all these factors lead for and towards the new arrangements made for education, the utilization of religious institutions for providing education in every corner of country. Later on this type of regional sectarian education, resulted because of this new arrangement make the way for different kinds of philosophic concepts especially in Brahmanic religion and became a striking feature of later period. But the growing importance of Brahmadeyas in education and society started decreasing with the advent of Muslim rulers in India in later period.

BIBLIOGRAPHY

1. Aiyer K.V. Subrahmanya (1928, 1933). South Indian Inscriptions.(Vol – 2&3). Madras: Archaeological Survey of India.
2. Altekar A.S. (1957). Education in Ancient India. (5th edition). Varanasi: Gyan Publishing House.
3. Max Muller Friedrich (1860). A History of Ancient Sanskrit Literature (1st edition). London: Williams and Norgate.

4. Majumdar R.C.(edited) (2001) The Struggle for Empire (5th edition). Mumbai: Bharatiya Vidya Bhavan.
5. Singh Upinder (2009). A History of Ancient and Early Medieval India. New Delhi: Pearson Education Ltd.
6. Winternitz Moriz (1996). A History of Indian Literature, (Vol- 1). (Second edition). Varanasi: Motilal Banarasidass Publishers.

Chapter-15

A Study On Role of Peace Education in Secondary School in West Bengal

Arnab Chowdhury & Jayanta Mete

INTRODUCTION

In the present research paper, the researcher introduces an educational approach, by the name of "Peace Education Through study" as a part of Peace Education, which can undo certain basic negative effects of unrests taking place all round us. It attempts to do so by way of bringing in core human values essential for peaceful and health living. It provides a wide range of interesting and interactive stories which may be used as methods of teaching and learning and to deliver the curriculum effectively alongside with a focus on core human values. This study was aimed to evaluate the effectiveness of Peace Education at the Standard Ten level. Null hypothesis was formulated. The research was experimental in nature. The research design followed by researcher was One group Pre test Post Test Design. Data was analyzed using t-test. The conclusion is evident that Peace Education is an effective manner of providing Peace Education for Standard X students.

Peace education is not just about what happens in school. It is not about what you need to know for the test or memorize to please the teacher. Peace education is about how you can help build the future and make your world a more peaceful place to live.
Peace education asks you to ask yourself:

- What is PEACE?
- Is there peace in my life? Where? In my classroom? In my family? In my community?

- In my town? In my society?
- Where in my life cycle would I like to see more peace?
- What is important for me to LEARN about peace?
- What can I DO with peace and what I learn?

Lots of kids and young adults around the world are asking themselves what they can do to make the world a safer, healthier, greener, more fair and less violent place for everyone to live and grow. With so many challenges for the future, learning about peace in school is an important beginning.

What Is Peace Education?

'Peace is possible for life at all stages and it is up to man to choose his destiny or to suffer from the horrors of war. Today mankind is at the cross-road where he has to choose with courage, determination and imagination.'- Federico Mayor.

On reading this a teacher might wonder 'Is it really necessary to teach peace as such? Whole education is for peace. Isn't it already in the curriculum?' She may be right in a sense. But the questions remain: Are we giving adequate attention today to teach peace? Are our schools really interested in producing a peaceful young generation? Is it enough having mere peace concepts in the curriculum?

Under the present scenario there is a growing realization in the world of education today that children should be educated in the art of peaceful living. As a result, more and more peace concepts, attitudes, values and behavioural skills are being integrated into school curricula in many countries. There is also renewed interest to develop peace-related disciplines such as values education, moral education, global education, environmental education etc. In the past we seemed to have assumed that the more knowledge people have, the better they are. Accordingly, we stressed cognitive learning in schools at the cost of developing children's emotional, social, moral and humanistic aspects. The consequence of such imbalanced learning is evident today in the forms of youth unrest with their antisocial attitudes and behavioural problems.

Development of Peace Education

In tracing the recent development of peace education, we begin to see that in the past it had been an integral part of education at all times and in all cultures, every culture regards peace as a noble ideal to attain. However with the advent of Western secularism at the beginning of the 20th century through the guise of a positivist scientific outlook to education, moral and human values including peace were slowly discouraged away from school curricula.

However, in spite of such materialistic views, the thinking of such humanists like Rousseau, Henry Thoreau, Tolstoy and Maria Montessori kept the sense of education alive. With the witness of the horrors of the First and Second World Wars there was-a reawakening to the need of developing the humanistic side of education at least among a few educationists.

Peace education is more effective and meaningful when it is adopted according to the social and cultural context and the needs of a country. It should be enriched by its cultural and spiritual values together with the universal human values. It should also be globally relevant. Peace education is holistic. It embraces the physical, emotional, intellectual, and social growth of children within a framework deeply rooted in traditional human values. It is based on philosophy that teaches love, compassion, trust, fairness, co-operation and reverence for the human family and all life on our beautiful planet (Fran Schmidt and Alice Friedman, 1988)

Peace education is skill building. It empowers children to with creative and nondestructive ways to settle conflict and to live in harmony with themselves, others, and their world. Peace building is the task of every human being and the challenge of the human family (Fran Schmidt and Alice Friedman 1988)

Educational Power of a Study

Story has tremendous power to influence learning. It can be a very effective instructional tool. It can be easily integrated into different subjects. It can be applied in real life situations. It can be as a form of creative activities for many skills. It comprises of three terms – the teller, the story and the audience. Stories may be used as Entertainment, Education and for relieving distress. In their later avatars, manifestations, it has been experience of many educationists, therapists including this author, that a message is conveyed far more clearly through a tale, than a command or instruction. T.S. Eliot once wrote of written literature for young: "I incline to come to the alarming conclusion that it is just the literature that we read for „amusement" or „purely for pleasure" that may have the greatest and the least suspected influence upon us."

The study is an account of real events. It comes alive when it is tested and proved. The process of telling or explaining has been associated with study from the very beginning.

In study, real events are portrayed in words, images, and sounds. Since ancient times, human beings were using study to communicate a message or feeling or discover. Initially these images were also scratched onto the walls of caves. With the gradual evolution of human activities and technology, woodcarving, stone carving, painting on canvas, filmmaking or electronic digital messages were used to share these images. With the invention of writing, stories were recorded, transcribed and shared over wide regions of the world. These written studies have shown some of the humanity's most enduring message of struggle, hope and triumph.

In India conducting study is a part and parcel of Folk media, other forms of folk media being puppetry, proverbs, visual art, drama, concert, songs, drumming and dancing. A mythological study has been a part and parcel of every Indian Grandmother's food for thought for her grandchild. We all have grown up on this nutrition. The mythological study shows that the story shared by the elders in our families often motivates the us to perform certain special ceremonies daily or annually as our lives move through cycle of the seasons.

The word myth is derived from Greek word myths, which has a range of meanings from word to through saying and story to fiction. Myth has existed in every society. It is basic constituent of human culture. Mythology is a part of the study of religion and every myth fits in the total structure of the life of the society that believes in it.

The students would have heard some of these stories in the present context. Some such stories used by the researcher to infuse peace education are as follows:

- In India, environmental awareness dates back to the 14th century, in Rajasthan.The Bishnois are a small tribe in Rajasthan, who practice a religion of environmental conservation. They believe that cutting a tree or killing an animal or bird is blasphemy. In 17th century, during Aurangzeb"s time, a king of Jodhpur, wanted to cut the trees in the Bishnoi area and use it to build a new palace. The Bishnois protested and hugged the trees to protect them but the soldiers paid no heed. 294 men and 69 women were axed to death. When the king heard of this massacre he stopped the operation and offered protection to the Bishnois. The sacrifice of the Bishnois was the inspiration for the Chipko movement.

- Noah was asked by God to prepare a boat and take with him all his sons and their wives along with the male and female species of all living things clearly indicating emphasis on the interdependence of the species.

Peace Education through Study

Creating the Situation

- Teacher introduces the problem with help of a role play, dramatization, case study, anecdote, newspaper cutting etc
- Teacher asks probing questions in order to focus the attention of the Pupil on the problem
- Teacher with help of Pupils defines the problem/issue
Creating the Linkage
- Teacher narrates a mythological study based on story:

In Mahabharata, the Pandavas were exiled for twelve years, after having lost the kingdom in a game of dice. Arjuna went to the heaven to acquire the Divya astras to be used in warfare against Duryodhana. When he returned, the Pandavas were curious to know the strength of the astras, and requested Arjuna to demonstrate their use. But, just as he was about to use one of the astras, the devas stopped him. They said the use of such a powerful weapon just for exhibition or fun was strictly prohibited. The forest reserves cannot be targeted for casual experimentation.

Group Discussion

- Teacher with the help of developmental questions establishes a logical link of the story with the content to be taught.
- This mythology can be effectively used to integrate the need to use nuclear energy for peaceful purpose in the subject of Science as well as History. It can be used in the teaching of forest wealth in Geography and Economics.

The above procedure of study was used to Transact Peace Education to standard X students and the effectiveness of the same was studied.

Objectives of the study

Following were the objectives of the research.

- To prepare the students for transacting peace education among standard X students.
- To test the effectiveness of prepared study.

Variables of the study

- Independent variable: Peace Education Through Study
- Dependent variable: Awareness about peace education.

Operational definition

Awareness about Peace Education: It is defined as the extent of sensitivity about need and importance of peace at international level and skills required for sustaining unity in institution. (Mhatre, 2008)

Hypothesis

Following null hypothesis was put forward.

There will be no significant difference in the pre and post test scores on awareness about peace education.

Scope and limitation of the study

The study was limited to English medium students of standard X studying in a school situated in Ranaghat in West Bengal.

Significance of the study

The developed study will be useful to the teachers of the schools. The Study also will provide guidelines for developing pedagogy for transacting peace education. The use of study will enable students not only understand the Indian culture through mythology but also create an insight into the rich cultural heritage and the sound values of it.

III. Methodology

For the present study experimental method has been used. Researcher adopted single group pre-post test design.

Sample

Non-probability sampling method was used. Students from one class of standard eight were included in the sample. Fifty students were selected by incidental sampling.

TOOLS USED

Rating scale prepared by the researcher for measuring awareness about peace education was used. This is 4-point scale with 36 statements. Coefficient of reliability by Cronbach alpha is 0.50 and by split-half method is 0.66. The maximum possible score is 144 and minimum is 36.

DEVELOPMENT OF PETS

On the basis of operational definition following objectives were decided.

To create awareness about

1. Need and importance of peace education.
2. Importance of communication skill in maintaining peace.
3. Importance of co-operation in maintaining peace.
4. Making proper decisions in maintaining peace.
5. Importance of conflict resolution in maintaining peace.

Following points were taken into consideration while preparing activities.

1. All the activities were group centered.
2. Activities were based on the study.

Altogether 12 clock hours were required for implementing the study.

DATA ANALYSIS

Single group t-test was used for analysis of the data. TABLE 1 shows significance of difference in the pre and post test means.

Table 1: Significance of Difference Between Means of Pre and Post Test

Test	N	MEAN	R	SE_D	t-value	LOS
Test Post Test	50 50	92.98 92.98	0.27	0.67	11.79	0.01

Source: Primary Data

For df=49, calculated t is greater than tabulated t. Hence null hypothesis is rejected at 0.01 level. It shows that Peace Education on Study was effective in creating awareness.

Discussion: Since students had given opportunity to think and reflect on the study, it may have helped them to realize the importance and maintenance of peace. That may be the reason for effectiveness of the prepared Peace education through study.

SUGGESTIONS FOR TEACHERS

From the above conclusion it is evident that simple Study are useful for giving the message of peace. There is no need to include peace education as a separate subject in the syllabus. One can plan such simple stories and implement them during proxy periods or value education period. Wherever possible teacher can use integrated approach. For example while teaching about atomic energy in Science class teacher can have discussion about use and misuse of it. The teacher has a key role, facilitating the process by which students hone their social competency skills. More specifically, this methodology includes five techniques:

1. Model skills such as reflective listening, I-Statements and problem-solving on an regular basis.
2. Teach skills by promoting basic understanding and recognition of the skills as well as providing an opportunity to practice the skills in low-stress situations.
3. Coach students by supporting their efforts to translate mental knowledge into practical application and providing feedback regarding their efforts.
4. Encourage students to use skills appropriately by providing brief prompts and reminders. Reinforce students" efforts through praise and recognition of intrinsic rewards.
5. Export students" skill proficiency by involving them in opportunities for meaningful participation such as service learning projects or mentoring less-experienced students.

Benefits

The report drafted in 1996 by the UNESCO commission for Education in the 21st century entitled "Learning: The Treasure Within" reflects on four pillars of Education; two out of the four pillars of education suggested are "Learning to Live Together" and "Learning to be", are related to peaceful living. At matters is integrating peaceful attitudes, values, and skills into the teaching and learning process in school and makes it a part of the total curriculum. Certain countries and institutes have it in the form of subjects such as Values Education, (Malaysia and Philippines), Citizenship Education (U.S.A.). Education for Mutual Understanding (Ireland) and Developmental Education (UNICEF). Through applying peace education and creating a peace culture, it has been observed that educational institutions can have the following benefits

Educational Institutions can:

- Develop a more humanistic management approach.
- Improve human relations between, teacher-student, teacher-teacher, student-student, etc.
- Help develop good attitudes in students and teachers as well, e.g. co-operation, mutual respect.
- Help healthy emotional development in students.
- Facilitate socialization through participation in interactive and co- operative learning activities
- Improve students' discipline and moral behaviour.
- Develop creativity both in students and teachers.
- Improve standard of quality of teaching and learning.

CONCLUSIONS

No education system is complete without some form of component similar to peace education. It may take such forms as moral, value or citizenship, democratic or global education. The differentiating feature of peace education is the focus it has on the problem of human violence. In short, peace education can be defined as an educational response to the problem of human violence. It has the following basic features: It aims at protecting children's minds from being imbued by violence in the society. It prepares them for building a peaceful world by empowering them with necessary knowledge, attitudes, and skills. It humanizes the child, teaching and learning, and school.[4]

Educational institutions can directly benefit by adopting peace education. There is ample evidence to show that it improves the quality of teaching and learning, discipline, and helps emotional development in children. [5]

It is interesting to mention here an evaluation done on affective learning techniques such as using stories to infuse Peace Education has resulted in the following major outcomes:

- Better learning of cognitive material.
- Heightened motivation and response to learning situations.
- Greater appreciation of self, nature, others, feelings, etc.
- Greater pupil responsibility

Hence to conclude one may say that stories are a wonderful resource for Teachers, Parents, Grandparents, Mentors, coaches, Mental health professionals and even political speakers to convey a point and drive it home.

BIBLIOGRAPHY

1. New Era Development Institute. Peace Education Activities for Children: A Teacher"s Guide. Panchgani, India: New Era Development Institute, 2002.
2. Synder, C. R., Lopez S. J., (2007) *Positive Psychology the scientific and practical explorations of human strengths* Sage South Asia edition, New Delhi.
3. Stephen P. Robbins. (2004) *Organizational behavior* Prentice Hall of India, New Delhi.
4. Banks, James A. (Editor). (2003). *Diversity and Citizenship Education: Global Perspectives*. San Francisco: Jossey-Bass.
5. Tiedt, P. (2001). In *Multicultural teaching* (6th ed.). Boston, MA: Allyn and Bacon.
6. Castro, Loreta Navarro and Jasmin, Nario-Galace(2008): „Peace Education: A Pathway to a Culture of Peace", Centre for Peace Education Miriam College: Quezon City, Philippines.
7. Dar, Altaf Ahmad (2013): "Imparting Peace Education children affects most", March 9, Greater Kashmir: Srinagar.
8. Wani, Showket Rashid (2010): "Peace education in schools" www.jandknow.com 25 Sep. 2010.
9. Srinivasan, Anupama(2008): "A Survey of Civil Society Peace Education Programmes in South Asia",Educational Policy Research Series, Volume I, Number, 2 August.
10. This study was conducted by Chennai based NGO The Pranjya Trust which is working for peace, justice and security
11. Desai, Mihir (2004): „Peace Education" AAKASH, AshaStanfords Quarterly Newsletter, Volume1 issue 3.

12. Mahapatra, DebidattaAurobinda and Shekhawat, Seema(2008): The Peace Process and Prospects for Economic Reconstruction in Kashmir", Peace and Conflict Review · Volume 3 Issue 1
13. I have personally participated in this seminar in March 21, 2011, for more information The Hindu(Chennai edition) March 22, 2011.
14. It was said by one of the respondent during interview in Govt Degree College Anantnag Kashmir on Dec. 20,2011
15. Youth Entrepreneurship in Kashmir: Challenges and Opportunities, SKYE Project,www.mercycorps.org/sites/.../youth_entrepreneurship_in_kashmir.pd, accessed on March 10,2012
16. Saadut, Economic opportunities denied: Kashmir, http://www.saadut.com/2011/11/economic-opportunities-denied-kashmir.html, accessed on March 2, 2012.
17. This view was expressed by one of the respondent during interview in Govt Degree College Anantnag Kashmir on Dec. 20,2011
18. As per the results of the Questionnaire

Chapter-16

Conflicts of South Asia and Human Right

Prodip Adhikari

INTRODUCTION

Before going to discuss, it is necessary to discuss what do we actually understand by human rights? Normally people say, 'Rights of Human being is called Human Rights' Many researcher also say, 'To live in a healthy way is Human Right'. Is it so? To live in a better way by causing harm to anybody is Human Rights. The matter is not like that. Every region or country has some socially approved principles. The right to alive in a healthy way through the work which is supported by the socially approved principal is called Human Rights[1].

According United Nations Human Rights Office of the High Commissioner Human rights are rights inherent to all human beings, whatever our nationality, place of residence, sex, national or ethnic origin, colour, religion, language, or any other status. We are all equally entitled to our human rights without discrimination. These rights are all interrelated, interdependent and indivisible.[2]

According to Robert Niven Human Rights is "Rights arise from the fact that man is a social being.[3] Thomas Hill Green said "Without society conscious of common moral interest, there can be no right".[4]

According to Ernest Barker, "Rights in there are the result, and the embodiment in particular person, of the general system of rights or justice on which the state and its law are based".[5]

Universal human rights are often expressed and guaranteed by law, in the forms of treaties, customary international law, general principles and other sources of international law. International human rights law lays down obligations of Governments to act in certain ways or to refrain from certain acts, in order to promote and protect human rights and fundamental freedoms of individuals or groups.[6]

Human Right violated is south area? If we want to get the answer, we have look into the present political condition of South Asia.

South Asia is important for geo politically and it is the region for discussion again and again. But its political history is not old. History of human rights no linked with this. Basically when political news is published in world's mass media, it is picture of violation of Human Rights become clear to us violation of Humans Rights is echoing from country to country all over the world which also influence South Asia. So, the people of South Asia involve themselves in struggle for Human Rights. But in many cases it fails. As days goes on. Violation of Human Rights is increasing. Kidnapping of human being, child problem, child labour, murder in border politically arrest, death in police custody, crossfire rape, assault of female, environmental al problem is going on[7]. The number of people is increasing day by day whereas national income does not increase side by side which create many problems. Though this type of incident occurs every year in every country Government of any country, Rules and Judgmental of South Asia have to take proper step united on the issue of the violation of Human Rights.

South Asia is the poor of and politically instable region of the world. Day by day the condition of Human Rights becomes world for the country Bangladesh, India, Pakistan, Srilanka, Nepal Afganistan along with south Asia[8]. The role of Taliban in Afganistan, Collision between different groups in Pakistan which takes many lives, Terrorist activity in Bangladesh and political instability in Nepal proves the violation of Human Rights.

Mass media empress its concern for murder, rape terrorism and condition of Human Rights in India. Though at present in India, there are more than 3,000 Human Rights Organization, they fail to take proper role. The department of Rules and Regulations accepts a small number of allegations, Muslims and Dalits are worst victims. It is a matter of concern for the protection of Muslims and Dalits as the incident of importance is increasing.

The news of violation of Human Right in Asia which we heard are extramarital murder prevent to express own opinion, prevent to organize peaceful meeting. Attack, on Judge and lawyer make Judgmental system weak. The incident of impatience against Muslim and Christian is worrying the protection for minority recently. There is an urge for international investigation for the violation Human Rights during the civil war in Srilanka. But Srilankan Government failed to take proper step against the allegation of violation of Human Rights.

There are people against whom there are allegations of violation of Human Rights. Give freedom from such allegation means deprive of thousands of Napalist the way to make peace. Nepal Government passed a rule to make a commission which investigates the allegation of violation of Human Rights from 1996-2006[9]. During this one decade takes lives of thirteen thousand people and many people are missing.

In Bangladesh, recently we see a tendency of public beating along with terrorist attack. Bangladesh is Human Organization Ask gives a report where we notice that death by public beating is increasing in 2014 where the number increases by 123 in 2015 total 135. People often take the rules in their in their hands which worries Human Rights. A rapid assessment of 675 commercially sexually exploited children and adolescents conducted in 2008 found that the number of trafficked women and children rescued has increased (from 93 persons in 2007 to 190 in 2008), while rehabilitation efforts are also increasing (from 104 in 2007 to 207 in 2008). This highlights increasing social awareness of trafficking and sexual exploitation of women in Bangladesh.[10]

Dr. Barkat, professor of Dhaka University says in his research, the missing number of Hindu is not same all the time. According to Dr. Barkat, During 1964-1977 Total Hindu Missing 705, during 1971-1981 Total Hindu Missing 521, during 1981-1991 Total Hindu Missing 438, 1991-2001 Total Hindu Missing 667 and 2001-2012 Total Hindu Missing 674. Dr. Barkat says in his research during 1964-2013 total Hindus left Bangladesh to India 1crore and 13 lacs.[11]

Year	Number of Missing Hindu per day
1964-1971	705
1971-1981	521
1981-1991	438
1991-2001	667
2001-2012	674

In Every year 230612 Hindu people are missing or they are fared to leave country.632 Hindu people are forced to leave per day.

Caption: A Protest by Women of Bangladesh Source: http://www.kolkata24x7.com/minority-hindus-living-from-bangladesh.html

In Kashmir is another reason for the violation of Human Rights, Government of India must stop the violation of Human Rights by Armed Force under Armed Force Special Power Act. In the age of globalization, where the whole world is thinking about properly and future Kashmir is worried for protection and fundamental Rights most of the country in India is in indiscipline.Condition and everybody is involved in a movement for the fulfillment of self motive. As a result, a country break into small region, India does not get rid from this. A terrorist movement starts for the claim of Gorkha and in Uttarbongo. Even the soldier of Gorkha, Gorkha Regiment of India claims for 'Gorkhaland' and they also say, 'Gun is also in our hands'. National Democratic front of Bodolands paresh Boruya group, PJACBM and ABASU, NDFBsupport the claim for 'Gorkhaland'. Minister does not solve the people who involve themselves in this movement. They are in search of a path of peace, but this will not stop in this political advantageous political system.

Bhutan is considered to link with globalization In South Asian country, we notice monthly the difference of nation, religion and color. In every country of the world, there is contrast of political, social and religion.

The country of western country united them economically. The politician of South Asia failed to create any region based unity. Though they tell about unity but they work against unity.

There are some reasons why south Asian Politician does not solve the problem but they keep up the problem.

First, to keep up war like mentality among the people of this region against appoint. For this reason people think the opponent is looked as winner country whereas neighbor country is looked as enemy country and neighbor is written such as except two or three characters, all characters are involve them into terrorist activity. Seeing this type of film, people starts to believe the neighbor country as enemy country. Even in India Pakistan Cricket match, if Pakistan players well, India hesitate to say the true. In a champion League India is Defeated by Pakistan where Mir says that if celebrity like

According to Artist Meer, "Sachin and Sourav comment on the defeat, it does not a matter of blame for them. What is problematic for the local people's reaction on the defeat?" Impatience is defeated by India by the Pakistanese by breaking T.V Why is it? Researchers think. That here religion is not a barrier. Was there not friendship between the two countries? Actually there are some people in both the country who never want friendship they just fulfill their motive.

Second, there is an excuse that that threat may come from neighbor country so that people are keeps away from Human Rights.

Third there is lack of daring among the present politician. The things are kept as it is we find many people with this type of mentality who does not like any change.

CONCLUSION

Combination of cooperation of people from region is much needed to establish Rights. Conflict within its own country is the main barrier. We have to be united for the sack of democracy. We has to solve the entire problem by discussion. Leo Borman said, if there is no Human Right, People will not be happy. But there are many countries where there are Human Rights but the People of this country are not happy. The employee of all Human Rights has to work cordially. It needed discussion should be done with Government. This barrier should be drive away. The problem is not for one person, it is problem for all.

BIBLIOGRAPHY

1. Rai Chowdhury, P. (September, 2015). Manab Adhikar O Manab Unnayn. Kolkata: Progressive Publishers. pp. 13.
2. Retrieved http://www.ohchr.org/EN/Issues/Pages/WhatareHumanRights.aspx
3. Gilchrist, R.N. (1921). Principles of Political Science. pp. 135.
4. Rai Chowdhury, P. (September, 2015). Manab Adhikar O Manab Unnayn. Kolkata: Progressive Publishers. pp. 15.
5. Rai Chowdhury, P. (September, 2015). Manab Adhikar O Manab Unnayn. Kolkata: Progressive Publishers. pp. 16.
6. Ibid.
7. Retrieved https://www.unicef.org/rosa/protection_7735.htm
8. Retrieved https://www.amnesty.org/en/latest/news/2017/02 human-rights-violations-endemic-in-south-asia

9. Retrieved https://www.revolvy.com/topic/Human%20rights%20in%20Nepal&item_type=topic
10. Retrieved Women and girls in Bangladesh. United for Children.UNICEF. https://www.unicef.org/bangladesh/Women_and_girls_in_Bangladesh.pdf
11. Retrieved http://www.bdtimes365.com/news-others/2017/05/31/158532

Chapter-17

Contribution of the Kothis to the Promotion of World Peace with Special Reference to Kothi Raushan UD Daula

Amrita Sen & Prodip Adhikari

INTRODUCTION

Lucknow, earlier known as the "City of Nawabs" or "the Constantinople of India" has been ornamented with various magnificent buildings better known as "kothi" such as "Gulistan-e-Irum", Darshan Vilas and so on. However these buildings although in dilapidated condition (though some conservation work has started) is vocal about the thought process of the people and the culture they housed and the amount of architectural excellence, time and energy they invested in beautification keeping tandem with the needs of the time. Very skillfully the artisans and the architects adopted and incorporated the gothic styles and Islamic style of architecture to give birth to the indigenous style of their own.

Keywords: Awadh; kothi; lucknow; indo-islamic style of architecture; Gothic Architecture

Awadh, with its capital at lucknow, for long had commanded an esteemed position in the society as the cultural hub of India especially throughout the Medieval period in the northern India. This place has a history of immense contribution to the development of new genres of architecture, music (thumri), literature (ghazal) and unique style of dance form *(kathak)*.

W. H. Russels, in 1858 described the city as –

"a fairy tale city, more vast and brilliant than Paris; a vision o palaces, domes azure and golden cupolas, colonnades long facades of fair perspective in pillar and column, terraced roofs- all rising up amid a calm still ocean of brightest verdures. Look for miles and miles and miles away, and still the ocean spreads, and towers of the fairyb city glean in its midst, spires of gold glitter in the sun, turrets and gilded spheres shine like constellations."

In 1722, the Mughal Emperor appointed Sadat Khan, a Persian Shi'a nobleman, as the Subehdar of Awadh and till 1856 his successors who ruled the land was popularly known as the "Nawabs". They are known to have enhanced the cultural tradition of this place and took it to a great height which is still contributing to the economy of the state through the tourism industry.

OBJECTIVES

The objective of this study is to understand and analyse the unique style of architectural features of the monuments (kothis) of the Nawabs in Quaiserbagh in lucknow with special reference to "kothis"- raushan-ud-daulah and see how it was responsible in producing a society that believed in international peace and harmony

METHODOLOGY

Field Survey

A group of 5 students of Archaeology had gone to survey the area in Quaiserbagh, specifically 3 "Kothis" namely- "Raushan-ud daulah", "Gullistan e Erum" and"Darshan Vilas" for photography

Interview of the local people

The local people were interviewed to know the history of these buildings that revealed interesting turns.

Use of secondary sources of information

This paper relies mostly on the secondary sources of information (such as newspaper articles, books and articles etc.) regarding the position of women living in the kothis, in the society and the Nawabs.

Limitation

Reliance on the secondary sources of information can be considered to be a limiting factor as the biasedness of the authors can prove to be influential.

The basement chambers of the monuments could not be reached as they were dumped with garbage so could not be examined properly.

The personal interviews of the local people included various stories of their own which might be a deviation from the actual events.

Study Area

Roshan-ud-Daulah Kothi (26⁰ 51'8.28" North latitude and 80°55'46.82" East longitude), is situated at an elevation of 120 m above sea level at a distance of 0.22 km from River Gomati which lies to its north. This "*kothi*" is situated in the locality of Qaiserbagh Bus Terminus, towards the northwest of the city of Lucknow of about 4 km from Charbagh Railway Station, on the Kanpur Road.

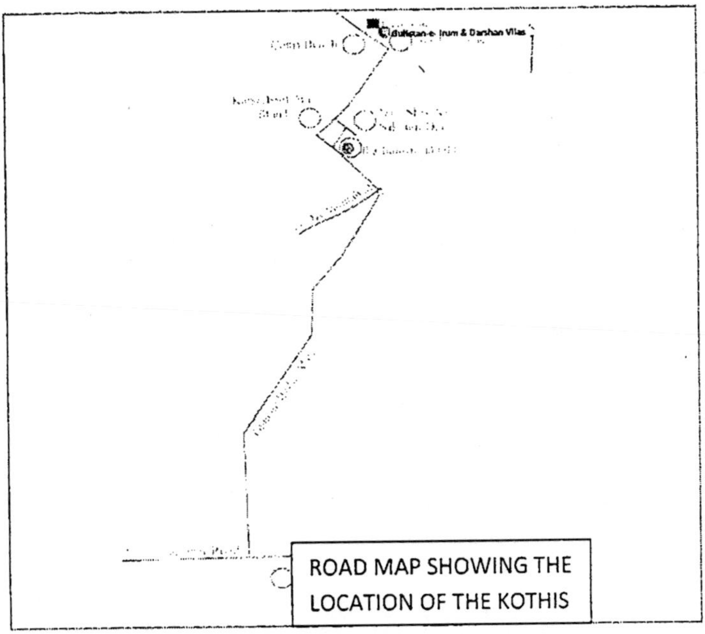

ROAD MAP SHOWING THE LOCATION OF THE KOTHIS

Discussion

While conducting the survey in March, 2013 it was found that out of the 3 building, 2 building namely- Gulistan-e erum and was completely locked as they were in dangerously dilapidated condition. And Kothi Raushan –ud-daulah is currently housing the State Archeology Department along with other public offices.

Background of Roshan-ud-daula Kothi

The Roshan-ud-daula Kothi stands as an excellent example of the Indo-French style amalgamated with the Islamic style of architecture. It was built by Wazir Roshan-ud-daula, the then Chief Minister of Ruler of Awadh, Nawab Ghazi-ud-din Haider (r.1827-1837) as his own personal residence around 150 years ago between1827-1837.

The Kothi of Roshan-ud-Daula fascinated the last King of Awadh, Wajid Ali Shah so much that he made it his residence, his then most favoured keep named Mashooq-ul-Sultan. The kothi and the woman gained so much importance in his life that he gave another name to this kothi, Qaiser Pasand (Quaiser's choicest).

Then with the gradual establishment of the British rule on Indian soil, the city of Nawabs too went into the grabs of the English rule. This automatically points out undoubtedly to the fact that the concerned monument too went under the English rule. Under this rule however the importance of the kothi got enhanced as it became the District Court but unfortunately, they demolished the two of its upper storeys.

Nevertheless it is really fascinating to be aware of the fact that the monument is still in the working condition and has not yet become defunct. The Kothi Qaiser Pasand or Roshan-ud-Daulah kutchery (as it is more popularly known, since the British rule) presently houses the office of the State Archaeology Directorate and the District Election Office.

Architecture

This kothi facing north, oriented in the east-west, is a triple storied rectangular structure, majestically representing the rich heritage and wealth of the yester years. According to the Government publications, in the Medieval times, it used to cover a vast area of open space in front of the building. However, due to recent modernization, it has now been restricted to a much lesser area.

On **plan**, the elaborate Kothi is rectangular but has acquired a "complex polygonal outline", as it has "canted corners" in the north, projecting rectangular bays on the east and the west, a grand "hexastyle" portico on the south, and yet other tiny balconies, colonnaded verandahs and staircases on each and every front. This structure is bordered by fluted pillars. On the north-east and the north-west corners, were two edifices designed in the standard Nawabi-mosque-form of which the northeast one is functional while the other one serves as an office of the Election Control Board.

The **structure** of the Roshan-ud-daula kothi comprises of 4 big halls and 9 rooms on the first floor while the second floor consists of 3 big halls and 5 rooms, of varied shapes and sizes. On the first floor, it has two openings on the northern and the southern sides each and one each on the eastern and western side. Elaborate staircases are provided with every opening of the first floor. The second floor too has almost equally distributed rooms and halls with staircases. The most striking feature of this kothi is its balconies which are present on all the sides and obviously the rooms which are all interconnected with each other.

As far as the **elevation** is concerned, the Roshan-ud–daula kothi exhibits the most turbulent composition which had a confused design, combining an astonishing range of disparate elements. It was a huge edifice with atleast one (and possibly two) basement level(s), and (now) three, (originally five) levels above ground. On its northern front, the kothi is overshadowed by a vast portico which has gigantic, fluted columns. Its second and third levels are marked by half columns employing the looser version of the same order, and were offset on the third level by rectangular corner-turrets with cupolas; (now) the final (but once penultimate) level had rectangular door openings with superimposed (clumsily executed) pediment, which was in turn surmounted by an intriguing metallic half-circle of an inharmonious outline.

Style of architecture

This structure much interestingly incorporates and balances the fusion of occidental and oriental style of architecture with fish motif at the gates, domes with golden umbrellas, vaulted halls, arcaded pavilions, underground chambers (connected to River Gomti) and labyrinths. On one hand it showcases the French style by the marvelous display of fluted colonnades, hanging balconies while on the other, it focuses the Islamic style with large vaults (domes) and arches.

This structure also portrays the interesting use of passive solar concept of heating and cooling which ensured the natural cooling system of the interiors and also allow sufficient light to enter into the floors through the roofs.

Building materials

- Lakhauri brick – 1.87 cm thick and normally 10 to 15cm in length.
- Curved brick for making elaborate balustrade.

CONCLUSION

The City of Nawabs thus canvasses an excellent example of globalization and upholds the in depth understanding of the international peace and harmony through its marvelous structures. Quite interestingly it crosses the confines of a political boundary to exhibit how the people from different cultural backgrounds came together to give a new shape to the existing culture. The architecture not only symbolizes the par excellence of the artisans and the aesthetic sense of their patrons but also the immense syncretic and synthetic attitude dominated precisely by tolerance and mutual respect that each religion had towards the other. And so it commands to promote a similar kind of hegemony amongst us for propelling a better society for our future.

BIBLIOGRAPHY

1. Choudhary, M. (2012). *Domesticity, Religion and Politics: Exploring Life in Royal Palace of Awadh.* International Journal of Social Science Tomorrow, *Vol.1 (no. 4) SPIRI.*
2. Franki, P. (1962). *Gothic Architecture:* Penguin books.
3. Scott, R.A. (2003). *The Gothic Enterprise:A Guide to Understanding the Medieval Cathedral, University of California Press.*
4. Kamal, M. A. (2012). An overview of Passive Cooling techniquesin buildings: Design Concepts and Architectural Interventions. Acta Technica Napocensis: Civil Engineering &Architecture, Vol.55(No.1)
5. Gulati, R. (2013). Vernacular Houses of Lucknow: Customized Comfort Within. Internatinal Journal of Technical Research and Applications. Vol 1(4), pp.06-10.

Chapter-18

Culture of Bengal Refugees: Past to Present- A Study

Prodip Adhikari

INTRODUCTION

Now this is the most important Question, Who is Refugee? Refugee is a person who flees for refuge or safety, especially to a foreign country, as in time of political upheaval, war, etc.[1] According to UNHCR, A refugee is someone who has been forced to flee his or her country because of persecution, war, or violence. A refugee has a well-founded fear of persecution for reasons of race, religion, nationality, political opinion or membership in a particular social group. Most likely, they cannot return home or are afraid to do so. War and ethnic, tribal and religious violence are leading causes of refugees fleeing their countries.[2]

In 1951, Geneva Convention is the main international instrument of refugee law. The 1951 Convention clearly spells out who a refugee is and the kind of legal protection, other assistance and social rights he or she should receive from the countries who have signed the document.[3]

Now researchers try to discuss Socio-economic condition a Refugee Group who came to West Bengal from Bangladesh during 1946 – 1977 those maximum belong to Namasudra Scheduled Caste community or Dalits.

- "Excuse me, Sister
- Can you give me a bowl of flour?
- Next morning I'll return after grinding wheat."

This was the common conversation between Namasudra Scheduled Caste Community groups who came from Bangladesh or Purbabanga as refugees.

A night is spent by borrowing flour from the neighbor about aunt. The aunt also borrowed when she needed something. This give and take policy was going on between the homeless people who came from East Pakistan (East Bengal or Purba Banga) since pre-independence they are called 'Bengal'. Every day is in same condition, they live in occupied land. So it is called 'Colony', the same practice of borrowing from neighbor prevailed in the refugees coming from West Pakistan also. There is a pathetic story of communal riot behind the scene that nobody knows who feels the pain of leaving native land? Those who have sharp brain cannot feel that pain. The upcoming generation also does not feel the pain of their ancestors – how they survived, how they struggled or how they adapted themselves with a new country, new environment, and also with different culture. So, is it possible to feel the pain by the inhabitants of West Bengal who are living since many years?

After the riot of Noyakhali in 1946, many people came to Kolkata and nearby districts selling their properties in East Pakistan (East Bengal or Purba Banga). Amrita Bazar Patrika on October 23, 1946 reported, "For the 13th day today, about 120 villages in Raniganj, Lakshmipur, Raipur, Begumganj and Senbag thanas (police stations) in Noakhali district with a Hindu population of 90,000 and nearby 70,000 villagers in Chandpur and Faridganj thanas in Tippera (Comilla) district remained besieged by hooligans. Death stares the people of these areas in their face and immediate rushing of supply to these areas with the help of military, which alone could do it, would save the lives of these people, most of whom have been without food for the last few days."[4]

But those who stayed they got a shock when they came to know the clash between Neheru and Jinnha. Perhaps only the permanent inhabitants of West Bengal enjoyed the independence of 15th August, 1947. Those who have witnessed the bloodshed of riot were not able to enjoy the independence. Riot was started again in 1949. It spread on the districts of Barishal, Chhitagaong, Dhaka,Khulna, Maimansinha, Rashshahi the feared people went to the safe place which was inhabitated by 'our men' and thousands of refugees came to West Bengal. Few of them took shelter in their relative's house, few in refugee camp and few who did not get place in the platform of Sealdah station and Howraha Station.[5] Many people went to Paschim Dinajpur, Jalpaiguri, Coochbehar also. Many refugees were sent to Andaman and Dandakaranya. This flow of coming refugees to India, from 1947 in still going on though the government does not accept the people who are coming presently as refugee. The colonies near Kolkata were set up in between 1949-1950. They started inhabiting by occupying the extended land of the land – lords at Tollygang, Jadavpur and Baghajatin, Bongaon, Ranaghat, Kalyani. In 1957, 70,000 refugees gathered in Coopers Camp in Ranaghat from Bangladesh.[6] At present in Bangladesh Muslim population growing heavily then Hindus. In everyday life in Bangladesh Hindu population are decrease. (See Table 1: Ration of Hindus and Muslims in Bangladesh).

Table 1: Ration of Hindus and Muslims in Bangladesh

Year	Hindus (%)		Muslim (%)	
	East Pakistan (Bangladesh)	West Bengal (India)	East Pakistan (Bangladesh)	West Bengal (India)
1951	22.8	79.8	76.8	19.5
1961	19.2	79.4	80.4	20.0
1971	14.1	78.9	85.4	20.5
1981	12.7	77.9	86.6	21.5
1991	11.1	75.8	88.3	23.6
2001	8.0	74.1	91.0	25.2

Source: http://janasangh.com/jsart.aspx?stid=193

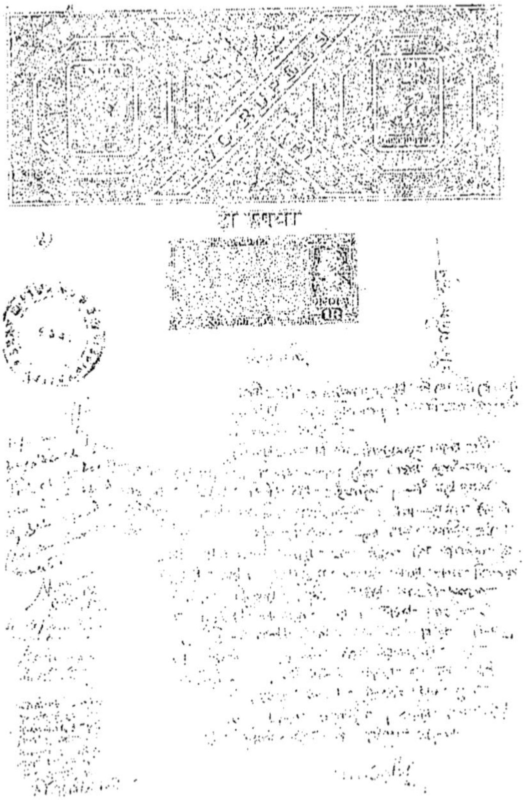

Caption: An affidavit by a Downtrodden Hindu Shree Jadish Chandra Shur (May 26, 1947)

The people of colony live in a group. Many of them were small and middle farmer who left their ancestors, house and took shelter here. Moreover, many homeless refugees came at that time also the discrimination between native farmers and homeless family was stopped in the colonies. The daily activities of Fullarar Baromasya were heard in every family. Besides borrowing something from neighbor, they used to share some exceptional new items of food among themselves. Many of them did not have watch and they asked time from the neighbors who have they used to share newspaper with other neighbors. The enthusiastic juniors use to ask their seniors about the score of East Bengal. Hearing Radio was luxury. In Sundays and

Wednesdays, they used to go to another colony to listen music of request. A group of people listen music from radio beside the road owned by roadside owner. They listens drama, folk song like Kabi gaan, Jari Gan, Jatra, Baul, Lokasangeet etc with the permanent inhabitants. In every Wednesdays, hundreds of refugees gathered in the open field or beside the pond or the Cannel. They gossiped and joked each other. They belonged to a world of love at that time. There was no less of feeling brotherhood if they get food or not. Old grand fathers of the colony started narrative story when radio had no programmes.

This apart, their jointly struggle of occupying land hold their unity. The Jamindars of the colonies were so desperate. They sent hooligans at night to uproot the refugees from their land. But the dwellers of colony jointly prevented them. Their motto is to hold their shelter.

For example, the scheduled caste refugees of South Chandamari prevent the Muslims of North Chandamari. Most of the Muslim of North Chandamari lived in village of Charjadubati. Being agitated by their torture, the Hindus of Bind Mahato attacked Muslims.

The environment of the Colony was not different from that of East Pakistan. Greeneries, field, pond, fences and housing of tin were well known to them. They had not ploughing field and certainty of food. They were satisfied despite not having sufficient things and this satisfaction was achieved by maintaining the discipline of seniors there basic forefathers drove them by providing the formula- 'express yourself in this society by education'.

The Bengal refugees are always strange human beings to the rich people of Kolkata. In Kalyani, there are some personal properties of rich people from Kolkata – Krishnanagar beside the government residence. These residence and houses were built in barren land in seventies. From the conversation of two people we can know –

"Where are the bushes of arums?
It is cleared by Bangals by eating them"

They (Refugees from East Bengal or Purba Banga) are strange people near Kolkata.

According to Mangal Adhikari, a refugee from East Bengal or Purba Banga, Once a classmate, coming from a family of well culture and frequent English speaking family, Chakraborty of North Kolkata, asked him in the field –

"You know a lot of slangs tell me something. At first I could not understand, but later I can understand that he wants to know 'Khisti' which is the dialect of East Bengal. They are not only 'Bengal' but also refugees. Their mother tongue becomes 'Khisti' in the view of others culture. Now the distance is a made. Though all the people of Kolkata is not like that. There are so many people in West Bengal who can realize the refugees and they sympathized on them. There is a person who is kind hearted for labourars and a true friend of environment often says about their cordiality while welcoming guests. Perhaps the inhabitants of Kolkata are divided into two by the process of man-making and the difference of views. So, it is not possible to see all as same."[7]

They still had a fear humiliation – humiliation of own culture. It has chased them once. People said them jointly-

"Bangladeshi Lok
Dhala Dhala Chokh
Atob Chouler Bhat Kheye
Camper Modhye Dhok"[8]

'Bastuhara Parisad' was set up by their collective straggle in 1950. Later this parisad was transformed into United Central Refugee Council (UCRC). There were many associating in Kolkata, 24 Parganas and Nadia like Nikhil Banga Bastuhara Karma Parisad, South Calcutta Shahartali Bastuhara Samiti, Nadia Bastuhara Parisad etc. They form UCRC. Their rights on land had been being granted for 35 years by many movements. They were provided the land record paper in 1985 from the relief and rehabilitation centre. Later they were provided the paper of ownership of land and from them, their unity become loose. The causes are that many years become successful in future by nature having higher education or vocational or technical training. Then they need not borrow flour from neighbor those who were not established, they started promoting business by building five-storyed on their own land and earned a lot. The new comes of these houses do not know struggle history of the colony. They are not sympathizer to each other.

CONCLUSION

The refugees who came from East Pakistan were uprooted characters by many means. They were uprooted from their native land. They were separated from immovable property and ploughing field. They left the culture of East Bengal and set themselves in near Kolkata like Kalyani, Ranaghat Coopars Colony and Kolkata was like Gujrat or Karnakata to them. There were a clash between different cultures in every where Kolkata is the land of the mother tongue, and here the refugees were suffering from identity crisis. It was so painful to them. From where, these refugees are coming? Before 1947, they were in India, again in 1950, there were in India, It is not a fears.

According to researchers, the Bengali refugees are inhabitants of this Bengal. They should be respected, not only by providing rice or food, but also providing a job for main earning person or helping them to get admission in school for their children, one day they will take important role to progress their Bengal.

BIBLIOGRAPHY

1. Bandhyapadhya, T. (1995, May). *Unish Sataker Ranaghat Subdivision.* Ranaghat: J. Publication.
2. Bhattacharjee, U. (1359). *Bharater Nari.* Kolikata: Modern Book Agency.
3. Biswas, A. (2014, April). *Udbastu – Panjika Desh Bhag: Part III.* Kolkata: Gangchil.
4. Biswas, H. (1417, Aghrahayan). *Alochana Prasange P.R. Thakur Smritikatha.* Chandpara: Damayanti Bhaban.
5. Biswas, N.B., & Roy, N.R. (2014). *Education of the Scheduled Caste People Namasudras of West Bengal.* New Delhi: Shipra Publications.
6. Biswas, T. (2007, August). *Lokodarpan.* Kalyani: Department of Folklore, University of Kalyani.
7. Chattapadhya, B. (2001). *Bangla Bangali Bangladesh.* Kolkata: Sristi Prakashan.
8. Das, S. (2008, November). *Udbastu Nagarir Chand.* Kolkata: Day's Publishing.
9. Ghosh, N. (2004, March). *Kalyani: Sekal O Ekal.* Kolkata: Sumati Publishers.
10. Ghosh, N. (2009, February).*Kalyanir Ash-Pash: Pathe Prantare GhureDekha.* Kolkata: Pustak Bipani.
11. Ghosh, N. (2008). *Nadiar Gaurab.* Kolkata: Pustak Bipani.
12. Ghosh, N. (2012, March). *Itihaser Prekhapate Nadia.* Kolkata: Pustak Bipani.

13. Jela Prakalpa Adhikarta.Gram O Ward Shikhsa Commitir Hat Boi. (February, 2009). Krishnanagar: Nadia Jela Sarva Shikhsa Mission.
14. Mandal, M. (2011). *Settling the Unsetteled A Study of Partition Refugees in West Bengal.* New Delhi: Manohar Publishers & Distributors.
15. Mukhapadhya, P.K. (1989, May). *Sekalbhanga Sanskriti.* Kolkata: Utsa Manush Sankalan.
16. Pal, M. (2011, January). *Nijer Kathay Marichjhanpi.* Kolkata: Gangchil.
17. Ray, K.B. (2014, July). *Status of Women Migrants from Bangladesh to West Bengal and Orissa During 1971-2001.* Kolkata: Smriti Publishers.
18. Raychowdhury, S.K. (1991, April). Sheser Dinguli. Kolkata: Dr.B.R.Ambedkar Library & Research Centre.
19. Rudra, K. (2007, January). *Paschimbanger Krishichitra Shilpayan O Krishaker Bhabisyat.* Kolkata: Mreettika.
20. Sarwar, M. (1997, February). *Bangabandhu Shekh Mujib Kache Theke Dekha.* Dhaka: Agami Prakashani.

End Notes

1. Retrieved http://www.dictionary.com/browse/refugee
2. Retrieved http://www.unrefugees.org/what-is-a-refugee/
3. Ibid
4. Retrieved http://noakhali1946.blogspot.in/
5. Chakraborty, P. (1997). Prantik Manab. Kolkata: Pratikhyan Publication Privet Limited. pp.87.
6. Chakraborty, P. (1997). Prantik Manab. Kolkata: Pratikhyan Publication Privet Limited. pp.95.
7. Interview Scheduled (10 March, 2017) with Mangal Adhikari.
8. Interview Scheduled (10 March, 2017) with Kalipada Adhikari

Chapter-19

Cultures of Violence Against Women and Social Reality in India

Dr. Nabanita Dutta.

INTRODUCTION

This article presents the theoretical and narratives foundation for the claim that societal acceptance or rejection of violence is shaped by those in positions of power and influence. An account of the evolution of privacy in India is presented here by tracing the conceptual trajectory of privacy through the filter of family regulation. The modern state is uniquely invested with power to politically determine and mediate culture narratives as it can legitimize ethos, values and practices through both legal and political machinations, as well as action and – more crucially – inaction. The state is thus imbued with the responsibility to encourage and create cultures free of domestic violence. What makes the inquiry of Indian notions on the subject interesting is that among all the social institutions in India, the family enjoys an iconic place in the social imaginary as an ideal unit. Often singled out as a cultural trope with an historic, natural and private existence, it stalls scrutiny into its intimate and sacrosanct space. Hence the long- standing struggle against the family's privacy is replete with tussles among religious jurisprudence, cultural norms, modern legislation, notion of community identity and individual autonomy, justice and human rights' discourse. The discussion here point outs the state's response to the family's class sexuality, religious, orientation, and so on; furthermore, it argues how the state and the family is responsible to maintaining the culture of violence and as well as silence doing so. The culture defense discourse and the right to family and privacy, act to seal the family as an isolated and autonomous unit. A human rights perspective is needed to re-situate the family within the justice system. Violence against women is reinforced by the state conception of family as a private domain, as well as the notion of the harmonious family being the foundation of the nation.

Violence is embedded in any one culture must be challenged to expose it as a practice supported and re-enacted through cultural narratives. Rather than essentializing domestic violence as culturally embedded, it is more constructive to acknowledge that it is a culture in and of itself. Culture is a socio-political symbolic discourse that changes over time with the state playing a role in its incarnation. Consequently, even if violence exists as an oppressive and reprehensible practice within cultures, it should not be preserved, respected and perpetuated. An analysis of how and why violence (domestic and public) continues to be erroneously placed within culture, as well as the consequent difficulty in challenging it due to intersecting issues of privacy, culture and honour. The claim that contestation of rights to privacy within the family and rights of victims of domestic violence cannot be resolved in favour of the former. An examination of the pattern of state action and inaction that condone and even encourage domestic violence. This discussion concludes by reiterating the primacy of eradication of violence in the construction of society and the nation state. In the endeavour to eliminate domestic violence, culture must be deconstructed; instead of justifying domestic violence in the name of culture, culture should be enlisted to create a non-violent society.

The persistence of gender inequality is most starkly brought home in the phenomenon of "missing women." It is estimated that 6 million women are missing every year (World Bank 2011). Of these, 23 percent are never born, 10 percent are missing in early childhood, 21 percent in the reproductive years, and 38 percent above the age of 60. Stark as the excess mortality is, it still does not capture the fact that throughout their lives, even before birth, women in developing countries are treated differently than their brothers, lagging behind men in many domains. For each missing woman, there are many more women who fail to get an education, a job, or a political responsibility that they would have obtained if they had been men. From this situations the question arises that is it our culture that girls cannot born and if they are born somehow society have the right to violence against girl's child or women? Is it our social culture that the state has the right to criminalizing women who were victimized by the society or the state anyhow?

The conceptualization of family as sited within both public as well as private domains; and herein lies the source of its ambiguity. When the state intervenes in family matters the family is treated as a public concern. However; the state takes a liberal stance on respecting individual human rights or even multicultural rights, when the sacredness of family as a private domain is emphasized. There are also extremes in degree of state intervention upon the family. As has long been acknowledged the family is no longer seen as primarily a site of production and reproduction, but also as a focus of tension and conflict, with violence among intimate partners being one of its manifestations. This research articles aims to uncover some of the sources of the difficulties and paradoxes in understanding violence against women as well as domestic violence as an all-encompassing problem, from its legal to its cultural dimension.

The clash between traditional culture and modernization in the discourse of domestic violence is misplaced. Domestic violence is a systemic global practice embedded in masculinities, patriarchy and domination of women that is then justifies in the name of hohour, culture and religion; in the process, this re-conceptualizes women not as victims of violence, but as violators of culture and family honour. Dominant societal notions of manhood depend on male superiority over and entitled to govern, women. Cultural justification of domestic violence obscures the fact that it is steeped not in culture, honour or religion but in practices of violence. As long as men's 'conjugal mastery' over women can be rationalized as being rooted in tradition and culture, the right to maintain and enforce this mastery through domestic violence will remain unquestioned.

In cases of domestic violence – through inaction – the state perpetuates a culture of domestic violence. Ironically, such inaction is an aberration, as the state has an interest and duty in confronting and eradicating all forms of violence. According to dominant theories of political philosophy, rules against violence and the use of force are the historical impetus for society-formation away from the Hobbesian "state of nature". Therefore, confronting violence is and must be the primary duty of the nation state. When the state assumes the right to punish transgressors in the name of society, the individual simultaneously gives up his right to do so. The 1990s and early 21st century have seen debates around the women's reservation bill, discussions on reproductive and sexual rights including alternate sexualities and an increasing attempt at using culture as the grounds for policing women's sexuality.

LEGISLATION AND QUESTION OF VIOLENCE

Discussions on feminism and the law inevitably raise a whole host of complex theoretical and political debates, not the least of which are those regarding how far the law can be utilized as a mechanism towards the empowerment of women law has occupied a central role in various organized efforts to improve women's status in India. These efforts have had different foci at different points in history. They include a preoccupation with protectionism during the social reform movement of the 19th century; a quest for constitutional and formal equality during the struggle for independence and finally the attack on patriarchy mounted by the contemporary women's movement.[1]

It was the widespread campaign during 1979-80 against the Supreme Court judgment in the Mathura rape case that brought women's issues on to the public agenda. In the wake of the Mathura fury, the magnitude and tenor of press coverage of incidents of police rape and protests suggested that there was a surge of anger all over the country. Given this apparent mass support, women issues assumed political significance and political parties could no longer afford to ignore them. The thrust of the campaign was to raise awareness and to lobby for a change in the rape laws. The campaign was well under way before questions of representation were raised. Until this point, it had not occurred to anybody to find out whether Mathura herself wanted the protest. There were some discussions on what they would have done in the event that she had objected but the key questions of who had voice and who had the right to speak for whom were not raised.

One of the major flaws in the amendment was that the campaign had been unable to dispel conservative assumptions about virginity and chastity. The demands for reforms were co-opted by more conservative political voices and eventually caste within the more traditional discourses of shame and dishonor.[2] This is apparent form of a particular clause in the amended law which made publishing anything related to a rape trial an offence. This stipulation was clearly connected to the perception of 'social stigma' that attached to the victim and the need to protect her identity. Mostly recently, Menon (2000) raises questions about the universality of women's experience of sexual violence, suggesting it is possible that in different cultural contexts codes which enable the recognition of 'sexuality' and 'sexual violence' may not be the same.[3] This line of argument also suggests that the law locates women's selfhood in the finite and bounded body and would be unable to address a philosophy of emancipation that seeks to transcend bodily notions of selfhood. The protests began to be recognized as mainstream political action.

The anti-dowry agitation marked the feminist assertion of the personal as political through an activist agenda. Atrocities that took place in the private spaces of the homes and were passed off as, among other things, 'kitchen accidents' were brought to public light. This agitation witnessed an unprecedented public uproar, touching the imagination of the people and focusing the attention of both Indian and international media on the atrocities against women. The activists in the fight against dowry were driven by an energy which in the time was "transformed' into a brand of activism which asserted women's agency in social change."[4] Various women's organizations vocalized that dowry was not an isolated phenomenon, but was linked to the inferior status and position of women in society. The protest actions had the effect of subverting the notion of stigma and shame which traditionally attached to 'bad' women on to the families that murdered their daughter in law for dowry. Social ostracism and visible campaigning outside their homes marked them out as murderers, a strategy which was extremely effective. Unfortunately, however, the effects of such shaming often did not last for long. In many cases the husbands of the murdered women remarried a few years later. In 1984, the 1961 Act was amended changing the definition of dowry by substituting the word 'as consideration for the marriage' to 'in connection with the marriage'. In 1986, the law was amended again to bring more stringent punishment, making the offence non-bailable and shifting the burden of proof on to the accused. Despite this there were hardly any convictions and the ground realities did not change.[5] Young women who were harassed for dowry found that their parents' fear of social stigma did not allow them to return home. Women continued to be murdered for dowry or committed suicide in despair.

JUDICIAL RESPONSES AND RIGHTS OF WOMEN

In order to analyze the practice and prevalence of domestic violence, it is important to inquire not only into the subordination of women, but also into relationships between men. The continuous competition for social status and hierarchy between men has given rise to what anthropologist calls a "culture- of- honour" stance. This stance links the idea of male honour to physical prowess, toughness, and courage. It also requires men to define themselves as dominant to women, using violence if necessary. Consequently, while other expressions of culture-of-honour are circumscribed by the state, violence against women generally, and domestic violence specifically, remain surviving expressions of culture- of – honour violence.

The debate over privacy and rights has raised its head in Indian courtrooms and some judgments reveal the varied stance. In 1984, the Delhi High Court passed a judgment on a case that: "*Introduction of constitutional law in the home... is like introducing a bull in a China shop... in the privacy of the home neither Article 21 nor Article 14 has any place.*"[6] The Protection of Women from Domestic Violence Act (PWDVA) 2005 finally presented a clear definition of domestic violence, based it is on the UN Framework for model Legislation on Domestic Violence and the United Nations Declaration on Elimination of Violence against Women. Besides covering a gamut of physical, verbal, economic and mental abuses, the act also include sexual abuse, especially forced, non-consensual sexual intercourse.

To deal with gendered violence in diverse private domestic relationships, the act has taken the unprecedented step of including 'any relationship in the nature of marriage.' It can also be used in natal family relationships by mothers, daughters, widows and so on. There have been many pro-women judgments since the implementation of the PWDVA 2005, but cultural stereotypes and biased interpretations persist. Marriage and children are central to the projecting of the ideal woman. The good woman's most valued attribute is her silence. This sentiment is even reflected in several court rulings on rape - "*no self respecting woman would come forward in a court just to make a humiliating statement against her honour such as is involved in the commission of rape on her or the rapist degrades the very soul of the helpless female.*"[7] A majority of women interviewed during the last National Family Health Survey justified violence against them by their husbands. As many as 54% of women and 51% of men agreed that it is justifiable for a husband to beat his wife. UNICEF's *The State of the World's Children 2012* reported that among 15 to 19 year olds in India, 57% of boys and 53% of girls believed that a husband was justified in beating his wife under certain circumstances. It sees that notions of self-identity, shame and honour exert more pressure and influence on the collective consciousness of women than laws that promise them redress. Women continue to bear the cross for the family, community and nation's honour in India's patriarchal regime.

Central to unpacking the private- public divide will be a compelling re-conceptualization of privacy. The mid 1970s national family planning drive or the Government of India's Child Care Leave only for its women employees are examples of the state breaching boundaries. Perhaps Frances E. Olsen asserts that "*non-intervention (of the state) is a false ideal because it has no coherent meaning... the state is continuously affecting the family by influencing the distribution of power among individuals.*"[8] Olsen strongly disagrees with the popular view that the state should intervene only when necessary because it "*presupposes that non-intervention is a possible choice, and second, it usually accepts non-intervention as a norm or as an ideal.*"[9]

The argument of some scholars that "the institution of patriarchy operates in the name of culture for justifying child marriage of young girls" becomes problematic when we examine elopement cases. As against the socio-economic constraints of child marriage due to poverty, these cases concern marriages of choice by young girls. Here the legal provision becomes a weapon to control the expression of sexuality, and curb voluntary marriages, and is used to augment patriarchal parental power. The use and abuse of state power at the instance of parents in marriages of choice is in direct opposition to women's autonomy, agency and free will.

In a society ridden with prejudices against the lower castes and communal conflicts, a young couple who dares to disobey community dictates is severely punished. At times, the price for choosing a partner is death or public humiliation.[10] The notion that women are the sexual property of their communities is deeply internalized, leading to violence not merely by the girls' families but also the community.

Several judges have commented that many of the habeas corpus petitions filed for production of a girl in court are really cases to do with elopement. This is a serious concern for courts. In Ashok kumar vs State, the Punjab and Haryana High Court commented that couples marrying out of love are chased by the police and relatives, accompanied by musclemen. Often the state is a mute spectator.

In Payel Sharma vs superintendent, Nari Niketan, Agra, the Allahabad High Court rejected the father's contention that the girl was a minor and instead accepted her contention that she was a major. Further, the court declared that as a major she had a right to go anywhere and live with anyone. "in our opinion a man and a woman, even without getting married can live together, if they wish. This can be regarded as immoral by society bit it is not illegal. There is a difference between law and morality," the court commented. Since the girl had stated that her life was in danger, the court also ordered police protection to ensure her security.

These judgments serve as a benchmark for the liberal interpretation of the constitutional provisions of equality and individual freedom. At times, our judges, with a concern for social justice, have resolved the issue by resorting to the basic principles of human rights, and saved minor girls from the wrath of their parents and from state run "protective homes". The only way they could do so was by holding these marriages to be valid and by allowing the girls to cohabit with their partners of choice.

However, feminists and the women's movement in India have had a difficult and paradoxical relationship with law. Since law is inextricably involved in the very acts that it condones, controls and penalizes, it becomes a site of ambiguity instead of a force against these acts. As Nivedita Menon said, *"our attempts to transform power relations through the law tend rather to re-sediment them and to assert dominant values."*[11] This may create newer and alternative legal meanings that do not devalue subjectivities, and that imagine moving 'subject' from a passive recipient of law to an active agent of its creation. It still begs the question- even though the family needs to be protected from violence, what if the family needs protection from the violent state? Self-regulation by the family seldom works. On the other hand, the state tends to become panoptic.

Among all the social institutions in India, the family enjoys an iconic place in the social imaginary as an ideal unit. In this ideal family dowry related violence triggered a high-pitched women's movement that pushed the Indian government to amend existing laws and protect women from violence. Although law in India does not view domestic violence as a 'private' matter, the culture ideology that obliquely permits it, does.

ROLE OF THE STATE IN SHAPING CULTURE

The condoning of domestic violence by the entire state system serves to perpetuate the alleged basis and factors that sustain and encourage domestic violence. Culture may be thought of as a network of relationships. Through its legal and political machinations, states create and perpetuate a culture of domestic violence. If society sees no evidence of willingness by the state to take effective action to sanction against domestic violence, society will more readily associate domestic violence with its own cultural identity. When states fail to prevent or prosecute domestic violence, it is the state and not traditional practice or ethos that should be the focus of our inquiry. Examining domestic violence from the perspective of the state's role exposes domestic violence as a culture in and of itself. State inaction in enforcing the letter of the law coupled with signals given by the legal and judicial officers that domestic violence is tolerated; implicitly sanction the continued practice of domestic violence. Thus where a culture of domestic violence exists, domestic violence is transformed into institutional and structural violence, private and public arena, that is found formally or truly embedded in society.

In international law, states are required to act with due diligence to eliminate violence against women. Despite this and international and regional instruments investing states with the responsibility to eliminate violence against women, many states lodge reservations on the grounds of culture. These reservations, in so far as they apply to domestic violence, are made all the more serious in view of the argument that domestic violence should be understood and treated as a form of torture and, when less severe, ill treatment.

The prohibition of torture as a whole is a jus cogens that violates the demands of humanity and dictates public conscience. Any type of torture is just wrong and would be wrong whether positive law prohibits it or not. Acknowledging that violence can be torture, mainly domestic violence, or at the very least ill-treatment, elevates it into jus cogens prohibition in international law, which necessarily means that states are not able to derogate from their obligation to intervene, prevent, stop, sanction and provide remedies in cases of domestic violence.

As there can be no 'cultural defense' against torture, there can be no cultural defense against domestic violence.

The avoidance and prevention of violence constitute the basic purpose of lawmaking. The predominant model of addressing domestic violence both as discrimination and through the formal judicial system has borne limited success. Hence, it is essential that we broaden our understanding of domestic violence to emphasize the harm it causes. Domestic violence is an assault on human dignity, often seeking to reduce or eradicate a person's autonomy, destroy self-esteem and compel subjugation.

IN LIU OF CONCLUSION

Deconstructing culture in the context of domestic violence and violence against women, therefore, involves examining the identities of those claiming their rights to culture, the authorities that sanction these rights, and in the event culture is used to claim legal rights, the role of the states as the final arbiter in recognizing and perpetuating these claims. In this regard, it is more accurate to construct domestic violence as a culture in and of itself, rather than embedded in culture, and to scrutinize the role of the state in alternatively creating, tolerating, developing and encouraging a culture of domestic violence as well as the state's role and responsibility in its eradication.

Poor conviction rates in domestic violence cases and unwieldy court procedures have made legal remedies less useful for women. Hence, the passage of India's domestic violence law, the Protection of Women from Domestic Violence Act (PWDVA), did not radically transform the notion that family privacy is sacrosanct and confirm the popular perception that domestic violence is a family affair. The privacy of family will continue to sustain gendered hierarchies that are often dependent on the deployment of male domination and violence. In such a situation law becomes a site of ambiguity instead of a force against it.

Violence against women is a global phenomenon, rooted in the unequal balance of power between women and men, in which women suffer severe forms of physical, emotional, sexual and economic harm. Laws and policies must reflect this recognition. The anti-women's backlash spurred by the family violence approach may lead to the continuation of practices that put women's health and safety in jeopardy. Sexual literacy, legal awareness among women and gender awareness among law enforcers must be given special attention, as should education for girls and a ban on early marriages. As domestic violence takes place in the home and is often justified by patriarchal biases that stipulate that women should be demure, dependent and submissive, the fallacy of the harmonious family must be exposed.

The glorification of this family model hides its underling symbolic and physical violence. In India, the lesbian group Sappho for Equality, in collaboration with the Kartini Asia Network, documented 92 kinds of violence that lesbian women experience, ranging from abuse and ridicule to murder or double suicide.[12] For women in India, the normative family model is based on pre-marital virginity, chastity during marriage, and motherhood. Self-sacrifice and dependence upon males is glorified for women. These norms are anchored in religious values. The Indian 'divine family' should not be ruptured by divorce; marriage, particularly a woman's sexual obligation to her husband, is seen as a service to God. In India divorced women are heavily stigmatized; this stigma even extends to organizations that attempt to empower those women. Ideals of purity and self –sacrifice are often enforced by in-laws. The two major studies on our family system do not mention incest, [13] other then referring to it as a category of marriage avoidance.

Pre-marital virginity remains important in India; for instance, in Madhya Pradesh on 30 June 2009, virginity tests were conducted before a government-conducted mass wedding of rural women. Activists protested, but it is unlikely they made a dent in the underlying enforcement of virginity. The pressure to remain a virgin until the marriage dated leads to early marriages, particularly for girls in poor households who cannot afford to attend secondary school. Money matters are a source of much strife within the Indian households discussed here. The men are supposed to be the breadwinners and drive social standing and power within the household if they fulfill that role well. In popular understanding, women provide sex to their husbands, and men give their wives money and social identity. The housewife-breadwinner ideology does not hold up in poor households, where both women and men have to work, yet in anticipation of man's breadwinner role, boys receive better education than their sisters if there is not enough money to provide schooling for all siblings.

Hetero-normatively presents the heterosexual family as the ultimate goal in life for women, where they will attain the bliss of a 'normal', 'harmonious' family life.[14] However, in reality, the family is often not the safe haven promised to them. Once cracks become permanent, women are supposed to adjust, emotionally, intellectually and financially. Passionate aesthetics involve various modes of control, objection and violence, rendering the non-heterosexually-married space for women highly unattractive or even dangerous. However, there is danger within the 'normal' heterosexual family too. The success of these aesthetics lies in the way of women, even in non-heterosexual relationships, aspire to its values, while women who have experienced various forms of violence themselves continue to live, or a least live with, the perpetrators of that violence.

Perceiving violence against women as a private issue may have the effect of making structural factors that fuel this violence invisible. Hetero-normatively is not limited to the bed-room but extends its tentacles into courtrooms, boardrooms and into all locations in which societal institutions operate. It has always struggled to create space for women to fight against cultural impositions and religious restrictions, which underline and reinforce the economic, social, political and psychological suppression. In this paper, I examine violence against women first on a macro scale, focusing on the origins and persistence of violence through history and society, then on a micro scale, through the narration and discussion of the 2012 Delhi rape case. Underlying this analysis, the paper studies the major tension between institutional attempts to address violence against women, and the resistance to progress brought upon by cultural and historical norms. Public outcry of the rape ultimately resulted in the creation of the Verma report, a comprehensive report outlining recommended laws for rape, sexual harassment, and trafficking, medical examination of victims and other aspects of violence. Amendments failed to include any formative recommendations from the Verma Committee report, instead continuing to leave women unprotected from discrimination and violence. The shortsightedness of the Verma report itself is caught in the aforementioned tension, and to some degree, works to reinforce it. Examination of the 2012 rape case discloses why this case in particular developed a mass outcry, and moving forward, how long must stories of such horrific suffering continue before significant legislative and societal change takes place. At this end, the paper offers deeper comprehension of how government inadequacies and the normalization of gender injustice fuel the violence epidemic in India. In highlighting the foundation and societal development of violence, this research calls attention to the very sectors that demand future reforms.

BIBLIOGRAPY

1. Ratna Kapur and Brenda Cossman (1995), *Communalizing Gender, Engendering Community: Women, Legal Discourse and the Saffron Agenda* in Tanika Sarkar and Urvashi Butalia (eds.), *Women and the Hindu Right*, Kali for Women, New Delhi, pp-82-120
2. Ibid, Kapur and Cossman, (1995)
3. Nivedita Menon,(2000), *Embodying the Self: Feminism, Sexual Violence and the Law*' in Partha Chatterjee and Pradeep Jaganathan (eds.), *Community, Gender and Violence, Subaltern Studies XI*, Ravi Dayal, New Delhi, pp-66-105
4. Indu Agnihotri and Vina Mazumdar (1995), *Changing Terms of Political Discourse: Women's Movement in India, 1970s-1990s,* EPW, vol-30, no-29, July 22, 1869-78.
5. Flavia Agnes (1992), *Protecting Women against Violence: Review of a Decade of Legislation, 1980-89*, EPW, April 25, WS 19-33.
6. F. Agnes, '*Hindu Conjugality*', in A. Parasher and A. Dhanda (eds.), *Redefining Family Law in India*, Delhi, Routledge, p-245
7. S. Goonsekere, (2004), *Violence, Law and Women's Rights in South Asia*, Delhi, Sage p-336.
8. F. E. Olsen, *'The Myth of State Intervention in the Family'*, in S. Moller Okin and J. Mansbridge (eds.) 1994, *Feminism, School of thought in Politics,* Series No. 6. Cambridge University Press, pp-835-864.
9. P. Chowdhury, *Private Lives, State Intervention: Case of Runaway Marriage in Rural North India, Modern Asian Studies*; Vol-38, No-1, pp-55-84.
10. N. Menon, Ibid, p-863.
11. N. Menon,(2004), *Recovering subversion: Feminist Politics beyond Law*, Delhi, Permanent Black, p-206.
12. See S. Ghosh, (2011), *Vio-Map: Documenting and mapping violence and rights violations taking place in lives of sexually marginalized women,* Kolkata: Sappho for Equality.
13. T. Patel, (ed.) 2005. *The family in India, Structure and practice.* New Delhi: Sage; Uberoi, P. (ed) 1994. *Family, kinship and marriage in India.* Oxford: Oxford University Press.
14. Ibid.

Chapter-20

Domestic Violence in India: A Critical Review Including the Protection of Human Rights and Legislations

Lopa Sarkar & Arnab Das

INTRODUCTION

Domestic violence becomes an important issue in this 21st century. Various factors, i.e. economic conditions, social problems, cultural and psychological issues are mainly liable for the situation. Lack of peace education to the diverse sections of population in the society and unconscious activities lead to increase in the domestic violence in our country. The uses of various social networking sites, mobile phones and internet are increasing day by day due to population increase and it plays a significant role in domestic violence such as violence in home or in the society. Behind closed doors of homesor any other places, people are being tortured and killed. It is happening in urban areas, rural areas andas well as in metropolitans. It is crossing all social classes, genders, and age groups. It is becoming a heritage being continued from one generation to another. The term 'Domestic violence' stands for the violence within our home or family members towards the relationship such as mother, father, son, brother, sister, cousin, uncle, husband, wife etc. This paper is based on psychological, social and cultural issues that lead to domestic violence. It also focuses on the present scenario of domestic violence, its effects and various human rights and laws to protect the victims.

India is a developing country where literacy rates are not very high. It discriminates among various states. There are various religious people with their own traditions and cultures living in our country. Some of them belong to the diverse section of the society where the education could not reach to them yet. They are not conscious about protecting the human rights and executing the constitutional laws. The term 'Domestic violence' arises when any activity takes place within the family amongst its members and it harms them. Definitions of domestic violence are socially constructed, have developed over time, and reflect prevailing understandings, interests and power distributions (Muehlenhard & Kimes 1999). The origins of domestic violence are linked to power and control. The concept of domestic violence is not a new phenomenon in the contemporary world that we live in. Mental and physical tortures, unconstitutional behavior which involves violence or other abuse by a person against another person within the family fall under the Domestic violence category. Domestic violence can take place in various family relationships, and can involve violence against children in the family. It forms as abuse, domineering, economic deprivation, threats, intimidation, stalking, etc. The abuse may take the form of physical violence, emotional abuse, sexual abuse, psychological abuse, economic abuse, incest and ultimately death **(Chalk & King, 1998)**. It has been found that the vast majority of cases involve violence from men to women. Some issues of terminology remain actively contested, such as whether domestic violence should be a gender-specific or neutral referent and/or encompass all forms and incidence of abuse in all types of intimate relationships (Muehlenhard&Kimes 1999, Mullender 1996). All forms of domestic violence constitute violations of human rights and freedoms which all public bodies have a proactive duty to prevent under the Human Rights Act, 1993. A key unifying feature of the human rights framework is the universality of these rights, which are not qualified by, or subordinate to,the norms and values of any particular culture or tradition (United Nations 1993, Council of Europe 2002, Amnesty International 2004). Viewing domestic violence within a human rights framework shifts responsibility for prevention from the private to the public sphere and focuses not only on public bodies' responsibility for the rehabilitation of the abused and the abuser, but also on broader public health, education and gender socialization responsibilities (Walker 1999).

CAUSES THAT CONSTITUTE DOMESTIC VIOLENCE

- **Abused as Child:** Some people think that they have the right to ignore children as they are smaller in age. Children often get physical punishment by their parents or other family members that constitute a fatal blow. These kinds of tortures due to inadequate knowledge may create physical injury, impairment of bodily function, or even *death. Lack of psychological knowledge and peace education lead such family members to mistreatment the children.*

- **Abused as woman:**Men dominated society often think that women are not equal to men. They have been learning this behavior in a family where domestic violence was accepted as a normal part of life. Boys who have been learning that women are not to be valued in our society or family and seeing the violence directed against women during their growing up within the culture or society. Ancient history of India disclosessomedehumanized cultural practices such as immolation of a Hindu widow on the funeral pyre of her deceased husband. Such kind of practices are obsoleted now but the dowry related violence has become a critical issue where the women behind closed doors of homes are being suffered. Some of people traditionally think that they have the right to control their wives. Girls who witness or are the victims of violence are more likely to be victimized by their own family members such as brother, sisters or by the husband after the marriage.Although women are most often the victim of domestic violence, the gender roles can be reversed sometimes.
- **Alcohol and drugs:** Alcohol and drugs are being misused in many households, as a result, lack of control plays a vital role in domestic violence. Keeping such drinking and drug usecan't be responsible, the main cause that constitutes domestic violence is uncontrolled behavior or activities. It is not just about physical violence, it's an organized pattern of controlling behavior ranging from controlling household management to not forcing their family member to commit suicide.
- **Mental disorder:** Mental health problem may constitute domestic violence. Although it can't be a cause of domestic violence always, it depends on particular situation where the abuse is planned only to specific family members within the households. Sometimes, it can be uncontrolled and leads to violent activities. It has been found that the people with mental disorders are more likely to be victims of domestic violence by their family members.

- **Socio-economic factors:** Due to economic depressions, domestic violence can be arisen. Unemployment, poverty, Job loss or debt can be the factors related to higher stress level and that can lead to domestic violence. On other aspect, woman having high socio-economic status than her partner can cause inequality between them. Higher socio-economic status has generally been found to offer some protection against the risk of domestic violence. Internationally, studies indicate that whilst violence to partners cuts across all groups, women living in poverty are disproportionately affected (WHO 2002).
- **Violence against women in India during 2013-2014:** According to the report by National crime records bureau, A total of 3, 37,922 cases of crime against women (both under various sections of IPC and SLL) were reported in the country during the year 2014. In 2013, it was 3, 09,546, thus showing an increase of 9.2% during the year 2014. Uttar Pradesh with 16.8% share of country's women population has reported nearly 11.4% of total crimes committed against women at all India level, by reporting 38,467 cases and West Bengal accounting for nearly 7.5% of the country's women population, has accounted for 11.3% of total cases of crimes against women in the country by reporting 38,299 cases during the year 2014. The crime rate under crimes against women was reported as 56.3 in 2014. Delhi UT has reported the highest crime rate (169.1) compared to 56.3 at all India level during the year 2014, followed by Assam (123.4), Rajasthan (91.4), Tripura (88.0), West Bengal (85.4), Madhya Pradesh (79.0) and Telengana (78.3).

Fig: (1) Crime against women during 2010 - 2014

Sl. No.	Crime Head	Year				
		2010	2011	2012	2013	2014
1.	Dowry deaths	22172	24206	24923	33707	36735
2.	Kidnapping & abduction of women	29795	35565	38262	51881	57311
3.	Assault on women with intent to outrage her/ their modesty	40613	42968	45351	70739	82235

4.	Insult to the modesty of women	9961	8570	9173	12589	9735
5.	Cruelty by husband or his relatives	94041	99135	106527	118866	122877
6.	Abetment of suicide of women	-	-	-	-	3734

Star () mark mainly stands for domestic violence.

VIOLENCE AGAINST CHILDREN IN INDIA

In 2007, the Ministry of Women and Child Development (MWCD) released a study report on child abuse. The report discusses incidence of child abuse nationwide. The study found that 69% of children reported to have been physically abused. Out of these 54.68% were boys. 52.91% of boys and 47.09 % of girls reported having been abused in their family environment. Of the children who were abused in family situations 88.6% were abused by their parents. Every two out of three school children reported facing corporal punishment. In juvenile justice institutions 70.21 % of children in conflict with law and 52.86% of children in need of care and protection reported having been physically abused. With regard to child labor 50.2% of children work all seven days of the week. 81.16% of the girl child laborers work in domestic households, while 84% of the boy child laborers worked in tea stalls or kiosks. 65.99 % of boys and 67.92% of girls living on the street reported being physically abused by their family members and other people.

According to the report by National crime records bureau, a total of 89,423 cases of crimes against children were reported in the country during 2014 as compared to 58,224 cases during 2013, showing an increase of 53.6%. Madhya Pradesh accounted for 16.9% of total crimes committed against children reported in the country. The next in order was Uttar Pradesh (16.6%), Delhi (10.5%) and Maharashtra (9.1%). The crime rate i.e. incidence of crimes committed against children per one lakh population of children (up to 18 years of age) was observed as 20.1 at all India level during 2014. The crime rate was highest in Delhi (166.9) followed by Goa (63.5), Chandigarh (52.0), Madhya Pradesh (50.2) and Sikkim (45.8) as compared to the national average of 20.1.

Fig: (2) Crime against children during 2012 - 2014

Sl. No.	Crime Head	Year		
		2012	2013	2014
1.	Murder	1597	1657	1817
2.	Infanticide	81	82	121
3.	Assault on women(Girl children) with intent to outrage their modesty	-	-	11335
4.	Rape	8541	12363	13766
5.	Kidnapping & Abduction	18266	28167	37854
6.	Procuration of minor girls	809	1224	2020
7.	Foeticide	210	221	107
8.	Prohibition of Child Marriage Act	169	222	280

Star () mark mainly stands for domestic violence.

CONSTITUTIONAL PROVISIONS, HUMAN RIGHTSAND LEGISLATIONS

We have observed that the women and children are most often the victims of domestic violence in India. This explanation is on The Protection of Women and children from Domestic Violence.

Constitutional Standpoint

Article 253 of the Constitution confers on the parliament the power to make legislations in international conventions, treaties, conference, etc. Based on the recommendations given by the United Nations Committee in the Convention on the Elimination of all Forms of Discrimination against Women, the domestic violence act was constituted. The Act contains all the provisions of the Specific recommendations which belong to part of General Recommendation no.19, 1992.Keeping in view the fundamental rights assured under Articles 14, 15, and 21, the act was passed.

Article 21 confers the right to life and liberty that may not be taken away except by the legislative procedure, if required, as a result of judicial decisions in specific reasons. With respect to the right to be free of violence, the Supreme Court stated that any act which damages or injures or interferes with the use of any limb or faculty of a person, either permanently or even temporarily, would be within the inhibition of the said article.This right is included in the act as physical abuse, which constitutes domestic violence (and is hence punishable under the Act). Physical abuse denotes such natures that include the activities which may harmthe life or health. Article 14 contains the equal protection clause. It affirms equality before the law and the equal protection of the laws. Article 14 prohibits class legislation, but permits classification for legislative purposes.

Protection of women from Domestic Violence. Act, 2005

The Protection of Women from Domestic Violence Act 2005 is passed in the Indian parliament to protect women from domestic violence. It was brought into force by the Indian government from 26 October 2006. The Act provides the definition of domestic violence that includes physical violence and as well as other forms of violence such as emotional, verbal, sexual, and economic abuse. It is a civil law meant primarily for protection orders and not meant to penalize criminally.

Protection of Children from Sexual Offenses Act, 2012

Itwas formulated in order to effectively address any sexualexploitation committed against children. The Protection of Children from Sexual Offences Act has been passed by both the houses of the parliament in 2012. The law provides for relief and rehabilitation of the child, as soon as the complaint is made to the Special Juvenile Police Unit (SJPU) or to the local police.

Protection of Human Rights Act, 1993

The Rights Commission (NHRC) of India was constituted on 12 October 1993 under the Protection of Human Rights Ordinance of 28 September 1993. It was given a statutory basis by the Protection of Human Rights Act, 1993. The NHRC is the National Human Rights Commission of India, responsible for the protection and promotion of human rights, defined by the Act as "rights relating to life, liberty, equality and dignity of the individual guaranteed by the Constitution or embodied in the International Covenants".

WAY TO OVERCOME THE SITUATION

1. Peace Education and empowerment of families

The child is the responsibility of the parents, the family and the nearby community. The families and the community must be educated, informedand empowered so that they can provide careand protection to their children. Psychological and peace Education among family members effectively develop parenting skills that can make a violence free stabilized environment.

2. Role of people

In absence of parents, the nearbyfamily members or the community must take care of the children, thus, they must ensure thatevery child is in school, receives basic health care (particularly immunizations, nutrition) and is protectedfrom abuse & neglect.

3. Role of NGOs

Various non-government organizations working in child and women protection must coordinate their welfare activities and need to work consciously.They also need to supervise the implementation of various government measures that are already in place. Those include basicright to health, education, protection of human rights and prevention of woman and child abuse.

4. Role of Government

The main responsibility to protect the women and children from domestic violence lies with the Government. The Governmentshould introduce appropriate legislative, administrative, social and educational measures to prevent and protect children and women from domestic violence. Various laws that are constituted by the government, i.e. Juvenile Justice (Care and Protection) Act 2000(amended in 2006),The *Protection*of *Human Rights Act*, 1993, Prohibition of Child MarriageAct (2006),Domestic Violence Act 2005, the formation of the NationalCommission for Protection of Child Rights(2005), the Child Labor (Prohibition & Regulation) Act, 1986 (two notifications in 2006 & 2008), expanded the list of banned and hazardous processes and occupation, to protect, promote and defend child rights in the country. However, there is a widegap between policy, implementation & outcome, and millions of victims fall through the gaps.

CONCLUSION

Published evidence concerning domestic violence may not fulfill all the gaps in the research literature. Instead of being abused, we must raise our voice against such activities. The hidden object of this paper makes us aware about our own values. We have to be strict at the time of taking judicial helps against family members who are involved in such felonious activities. Monitoring, prosecution, penalizing and sentence implementation policies and practices also need fuller comparative investigation to identify positive, negative and interactive impacts on Indian victims of domestic violence. Various strategies and practice initiatives that have implemented outside the country should also be attempted. Although the circumstances towards protecting those victims from domestic violence is critically discussed in this paper, we still have plenty of research and works to constitute in near future.

BIBLIOGRAPHY

1. Aggarwal K, Dalwai S, Galagali P, et al. (2010). Recommendations on recognition and response to child abuse and neglect in the Indian setting. Indian Pediatr; 47:493–504.
2. Amnesty International, (2004), it's in our hands: stop violence against women. Summary. London: Amnesty International Publications.
3. Annual Report (1993). of the National Human Rights Commission.
4. Chalk, R. & King, P. A. (eds) (1998). Violence in families: assessing prevention and treatment programs. Executive summary. Committee on the Assessment of Family Violence Interventions, National Research Council and Institute of Medicine. Washington DC: National Academy Press.
5. Council of Europe. (2002) Recommendation Red (2002) 5 of the Committee of Ministers to member states on the protection of women against violence adopted on 30 April 2002 and explanatory memorandum.
6. Crime against Children, chapter-6, (2014).retrieved from*ncrb.nic.in/StatPublications/CII/CII2014/chapters.*
7. Crime against Women, Chapter-5, (2014). Retrieved from*ncrb.nic.in/StatPublications/CII/CII2014/chapters.*
8. Muehlenhard, C. L. &Kimes, L. A. (1999), the social construction of violence: the case of sexual and domestic violence. Personality and Social Psychology Review.3(3). 234-245.
9. Mullender, A. (1996). Rethinking domestic violence: the social work and probation response. London: Routledge.
10. Srivastava RN. (2008). Child health & welfare, panchayats& rural development. CANCL News. 8(1):3–4.
11. Study on Child Abuse: India (2007). Ministry of Women and Child Development, Government of India, Retrieved fromwww.wcd.nic.in/childabuse.pdf.

12. The Protection of Human Rights Act, (1993) as amended by the Protection of Human Rights (Amendment) Act, 2006.
13. The protection of women from domestic violence act, 2005 No. 43 of 2005, (2013)retrieved*from* https://web.archive.org/web/20130301005246/ http://wcd.nic.in/wdvact.pdf
14. Third and Fourth Combined periodic report on the Convention on the Rights of the Child (2011). Retrieved fromwww.wcd.nic.in.
15. United Nations. (1993) Declaration on the elimination of violence against women.General Assembly resolution 48/104 Of 20 December 1993. United Nations.
16. Walker, L. E (1999). Psychology and domestic violence around the world. American Psychologist. 54(1). 21-29.

Chapter-21

Gender Equality: A Pre-Condition for Peace Building

Shyamasree Sur & Jayanta Mete

INTRODUCTION

"In war torn societies, women often keep societies going...... We must ensure that women are enabled to play a full part in peace negotiations, in peace processes, in peace missions."

-Kofi Annan. United Nations Secretary General

Gender conflict is found in societies around the globe, and gender discrimination and conflict is a leading cause of violence. A number of gender training initiatives have begun to address the prevention of violence against women, and alternative ways in which gender conflict may be handled. These initiatives promote attitudes and values that emphasize the rights of girls and women to safety, respect, non-discrimination, and empowerment. Some programmes focus specifically on boys, helping them better understand their relationship to girls, their roles and responsibilities in family life stereotypes about masculinity, and communication skills for dealing with conflict. Gender training initiatives have an essential perspective to add to peace education activities, which have sometimes tended to overlook the gender component in violence and conflict resolution.

Concept of Peace-building

Peace building is a relatively new term, but the ideas and practices behind peace building have deep roots in all cultures. All cultures and communities have ways of building peace. The tasks of those who desire to be peace building are; to help uncover the traditions of peace building within each culture, to borrow peace building ideas from other cultures, to adapt them to local contexts, and to empower people to engage in peace building processes. In simple terms, peace building is all activity aimed at improving the quality of life. Peace building prevents, reduces, transforms, and helps people to recover from violence. Peace building includes a set of values, relational skills, analytical tools and processes to create sustainable, just and peaceful communities. Peace building is found in every community and in every culture, but many of our communities need help to explore and strengthen their capacity to building peace. Men and women in every community are already engaged in building peace, but their tasks are almost always different. Women and men both have their role to place in peace building. But empowerment of women is a challenge in building culture of peace in India.

Women and Peace

The protection of women in conflict-affected areas, as well as their participation in political decision-making, has been increasingly prominent in international policy over recent decades. But the development of new policy and approaches has not yet had the impact many had hoped for. Most peace agreements do not address the specific concerns of women. And women are still excluded from political processes. Global policy highlights the importance of women's participation in peace processes and peace building. Yet the impact of international commitments is not felt on the ground. Most peace agreements do not address the specific concerns of women. And women are still excluded from political processes. The underlining highlights the providing insights into what women peace builders can achieve, the challenges they faced, the opportunities they created and how they can be effectively supported in their efforts.

Violence against Women

Violence against women is a common and serious problem in India. There are various types of violence against women in India like child marriage, female foeticide and infanticide, sexual abuse, female child labour, domestic violence, dowry harassment and bride burning, sexual harassment at work, even teasing, violence against elderly women, violence against widows and women trafficking etc. If we look towards the statistics about crimes/violence against women and educational development (Literacy) in India, we can simply conclude that cases of violence against women are rapidly rising with educational development. The correlation between above both, it is any act of gender – based violence, which results in physical, sexual or arbitrary deprivation of liberty and violence of human rights of women variables should be negative but it is positive in India. Education is an empowering tool for women and it is the crucial criteria of social development. Current peace education does its utmost to be considered a unique educational practice, a field of research and a discourse that has its own philosophical, social, rhetorical and political aspects. Peace education, however, has no theoretical framework. The promotion of peace through education is at the heart of UNESCO's mission. Two fundamental concepts of peace education are respect and skills. For sustaining and achieving peace, the need for peace education is felt more and more. Peace does not simply mean the absence of war but the absence of fear, and structural inequalities. Justice is integral to peace – so peace with justice is what women fight for. The only lasting peace is just peace based on respect for human rights. Women should come forward to protect themselves by empowering themselves. Women are expected to work for peace building by peace Education. Women are half of every community and they can shoulder the responsibility of the tasks of peace building. We should provide the Zone to empower women to overcome threats and obstacles that may interrupt or prevent their peace building.

Women's Engagement in Peace building Policy

The UN Resolution 1325 recognized the relevance of gender and peace and security matters, and mandated all United Nations member-states to ensure full participation of women at all levels of decision making in conflict resolution and peace processes. It also called for the protection of women and girls against violence during and after conflict, and for the adoption of a gender perspective to prevent and mitigate impacts of conflict on women. While progress has been made at policy levels, translating the goals of Resolution 1325 into reality in conflict- affected countries remain a challenge.

In the education sector, more efforts must be made by Government to identify and strengthen the right methodologies for empowering both male and female teachers to create a safe and secure school environment for girls and boys. Synergies must be created between experience and policies.

In 1995, the Beijing Platform of Action recognized education not only as a human right but also as an essential tool for achieving the goals of equality, development and peace. "Literacy of women is an important key to improving health, nutrition and education in the family and to empowering women to participate in decision – making and society." The issues raised at the UN Beijing conference remain relevant. The conference identified twelve critical areas of concern. Each concern revealed that women's human rights are very much compromised and at risk in a discriminated against solely on the basis of gender. The difference between men and women could not be achieved unless the rights of women are fully respected.

The 2011 European conference "On the move for Equality" highlighted that women's civil society organizations are an important vehicle for the promotion of women's participation and gender friendly. Policies are important both for long term peace and democracy. Burundi and Nepal are two post-conflict countries that are notable for the large number of women engaged in civil society. In these countries, women's organizations have been a driving force behind women's engagement in public and political life, for the adoption of laws protecting women's rights. Yet, the impact and sustainability of these organizations are hampered both by a lack of political will, and by insecure and inflexible funding regimes.

Gender Equality and Women's Empowerment

Gender equality is a human right, but our world faces a persistent gap in access to opportunities and decision making power for women and men. Globally, women have fewer opportunities for economic participation than men, less access to basic and higher education, greater health and safety risks, and less political representation. Guaranteeing the rights of women and giving them opportunities to reach their full potential is critical not only for attaining gender equality, but also for meeting a wide range of international development goals. Empowered women and girls contribute to the health and productivity of their families, communities and countries, creating a ripple effect that benefits everyone.

The word "gender" describes the socially constructed roles and responsibilities that societies consider appropriate for men and women. Gender equality means that men and women have equal power and equal opportunities for financial independence, education and personal development. Women's Empowerment is a critical aspect of achieving gender equality. It includes increasing a women's sense of self worth, her decision making power, her access to opportunities and resources, her power and control over her own life inside and outside the home, and her ability to effect change. Yet gender issues are not focused on women shone, but on the relationship between men and women in society. The actions and attitudes of men and boys play an essential role in achieving gender equality.

Education is key area of focus. Although the world is making progress in achieving gender parity in education, girls still make up a higher percentage of out of school children than boys. Approximately one quarter of girls in the developing world do not attend school. Typically families with limited means who cannot afford costs such as school fees, uniforms, and supplies for all of their children will prioritize education for their son families may also rely on girls labour for household chores, carrying water, and childcare, leaving limited time for schooling. But prioritizing girls education provides perhaps the single highest return on investment in the developing world. An educated girl is more likely to postpone Marriage, raise a smaller family, have healthier children, and send her own children to school. She has more opportunities to earn an income and to participate in political processes, and she is less likely to become inflected with HIV.

Women's health and safety is another important area., HIV/AIDS is becoming an increasingly impactful issue for women. This can be related to women having fewer opportunities for health education, unequal power in sexual partnership, or as a result of gender based violence. Material Health is also an issue of specific concern. In many countries, women have limited access to pre-natal and infant care, and are more likely to experience complications during pregnancy and childbirth. This is a critical concern in countries where girls marry and give birth children before they are ready; often well before the age of 18. Quality maternal health care can provide an important entry point for information and services that empower mothers as informed decision-makers concerning their own health and the health of their children.

A final area of focus in attaining gender equality in women's economic and political empowerment. Though women comprise more than 50% of the world's population, they only own 1% of the world's wealth. Throughout the world, women and girls perform long hours of unpaid domestic work. In some places, women still lack rights to own land or to inherit property, obtain access to credit, earn money, or to move up in their work place, free from job discrimination. At all levels, including at home and in the public area, women are widely underrepresented as decision makers. In legislatures around the world, women are outnumbered 4 to 1, yet women's political participation is crucial for achieving gender equality and genuine democracy.

The world Economic forum recently ranked the United States as 19th in the world on its gender gap index. With women comprising less than one fifth of elected members of congress, the report identifies political empowerment as the greatest gender equity issue for the United States. The U.S. ranked higher in economic empowerments, but women's earning power remains approximately 20% lower than men's. Women in the United States have a very high ranking of educational attainment, though, with high levels of literacy and enrolment in primary, secondary, and university education. At present, there are more U.S. women attending college than men.

Globally, women country has fully attended gender equality. Scandinavian countries like Iceland, Norway, Finland, and Sweden land the world in their progress towards closing the gender gap. In these countries, there is relatively equitable distribution of available income, resources and opportunities for men and women. The greatest gender gaps are identified primarily in the Middle East, Africa and South Asia, However, a number of countries including South Africa, Sri Lanka etc. outrank the U.S. in gender equality.

Around the world, Peace Corps Volunteers are working with communities to address gender equality and empower women and girls. In 1974, Congress signed the **Percy Amendment** requiring Peace Corps Volunteers to activity integrate women into the economic, political and social development of their countries. Many Peace Corps Volunteers implement the camp GLOW (Girls Leading Our World) programme, to help girls develop self-esteem and leadership skills. Recognizing that men and boys must be equal partners in achieving gender equality, volunteers also teach leadership and life skills to boys through Teaching

Our Boys Excellence (TOBE) camps. Peace corps volunteers promote gender equality and women's empowerment through health education, business develop, and by raising awareness of women's rights and contributions to their communities.

Gender Equality in Education

Gender based discrimination in education is both a cause and a consequence of deep-rooted disparities in society. Poverty, geographical isolation, ethnic background, disability, traditional attitudes about their states and role all undermine the ability of women and girls to exercise their rights. Harmful practices such as early marriage and pregnancy, gender-based violence, and discriminatory education laws, policies, contents, and practices still prevent millions of girls form enrolling, completing and benefitting from education.

Gender must therefore be integrated at all levels of education, from early childhood to higher education, in formal and non-formal settings and from planning infrastructure to training teachers.

A culture of peace and non-violence goes to the substance of fundamental human rights; social justice, democracy, literacy, respect and dignity for all, international solidarity, respect for workers' rights and core labour standards, children rights, equality between men & women, cultural identity and diversity, indigenous peoples and minorities rights, the preservation of natural environment to name some of the more obvious thematic.

Education is a key tool in combating poverty, in promoting peace, social justice, human rights, democracy, cultural diversity and environmental awareness. Education for peace implies an active concept of peace through values, life skills and knowledge in a spirit of equality, respect, empathy, understanding and mutual appreciation among individuals, groups and nations. By educating women, society would be striving to get them out of the deep levels of illiteracy the world over. It would give them a chance to engage competitively in various issues that will invariably have a positive impact on sustainable peace.

Peace education would enable the girl child to have an equal platform in contributing to addressing form of structural and cultural violence and actively participating in seeking effective and sustainable ways of resolving the situation and enhancing all rounded peace.

EMPOWERING WOMEN IN REAL SENSE

Strategies emphasizes on placing women on the negotiating table and representation of women in the various committees which can contribute toward governance and peace building. Some initiatives like ensuring enhanced presence of women in elected bodies, reservation of women in government services, creation of strong women's pressure groups, larger women participation in national forums, employing more women in the para-military forces and designated women guards in relief camps during armed conflicts will go a long way in real empowerment of women and their role in conflict resolution and development of society.

CONCLUSION

It is only by critically addressing the cultural and structural hindrances that exist against women that sustainable peace and development can be achieved. In order to override these problems, we need to act to empower women by taking steps to eliminate inequalities by the promotion and fulfillment of women's potential through education, skill development and employment hence giving paramount importance to the elimination for sustainable development and positive holistic peace.

Education is the first building block of development upon which everything else, health care, social care, employment – must be founded. It is the key to holistic development in the economic, social and political spheres. The role of education in development and in the enhancement of positive peace cannot be overlooked. Thus, the education of the girl child can be used as an empowerment tool to address practices that institutionalize discrimination, injustice and equality. By educating the girl child, the society as a whole would have come one step further in addressing human security and ensuring better future for all its citizens. In order to grow as nation, then it must be resized the importance of bringing women and most specifically girl child to the same level as the men and boy children, then and only then, it can realize positive peace. The promotion of peace education is the way out of cultural and structural violence against women. Women also need to be represented at the decision and policy making level with in the education sphere. Educating women will further societal expectations in various ways including improved health and better socio-economic status. This is in striving towards the attainment of equity through education and in giving both genders the same opportunities to access education. Peace education for the women and girl child affects all spheres in society be the political, economic or social. If well implemented, it has the potential to promote sustainable development and positive peace.

BIBLIOGRAPHY

1. Basiga Brenda (2004) Article : *Globalization and peace Education,* University of Alberta. Journal : Canadian Social Studies, Volume 38, Number 3.
2. Brecher, J. & Castello. T (1994). *Global Village or Global Pillage* Boston: South End.
3. Carnoy. M. (1999) *Globalization and Educational reform : What planners Need to know*. Paris. UNESCO : International Institute for Educational Planning.
4. Brock – Utne.B. (1989). *Feminist Perspectives on Peace and Peace Education.* New York : Pergamon.
5. Eisler, Riane, 1997 : *Human Rights and Violence. in : Turpin,* Jennifer and Lester R.Kurtz. (eds), 1997 : The web of violence Chicago : University of Illijnoise Press.pp16/- -187/-.
6. UNDP, 1997 : *Human Development Report.*

Chapter-22

Gorkha Cessation – Cruelty and Endangered Childhood

Prodip Adhikari

INTRODUCTION

Now a day, What North Bengal area became enraged. Specially in Kurseong, Darjiling, Bhaktinagar, Kalimpong, Malbazar, Chalsa, Nagarkatta, Banarhat, Birpara, Madarihat, Jaigoan, Kalchini and Kumargram and so on. Almost ten years ago 'Gorkha Janamukti Morcha' was born on 2007[1]. At the end of 2011, they established a good relationship in between the chief minister of the state and the politicians of 'Gorkha Janamukti Morcha'. And in 2012, G.T.A. agreement was signed for the welfare of North Bengal. Respectable chief minister said, "The Mountains are laughing". But suddenly what happened that the citizen of North Bengal openly adapted the ferocious way and they are protesting? In the reason is that respectable chief minister selected bengali language as the first language in whole state, the language which 'UNESCO declares to be the World's sweetest languages'[2]. Or there is a deep plan behind this movement? The main problem is that, children have gathered for protesting instead of going school for education. Some students age below five years.[3] Alise a student of Class VIII, age near about 12, said "We want Gorkha. We will be good at that" "Amra Gorkhaland Chai, Tate Amader Vali habe".[4] Purabi Thapa, a mother of Rakesh Thapa (Nine years old) said, Eta Amader Adhikar Adayer Andolon, Ar alada rajya hole paraborti prajanmai sabchaite beshi upakrita habe, Sutarang ora michile hatle dos kothay?"[5] "This is our right to move the movement. And in the separate sate, the next generation will be benefited most, so where is the fault in the procession?" "We proved today that we can bleed for Gorkhaland," said Tilak Chhatri, one of the Gorkha youth.[6] Some question obviously arises. Are those little children were forced to gathered at this protesting? Or they gathered at protesting with their own wish? If we agree eventually that they gathered for protesting willfully, then we must say that our new generation are matured enough before a certain age. But according to psychology, after a certain age children's developed mentally and socially and they became adult. Actually in some cases they take part in some demonstration out of curiosity and to some extent out of enjoyment of this age which has been very clearly portrayed in the poem *'Atharo Bachar Bayas' (eighteen years old)* by Sukanta Bhattacharya.

Caption 1: A procession on demanding Gorkhaland of Nepali Professors like Binod Bhatariya, Surendra Sampang on July 2, 2017

But the question is on other side. When in front of the eyes of these children, the shops, government cools, houses, office, market are destroyed – how these affect the children? On the other hand, the travelers spend say and night with dread or panic. When is this wool the relatives of a little child lose their life in front of the child, how does this effected the child? How he mentally affected by the death? So, we can say that by this the future of the children is destroyed pathetically. They are observing death, murders from childhood. So, Environment led them to a way where they thought that "BLOOD ARE NOTHING". Death, murders, blood are becoming very normal subject for the children's of Gorkha. The Education Minister said, "Eta manab adhikar langhan, abang ei aganatantrik kajke samarthan kara jaina".[7] The pure heart of the children is poisoned by cruelty and the result is regional dissimilarity, from one India to vindicate India. We have to kept in mind that, few foreign countries want that are beautiful India turned into an indiscipline India.

There is debate over the inclusion of children's political activities in the world. In the hearing of a case in the High Court, the Chief Justice Jaynarayan Patel and Justice Ashim Kumar Roy ordered that no child be included in the political rally.[8]

Caption 2: Demand of Gorkhaland by Gorkha Children on Jun 28, 2017

WHO ARE THE GORKHA?

The 'Gorkhas' in the Indian context are Indian citizens of Nepali ethnicity, who live across the length and breadth of India. The term 'Gorkha' in the Indian context is used to differentiate the Indian citizens of Nepali ethnicity from the citizens of Nepal, who prefer to be called 'Nepalese.'[9] Many a time, people mistake the Indian

'Gorkhas' with Nepalese 'Gorkhali'. It is to be noted that in terms of Nepal, 'Gorkhali' refers to the people from the 'Gorkha' region. However, the use of the term 'Gorkha' in the Indian context is very different than in Nepal's context[10]. Therefore, the term 'Gorkha' refers to different groups of people depending on the country they are being used in reference to.

Majority of the people who identify themselves as 'Gorkhas' in India are sons and daughters of the soil, and their forefathers 'came with the land.' They did not immigrate to India. However, it is well recognized that there are many immigrants from Nepal, who have also settled in India, post-independence.

WHY GHORKHALAND?

Gorkha leader Tilak Chhetri said, "Our (Gorkha People) culture are deferent, lifestyle are different, so we want to separate"[11]. Yes we agree with that became until we understand that the people of Gorkha are also the people of Bengal, until that day the problem will not be solve. We remember the mountain area only on vacation like summer vacation, winter vacation or puja vacation. Is this right? No

The demand for a separate administrative unit (separate state in today's term) for the Darjeeling region had started as early as 1907. However, the influx of Bangladeshi refugees starting in 1965 and later state sponsored illegal immigrants from Bangladesh post-1971 for vote bank by subsequent West Bengal governments led to marginalization of the ethnic Gorkha, Kamtapuri and the Rajbanshi communities of the region. The demand for Gorkhaland is a demand to protect the identity, culture, history, traditions and the rich bond of people from Darjeeling region, which they share with their land. Furthermore, the Gorkhas from the Darjeeling region have continued to be labeled by the fascist and state sponsored Bengali organizations such as 'Bangla O Bangla Bhasa Bachao Samity', 'Amra Bangali', 'Jan Jagaran Morcha', 'Jan Chetna Morch'a as illegal immigrants and the demand for Gorkhaland illegal. They have rendered the ethnic Gorkha people as an intruder in his/her own ancestral lands. This has caused widespread socio-economic and political marginalization of the Gorkhas. All these factors have resulted in the Gorkhas being under-represented, stereotyped and communally discriminated in almost all sectors.Moreover, Bengal has always been colonial in its approach to this region. The large revenues collected from Darjeeling region have been used to develop other parts of Bengal, while neglecting even the basic infrastructure in the region.

Case in point: the National Highway 55, which used to be the artery connecting the hills of Darjeeling to the rest of India, has been closed due to land slide since 2009 and the West Bengal government has done nothing to rebuild it.

According to Manoj Giri (21 Jun, 2008) "Gorkhaland is non development area: he given example like-

- When the British left there were 180 tea estates in Darjeeling, now only 82 are left including some which are closed.
- In North Bengal there is presently 18 tea gardens locked -out and in these some 30 thousand workers are jobless.
- The wage of a labour in Darjeeling Dooars is the lowest in the country.

Tamilnadu	Rs.101/-,
Kerala	Rs. 92/-,
Karnataka	Rs. 92.85/-
Darjeeling- Dooars	Rs.68.70/-

(These are inclusive of fuel and rations of poorest standards).

It is below the minimum wage of Rs.100/-.

- During the British Rule five to six mail and passengers trains used to go up and down Darjeeling – New Jalpaiguri, and the whole night goods trains used to run in the narrow gauge line. But now there is only one train with 3 compartments that runs between the two stations.
- Almost all the ropeways constructed by the British, an easy way of transport and employment, which carried goods to far flung areas, are now defunct.
- Malbazar- Mateley- Dooars was part of Darjeeling Parliamentary constituency, it was cut away and Islampur Chopra with no Gorkha population was attached to this constituency. This was done by B C Roy. His intention was criminal as the Gorkhas could not send an MP on their own; they had to depend on the Bengalese Ruling class's whims and politics which always were detrimental to the interests of the Gorkhas.
- Drinking water problem is world famous:[12]

Now we discuss the chronologically demand of Gorkhaland. In 1782The Gorkhas captured Sikkim and most part of North Eastern states that includes Darjeeling, Garhwal hills, Kumaon, Nainital, Siliguri, Simla and Sutlej, that is, the entire region from Teesta to Sutlej, in 1835 British handed over Darjeeling to Sikkim, in 1907 The first demand for Gorkhaland is submitted to Morley-Minto Reforms panel and 2013 Declaration of Gorkhaland Territorial Administration (GTA) and Gurung is made its leader.

1780	The Gorkhas captured Sikkim and most part of North Eastern states that includes Darjeeling, Garhwal hills, Kumaon, Nainital, Siliguri, Simla and Sutlej, that is the entire region from Teesta to Sutlej.[1]
1816	The Gorkhas surrendered the territory to British in the Treaty of Segoulee after they lost the Anglo-Nepal war.[2]
1835	British handed over Darjeeling to Sikkim
1907	The first demand for Gorkhaland is submitted to Morley-Minto Reforms panel. After that on several occasions demands were made to the British government and then government of Independent India for separation from Bengal.
1952	The AGL (All India Gorkha League) submits a memorandum to then Prime Minister Jawharlal Neheu demanding separation from the state of Bengal.
1955	Daulat Das Bokhim submits a memorandum to the chairman. State Reorganisation Committee demanding the creation of separate state consisting of Darjeeling, Jalpaiguri and Cooch Behar district. Daulat Das Bokhim was a President of District Shramik Sangh
1981	Prime Minister Indra Gandhi receives a memorandum from Pranta Parishad, demanding a separate state.
1980	Under the leadership of Gorkha National Liberation Front supremo Subhas Ghising. The movement turns violent during the period of 1986-88, and around 1,200 people are killed.
1988	The Darjeeling Gorkha Hill Council (DGHC) is finally formed
1905	Centre and state government initiative for a permanent solution of this region by bringing it to the sixth schedule of the constitution giving some degree of autonomy to a predominantly tribal area. But the Gorkhas opposed this sixth schedule and demand statehood gains pace.

1907	The mass movement for Gorkhaland takes place under the leadership of Gorkha Janmurti Morcha (GJM) supremo Bimal Gurung
2013	Declaration of Gorkhaland Territorial Administration (GTA) and Gurung is made its leader.

Proposed Map of Gorkhaland

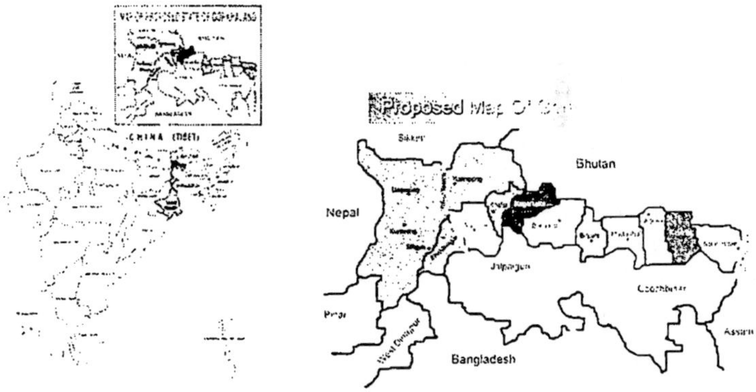

On the other hand, we have to think that, is the creation of the Gorkhaland is the end of all the problems? Will the people of mountains stay a peaceful life?

IS GORKHALAND STATE IS THE SALVATION FROM ALL THIS CRUELTY?

In 1989, the situation of the mountains people almost like present days. But is those days, the relation between central and state were very good. For that reason Rajiv Gandhi said to late chief minister Jyati Basu, "Basuji, Don't worry, Bengal will not be divided. We will be together but Ghisingh have to pay much more money for the mountain". Jyati Bosu gave huge money for the welfare of the mountains. In 1887, Jyati Bosu stands up for the question of Darjiling. Even the result was the co-operation in between central and state which led to the peace is the lives of the people of mountains. But now days, the relationship between central and state obstruct to the sediment. For this may be, central tried to an extreme level to save Kashmir, but they failed to keep Bengal unbroken.

Darjiling is economically much more developed were than other district of West Bengal. The citizen of Darjiling is more or less advanced on various fields more than the districts of South or West Bengal. So, the claiming of economic backwardness of Darjiling is not true.

If Gorkhaland state will establish, thousands of citizens in mountain will get a job which is totally a false pledge. In this very little state, in this little state place how this number of economical institution will standup which can give job to those huge number of workers? Not only that, if Gorkhaland isolate and established, for government it is almost impossible to make any recruitment for next ten to twelve years.

Not only that, the travelers business will be greatly affected. Maximum of travelers in Darjiling are bengali even now. After the first phase of Morcha movement, the travelers of Darjiling selected Sikkim as their next destination.

The main problem is, only for the high ambitions of few politicians, the future of the next generation are destroying.

CONCLUSION

For the salvation from this cruelty centric on Gorkhaland, the state government and central government co-operate and they must discuss with the citizens of Gorkha for their welfare. They should bring back the children to the environment of school and education. The children of Gorkha who educate in English medium, government must select English/ Hindi as their first language, Hindi/English as their second language and Nepali (Mother Tongue) as their third language. Although, chief minister of West Bengal announced at the moment of 'Gorkha Movement' that, for the citizens of proposed Gorkhaland (Kurseong, Darjiling, Bhaktinagar, Kalimpong, Malbazar, Chalsa, Nagarkatta, Banarhat, Birpara, Madarihat, Jaigoan, Kalchini and Kumargram) bengali is not compulsory, lit us optional.

APPENDIX: A

A Letter of Chief Minister of Sikkim to Hon'ble Union Home Minister

Pawan Chamling
(Honoris Causa)
Chief Minister of Sikkim

☎ 03592-202575 (O)
03592-202304 (R)
E-mail : cm-skm@[illegible]nic.in

Gangtok - 737103
Sikkim

D.O No. [illegible]/CMO/2017
June 20, 2017

Respected Shri Rajnath Singh Ji,

You are kindly aware of the recent outbreak of agitation in the Darjeeling hills in connection with the statehood demand of Gorkhaland. Unfortunately, on July 17, 2017 three young people have been martyred and several others injured in the firing. The past three uproarious decades of agitation for the statehood demand in the neighbouring hills has claimed over a 1000 lives and caused incalculable loss of property and constant threat to security of life.

It is common knowledge that the landlocked state of Sikkim has been suffering untold loss owing to the recurring blockage of its one and only lifeline NH10, during the last 30 years of Gorkhaland agitation. The blockage of the transportation of essential goods and general utilities causes unmanageable inconvenience. What is more the atmosphere of uncertainty along the NH 10 poses great threat to lives as well. Sikkimese students studying in Darjeeling and the rest of India along with people needing medical treatment, have no option but to take this tension ridden highway to travel to their destination. Given Sikkim's delicate geopolitical location within three international borders with China (Tibet), Bhutan and Nepal, the potential danger posed by such a sustained agitation in the neighbouring Hills to the peace in Sikkim cannot be ruled out.

The Sikkim Legislative Assembly had passed a resolution in 2011 and sent it to the Government of India seeking a permanent solution to the pressing and long standing problem of the people of Darjeeling Hills which would not only be in the interests of the region but also of the entire nation.

The Gorkhas have a glorious history of extraordinary patriotism in India. The martyrdom of the Gorkha freedom fighter, Major Durga Malla has been duly recognized by the installation of his statue outside the Indian parliament. Dambar Singh Gurung and Ari Bahadur Gurung were among the members of the Constituent Assembly and the latter was a signatory during the introduction of the Indian Constitution. Captain Ram Singh Thakuri, another prominent Gorkha freedom fighter, composed the music to Jana Gana Mana and composed a number of patriotic songs including Kadam Kadam Badaye Ja and Subh Sukh Chain.

The fulfilment of the constitutional demand of the people of the Darjeeling Hills which is deeply connected with national identity of the Indian Gorkhas will provide long-awaited justice to their patriotism, which has been second to none. Creation of Gorkhaland state will also restore permanent peace and prosperity of the region and Sikkim will be hugely benefited as her developmental tempo can be maintained undisturbed.

With regards,

Yours sincerely,

(Pawan Chamling)

Shri Rajnath Singh,
Hon'ble Union Home Minister,
Government of India,
New Delhi

BIBLIOGRAPHY

1. Chhetri, V. (Jun 28, 2017). Tubelight-and-blood protest in Darjeeling. Calcutta: The Telegraph.pp.8.
2. Chakraborty, C. (Jun 28, 2017). Kalam Chilo, Kali noi, GTA niye mat khubda Binayer. Kolkata: Eisamay.pp.2.
3. Chakraborty, C. (Jun 25, 2017).Trish hajar lok niye michil morchar. Kolkata: Eisamay.pp.1.
4. Giri, P. (July 9, 2017). Tapta Pahar Fer Mrityu Char Janer. Kolkata: Anandabazar Patrika.pp.1.
5. Chakraborty, C. (Jun 24, 2017).Pahar theke samatale neme elo poruyar dal. Kolkata: Eisamay.pp.2.
6. Chakraborty, C. (Jun 23, 2017).Ami-e Paharer bap: Gurung. Kolkata: Eisamay.pp.1.
7. Ri Chowdhury. (September, 2015). Manab Adhikar O Manab Unnayan. Kolkata: Progressive Publishers.
8. Sankrityan, J. (Jun 30, 2017). Toy Train Asole Khelna Noi, Darjeeling Jane, Paharer Rajniti bujhte Arthanitir Khonj nite habe. Kolkata: Anandabazar Patrika.pp.4.

Endnotes

1. Chakraborty, C. (Jun 28, 2017). Sei 11 ta 19 she GTA-er sheskritya. Eisamay Sangbadpatra, pp. 1.
2. Retrieved http://www.mouthshut.com/blog/cchbmplup/UNESCO-Declares-Bengali-To-Be-The-Worlds-Sweetest-Language
3. Anandabazar Patrika (Jun 29, 017).Sharire Shikal, Morchar Michile Shishurao. Anandabazar Patrika.pp.5.
4. Chakraborty, C. (Jun 29, 2017).Michile Shishudero Namiye Prashne Morcha. Eisamay Sangbadpatra, pp. 1.
5. Ibid.
6. Chhetri, V. (Jun 28, 2017). Tubelight-and-blood protest in Darjeeling. Calcutta: The Telegraph.pp.8.
7. Anandabazar Patrika (Jun 29, 017).Sharire Shikal, Morchar Michile Shishurao. Anandabazar Patrika.pp.5.
8. Anandabazar Patrika (Jun 29, 017).Sharire Shikal, Morchar Michile Shishurao. Anandabazar Patrika.pp.5.
9. Telephonic Interview with Surendra Sappang, Assistan Professor, Sikkim Govt. College, Gyalshing on July 16, 2017.
10. Telephonic Interview with Bikash Chettri on July 16, 2017.
11 Telephonic Interview with Tilak Chhetri on Jun 28, 2017
12 Retrieved http://www.srai.org/demand-for-gorkhaland-what-is-it-and-why/
13. Retrieved http://indpaedia.com/ind/index.php/The_Gorkhaland_movement
14. Retrieved http://indpaedia.com/ind/index.php/The_Gorkhaland_movement

Global Peace Index Ranking (2008-2016)

Country	2016 rank	2015 rank	2014 rank	2013 rank	2012 rank	2011 rank	2010 rank	2009 rank	2008 rank
Iceland	1	1	1	1	1	1	2	1	1
Denmark	2	2	2	2	2	4	7	6	5
Austria	3	3	3	4	6	6	4	3	10
New Zealand	4	4	4	3	2	2	1	2	2
Portugal	5	11	18	18	16	17	13	15	14
Czech Republic	6	10	11	14	13	5	12	16	18
Switzerland	7	5	5	5	10	16	18	11	4
Canada	8	7	7	8	4	8	14	9	6
Japan	9	8	8	6	5	3	3	4	3
Slovenia	10	15	14	13	8	10	11	10	13
Finland	11	6	6	7	9	7	9	7	7
Ireland	12	12	13	12	6	11	6	14	11
Bhutan	13	18	16	20	19	34	36	43	19
Sweden	14	13	11	9	14	13	10	5	8
Australia	15	9	15	16	22	18	19	19	16

Country	2016 rank	2015 rank	2014 rank	2013 rank	2012 rank	2011 rank	2010 rank	2009 rank	2008 rank
Germany	16	16	17	15	15	15	16	17	15
Norway	17	17	10	11	18	9	5	8	9
Belgium	18	14	9	10	11	14	17	13	13
Hungary	19	22	21	23	17	20	20	25	20
Singapore	20	24	25	16	23	24	30	18	21
Netherlands	21	20	20	22	28	25	27	29	28
Poland	22	19	23	25	24	22	29	28	33
Mauritius	23	25	24	21	21				
Slovakia	24	23	19	33	26	23	21	23	25
Spain	25	21	26	27	25	28	25	32	27
Croatia	26	27	26	28	35	37	41	40	52
Chile	27	29	30	31	30	38	28	20	17
Botswana	28	31	36	32	31	35	33	31	37
Bulgaria	29	32	32	35	39	53	50	46	46
Malaysia	30	28	33	29	20	20	22	22	23
Romania	31	26	35	30	32	40	45	26	26
Latvia	32	40	39	41	45	46	54	50	45
Costa Rica	33	34	42	40	36	31	26	27	31
Qatar	34	30	22	19	12	12	15	12	30
Uruguay	35	44	29	24	33	21	24	24	24
Estonia	36	38	31	38	41	47	46	41	32

Country	2016 rank	2015 rank	2014 rank	2013 rank	2012 rank	2011 rank	2010 rank	2009 rank	2008 rank
Lithuania	37	37	46	43	43	43	42	36	48
Madagascar	38	67	66	90	99	105	77	69	35
Italy	39	36	34	34	38	45	40	39	34
Zambia	40	55	44	48	51	52	51	58	52
Taiwan	41	35	28	26	27	27	35	33	40
Indonesia	42	46	54	54	63	68	67	60	64
Sierra Leone	43	59	66	59	52	61	53		
Ghana	44	54	61	58	50	42	48	55	55
Malawi	45	51	77	74	60	39	51	51	62
France	46	45	48	53	40	36	32	52	50
United Kingdom	47	39	47	44	29	26	31	41	48
Serbia	48	47	52	62	64	84	90	71	80
Panama	49	64	57	56	61	49	61	66	43
Mongolia	50	43	41	64	58	57	92	88	89
Kuwait	51	33	37	37	47	29	39	38	42
Laos	52	41	38	39	37	32	34	49	55
South Korea	53	42	52	47	42	50	43	42	40
Albania	54	52	65	69	66	63	65	70	71
Namibia	55	48	48	46	49	54	59	59	60
Timor-Leste	56	58	69	51					

Country	2016 rank	2015 rank	2014 rank	2013 rank	2012 rank	2011 rank	2010 rank	2009 rank	2008 rank
Montenegro	57	57	55	73	81	89	88	80	
Tanzania	58	64	59	55	55	56	55	53	56
Vietnam	59	56	45	41	34	30	38	48	42
Bosnia and Herzegovina	60	53	61	71	65	60	60	45	69
United Arab Emirates	61	50	40	36	46	33	44	30	29
Equatorial Guinea	62	81	93	89	87	75	68	56	69
Lesotho	63	63	50	50	53				
Tunisia	64	76	79	77	72	44	37	37	40
Moldova	65	70	71	74	66	59	66	74	78
Togo	66	71	80	67					
Argentina	67	60	43	60	44	55	71	61	55
Mozambique	68	80	82	61	48	48	47	47	45
Nicaragua	69	74	58	66	81	72	64	72	71
Senegal	70	49	72	85	78	77	79	75	74
Cyprus	71	68	51	49	73	71	76	34	37
Benin	72	77	100	104	114				
Liberia	72	78	84	80	101	96	99		
Oman	74	74	59	45	59	41	23	21	22
Kazakhstan	75	87	103	78	105	93	95	97	82

Country	2016 rank	2015 rank	2014 rank	2013 rank	2012 rank	2011 rank	2010 rank	2009 rank	2008 rank
Ecuador	76	84	85	83	85	90	101	105	100
Kosovo	77	69	64	72					
Nepal	78	62	76	82	80	95	82	76	
Gabon	79	66	68	76	75	81	74	44	50
Paraguay	80	89	73	84	76	66	77	73	69
Bolivia	81	90	70	86	84	76	81	82	76
Greece	82	61	86	68	77	65	62	62	58
Bangladesh	83	84	98	105	91	83	87	93	93
Trinidad and Tobago	84	97	89	90	94	79	94	77	89
Georgia	85	79	111	139	141	134	142	134	
Cuba	85	82	75	65	70	67	72	64	64
Peru	85	92	119	114	79	85	89	78	89
Burkina Faso	88	83	78	87	56	51	57	65	72
Haiti	89	98	99	92	107	113	114	120	114
Swaziland	90	101	87	88	85	69	73		
Morocco	91	86	63	57	54	58	58	63	60
Gambia	92	99	94	93	74	62	63		
Jamaica	92	109	107	117	113	106	98	89	89
Macedonia	94	71	87	79	68	78	83	86	76
Guyana	95	92	83	70	69	88	91	94	
Jordan	96	71	56	52	62	64	68	67	61

Country	2016 rank	2015 rank	2014 rank	2013 rank	2012 rank	2011 rank	2010 rank	2009 rank	2008 rank
Sri Lanka	97	114	105	110	103	126	133	126	120
Angola	98	88	102	102	95	87	86	84	100
Papua New Guinea	99	96	90	99	93	94	95	91	96
Dominican Republic	99	100	95	94	90	91	93	79	83
Uganda	101	111	110	106	98	96	100	103	110
Guinea	101	117	118	116	92	92			
United States	103	94	101	100	88	82	85	104	100
Cambodia	104	111	106	115	108	115	111	101	95
Brazil	105	103	91	81	83	74	83	87	93
Belarus	106	110	92	96	109	112	105	85	89
Turkmenistan	106	106	95	103	117	108	117	90	97
Algeria	108	104	114	119	121	129	116	110	108
Uzbekistan	109	113	104	124	110	109	110	109	113
Armenia	110	91	97	98	115	109	113		
Honduras	111	116	117	123	129	117	125	116	116
El Salvador	111	123	116	112	111	102	103	92	93
Niger	113	129	121	127	116	119			
Republic of the Congo	114	115	109	107	104	98	102	99	101
Myanmar	115	130	136	140	139	133	132	122	124

Country	2016 rank	2015 rank	2014 rank	2013 rank	2012 rank	2011 rank	2010 rank	2009 rank	2008 rank
Guinea-Bissau	116	120	145	132	95				
Guatemala	117	118	115	109	124	125	112	102	102
Ivory Coast	118	105	140	151	134	128	118	113	109
Ethiopia	119	119	139	146	137	131	127	130	126
China	120	124	108	101	89	80	80	83	82
Djibouti	121	102	74	63	56				
Tajikistan	122	108	126	118	99	103			
Mauritania	123	122	120	122	125	130	123	117	105
Kyrgyzstan	124	121	125	131	131	114			
Thailand	125	126	126	130	126	107	124	119	111
South Africa	126	136	122	121	127	118	121	112	95
Zimbabwe	127	125	148	149	140	140	135	131	134
Rwanda	128	139	137	135	119	99	75	81	66
Saudi Arabia	129	95	80	97	106	101	107	108	105
Cameroon	130	134	113	108	97	86	106	95	93
Kenya	131	133	132	136	120	111	120	111	118
Bahrain	132	107	111	95	118	123	70	57	57
Iran	133	138	131	137	128	119	104	106	106
Azerbaijan	134	132	123	126	132	122	119	114	108

Country	2016 rank	2015 rank	2014 rank	2013 rank	2012 rank	2011 rank	2010 rank	2009 rank	2008 rank
Eritrea	135	127	124	120	122	104			
Chad	136	140	142	138	145	141	141	135	134
Mali	137	128	135	125	102	100	109	107	108
Burundi	138	130	130	144	138	132	131	123	
Philippines	139	141	134	129	133	136	130	118	116
Mexico	140	144	138	133	135	121	107	98	89
India	141	143	144	141	142	135	128	125	123
Egypt	142	137	143	113	111	73	49	68	74
Venezuela	143	142	129	128	123	124	122	115	103
Israel	144	148	149	150	150	145	149	137	134
Turkey	145	135	128	134	130	127	126	124	119
Lebanon	146	145	146	142	136	137	134	128	127
Colombia	147	146	150	147	144	139	138	129	125
Palestine	148								
Nigeria	149	151	151	148	146	142	137	127	118
North Korea	150	153	153	154	152	149	139	133	129
Russia	151	152	152	155	153	147	143	138	131
Democratic Republic of the Congo	152	155	155	156	154	148	140	136	128
Pakistan	153	154	154	157	149	146	145	140	132
Libya	154	149	133	145	147	143	56	54	65
Sudan	155	156	157	158	156	151	146	139	136

Country	2016 rank	2015 rank	2014 rank	2013 rank	2012 rank	2011 rank	2010 rank	2009 rank	2008 rank
Ukraine	156	150	141	111	71	69	97	100	80
Central African Republic	157	158	156	153	151	144	136	132	130
Yemen	158	147	147	152	143	138	129	121	111
Somalia	159	157	158	161	158	153	148	141	137
Afghanistan	160	160	161	162	157	150	147	142	135
Iraq	161	161	159	159	155	152	149	143	138
South Sudan	162	159	160	143					
Syria	163	162	162	160	147	116	115	96	77

Global Terrorism Index: 2016

Rank	Country	Score	Change in score (2015 to 2016)
1	Iraq	9.96	▼−0.04
2	Afghanistan	9.444	▲0.229
3	Nigeria	9.314	▲0.075
4	Pakistan	8.613	▼−0.027
5	Syria	8.587	▲0.458
6	Yemen	8.076	▲0.607
7	Somalia	7.548	▲0.012
8	India	7.484	▼−0.059
9	Egypt	7.328	▲0.751
10	Libya	7.283	▲0.228
11	Ukraine	7.132	▲0.094
12	Philippines	7.098	▲0.071
13	Cameroon	7.002	▲0.504
14	Turkey	6.738	▲1.272
15	Thailand	6.706	▼−0.249

Rank	Country	Score	Change in score (2015 to 2016)
16	Niger	6.682	3.474
17	Democratic Republic of the Congo	6.633	0.209
18	Sudan	6.66	0
19	Kenya	6.578	−0.04
20	Central African Republic	6.518	−0.229
21	South Sudan	6.497	−0.273
22	Bangladesh	6.479	0.959
23	China	6.108	−0.206
24	Lebanon	6.068	−0.122
25	Mali	6.03	0.347
26	Colombia	5.954	−0.197
27	Chad	5.83	3.663
28	Palestine	5.659	0.658
29	France	5.603	2.02
30	Russia	5.43	−0.623
31	Burundi	5.417	2.156
32	Saudi Arabia	5.404	1.678
33	Israel	5.248	−0.302
34	United Kingdom	5.08	0.012
35	Tunisia	4.963	1.452
36	United States	4.877	0.358

Rank	Country	Score	Change in score (2015 to 2016)
37	Kuwait	4.449	4.43
38	Indonesia	4.429	−0.027
39	Nepal	4.415	0.063
40	Uganda	4.327	−0.615
41	Germany	4.308	1.582
42	Algeria	4.282	−0.377
43	Greece	4.218	−0.011
44	Bahrain	4.206	−0.299
45	Myanmar	4.167	0.364
46	Sweden	3.984	1.858
47	Iran	3.949	−0.226
48	Paraguay	3.84	0.286
49	Tanzania	3.832	−0.125
50	Mexico	3.723	−0.129
51	Mozambique	3.536	−0.551
52	South Africa	3.531	1.676
53	Sri Lanka	3.486	−0.194
54	Ethiopia	3.454	−0.007
55	Ireland	3.429	0.1
56	Tajikistan	3.086	1.368
57	Peru	2.984	−0.046
58	Jordan	2.858	1.363

Rank	Country	Score	Change in score (2015 to 2016)
59	Australia	2.742	−0.026
60	Chile	2.699	−0.659
61	Malaysia	2.691	−0.341
62	Bosnia and Herzegovina	2.675	△1.455
63	Burkina Faso	2.623	△2.316
64	Senegal	2.598	−0.638
65	Rwanda	2.589	−0.726
66	Canada	2.518	−0.084
67	Japan	2.447	△2.447
68	Finland	2.377	△2.377
69	Italy	2.363	−0.205
70	Kosovo	2.205	−0.357
71	Czech Republic	2.179	△0.25
72	Ivory Coast	2.177	−0.752
73	Denmark	2.152	△2.061
74	Nicaragua	2.093	−0.656
75	Norway	2.077	−0.656
76	Cyprus	2.04	−0.301
77	Venezuela	1.998	△0.357
78	Macedonia	1.86	△0.02
79	Djibouti	1.78	−0.691

Rank	Country	Score	Change in score (2015 to 2016)
80	Brazil	1.74	−0.306
81	Madagascar	1.671	−0.67
82	Bulgaria	1.631	−0.38
83	Dominican Republic	1.562	−0.649
84	Kyrgyzstan	1.445	0.134
85	Guinea	1.403	0.942
86	Belarus	1.357	−0.698
87	Georgia	1.257	−0.677
88	Belgium	1.245	−0.684
89	Spain	1.203	−0.701
90	Honduras	1.144	−0.666
90	Guatemala	1.144	−0.666
92	Albania	1.103	−0.498
92	Estonia	1.103	1.026
94	Kazakhstan	0.934	−0.658
95	Morocco	0.892	−0.445
95	Lesotho	0.892	0.892
97	Netherlands	0.864	0.586
98	Ecuador	0.793	0.313
99	Laos	0.695	0.657
100	Eritrea	0.534	−1.082

Rank	Country	Score	Change in score (2015 to 2016)
101	Argentina	0.499	−0.491
101	Trinidad and Tobago	0.499	−0.28
103	United Arab Emirates	0.422	−0.635
104	Zimbabwe	0.413	−0.61
105	Republic of the Congo	0.365	−0.47
106	Azerbaijan	0.346	−0.433
106	Ghana	0.346	−0.433
108	Switzerland	0.288	−0.323
108	Armenia	0.288	0.173
110	Iceland	0.25	−0.249
110	Liberia	0.25	−0.249
112	Hungary	0.23	−0.231
112	New Zealand	0.23	−0.231
112	South Korea	0.23	0.23
112	Qatar	0.23	0.23
116	Austria	0.182	−0.183
117	Montenegro	0.154	−0.153
117	Uzbekistan	0.154	0.154
119	Bhutan	0.115	−0.115
119	Jamaica	0.115	−0.115
121	Serbia	0.086	−0.135

Rank	Country	Score	Change in score (2015 to 2016)
122	Guinea-Bissau	0.077	−0.077
122	Cambodia	0.077	−0.077
122	Taiwan	0.077	−0.077
125	Mauritania	0.067	−0.125
126	Portugal	0.058	−0.057
126	Croatia	0.058	−0.057
128	Bolivia	0.038	−0.039
129	Moldova	0.019	−0.019
130	Angola	0	−0.168
130	Benin	0	0
130	Botswana	0	0
130	Costa Rica	0	0
130	Cuba	0	0
130	Gabon	0	0
130	Gambia	0	0
130	Equatorial Guinea	0	0
130	Guyana	0	0
130	Haiti	0	0
130	Lithuania	0	0
130	Latvia	0	0
130	Mauritius	0	0
130	Malawi	0	0

Rank	Country	Score	Change in score (2015 to 2016)
130	Mongolia	0	0
130	Namibia	0	0
130	North Korea	0	0
130	Oman	0	0
130	Panama	0	0
130	Papua New Guinea	0	0
130	Poland	0	0
130	Romania	0	0
130	Sierra Leone	0	0
130	Singapore	0	0
130	El Salvador	0	0
130	Slovakia	0	0
130	Slovenia	0	0
130	Swaziland	0	0
130	Togo	0	0
130	Turkmenistan	0	0
130	Timor-Leste	0	0
130	Uruguay	0	0
130	Vietnam	0	0
130	Zambia	0	0

The fourth edition of Global Terrorism Index was published in November 2016. The study covered analysis of 163 countries.

The Nobel Peace Prize: 2001-2016

The Nobel Peace Prize 1901

Jean Henry Dunant
Frédéric Passy

The Nobel Peace Prize 1902

Élie Ducommun
Charles Albert Gobat

The Nobel Peace Prize 1903

William Randal Cremer

The Nobel Peace Prize 1904

Institut de droit international (Institute of International Law)

The Nobel Peace Prize 1905

Baroness Bertha Sophie Felicita von Suttner, née Countess Kinsky von Chinic und Tettau

The Nobel Peace Prize 1906

Theodore Roosevelt

The Nobel Peace Prize 1907

Ernesto Teodoro Moneta
Louis Renault

The Nobel Peace Prize 1908

Klas Pontus Arnoldson
Fredrik Bajer

The Nobel Peace Prize 1909

Auguste Marie François Beernaert
Paul Henri Benjamin Balluet d'Estournelles de Constant, Baron de Constant de Rebecque

The Nobel Peace Prize 1910

Bureau international permanent de la Paix (Permanent International Peace Bureau)

The Nobel Peace Prize 1911

Tobias Michael Carel Asser
Alfred Hermann Fried

The Nobel Peace Prize 1912

Elihu Root

The Nobel Peace Prize 1913

Henri La Fontaine

The Nobel Peace Prize 1914

No Nobel Prize was awarded this year. The prize money was allocated to the Special Fund of this prize section.

The Nobel Peace Prize 1915

No Nobel Prize was awarded this year. The prize money was allocated to the Special Fund of this prize section.

The Nobel Peace Prize 1916

No Nobel Prize was awarded this year. The prize money was allocated to the Special Fund of this prize section.

The Nobel Peace Prize 1917

Comité international de la Croix Rouge (International Committee of the Red Cross)

The Nobel Peace Prize 1918

No Nobel Prize was awarded this year. The prize money was allocated to the Special Fund of this prize section.

The Nobel Peace Prize 1919

Thomas Woodrow Wilson

The Nobel Peace Prize 1920

Léon Victor Auguste Bourgeois

The Nobel Peace Prize 1921

Karl Hjalmar Branting

Christian Lous Lange

The Nobel Peace Prize 1922

Fridtjof Nansen

The Nobel Peace Prize 1923

No Nobel Prize was awarded this year. The prize money was allocated to the Special Fund of this prize section.

The Nobel Peace Prize 1924

No Nobel Prize was awarded this year. The prize money was allocated to the Special Fund of this prize section.

The Nobel Peace Prize 1925

Sir Austen Chamberlain
Charles Gates Dawes

The Nobel Peace Prize 1926

Aristide Briand
Gustav Stresemann

The Nobel Peace Prize 1927

Ferdinand Buisson
Ludwig Quidde

The Nobel Peace Prize 1928

No Nobel Prize was awarded this year. The prize money was allocated to the Special Fund of this prize section.

The Nobel Peace Prize 1929

Frank Billings Kellogg

The Nobel Peace Prize 1930

Lars Olof Jonathan (Nathan) Söderblom

The Nobel Peace Prize 1931

Jane Addams
Nicholas Murray Butler

The Nobel Peace Prize 1932

No Nobel Prize was awarded this year. The prize money was allocated to the Special Fund of this prize section.

The Nobel Peace Prize 1933

Sir Norman Angell (Ralph Lane)

The Nobel Peace Prize 1934

Arthur Henderson

The Nobel Peace Prize 1935

Carl von Ossietzky

The Nobel Peace Prize 1936

Carlos Saavedra Lamas

The Nobel Peace Prize 1937

Cecil of Chelwood, Viscount (Lord Edgar Algernon Robert Gascoyne Cecil)

The Nobel Peace Prize 1938

Office international Nansen pour les Réfugiés (Nansen International Office for Refugees)

The Nobel Peace Prize 1939

No Nobel Prize was awarded this year. The prize money was with 1/3 allocated to the Main Fund and with 2/3 to the Special Fund of this prize section.

The Nobel Peace Prize 1940

No Nobel Prize was awarded this year. The prize money was with 1/3 allocated to the Main Fund and with 2/3 to the Special Fund of this prize section.

The Nobel Peace Prize 1941

No Nobel Prize was awarded this year. The prize money was with 1/3 allocated to the Main Fund and with 2/3 to the Special Fund of this prize section.

The Nobel Peace Prize 1942

No Nobel Prize was awarded this year. The prize money was with 1/3 allocated to the Main Fund and with 2/3 to the Special Fund of this prize section.

The Nobel Peace Prize 1943

No Nobel Prize was awarded this year. The prize money was with 1/3 allocated to the Main Fund and with 2/3 to the Special Fund of this prize section.

The Nobel Peace Prize 1944

Comité international de la Croix Rouge (International Committee of the Red Cross)

The Nobel Peace Prize 1945

Cordell Hull

The Nobel Peace Prize 1946

Emily Greene Balch
John Raleigh Mott

The Nobel Peace Prize 1947

Friends Service Council (The Quakers)
American Friends Service Committee (The Quakers)

The Nobel Peace Prize 1948

No Nobel Prize was awarded this year. The prize money was with 1/3 allocated to the Main Fund and with 2/3 to the Special Fund of this prize section.

The Nobel Peace Prize 1949

Lord (John) Boyd Orr of Brechin

The Nobel Peace Prize 1950

Ralph Bunche

The Nobel Peace Prize 1951

Léon Jouhaux

The Nobel Peace Prize 1952

Albert Schweitzer

The Nobel Peace Prize 1953

George Catlett Marshall

The Nobel Peace Prize 1954

Office of the United Nations High Commissioner for Refugees (UNHCR)

The Nobel Peace Prize 1955

No Nobel Prize was awarded this year. The prize money was allocated to the Special Fund of this prize section.

The Nobel Peace Prize 1956

No Nobel Prize was awarded this year. The prize money was with 1/3 allocated to the Main Fund and with 2/3 to the Special Fund of this prize

The Nobel Peace Prize 1957

Lester Bowles Pearson

The Nobel Peace Prize 1958

Georges Pire

The Nobel Peace Prize 1959

Philip J. Noel-Baker

The Nobel Peace Prize 1960

Albert John Lutuli

The Nobel Peace Prize 1961

Dag Hjalmar Agne Carl Hammarskjöld

The Nobel Peace Prize 1962

Linus Carl Pauling

The Nobel Peace Prize 1963

Comité international de la Croix Rouge (International Committee of the Red Cross)
Ligue des Sociétés de la Croix-Rouge (League of Red Cross Societies)

The Nobel Peace Prize 1964

Martin Luther King Jr.

The Nobel Peace Prize 1965

United Nations Children's Fund (UNICEF)

The Nobel Peace Prize 1966

No Nobel Prize was awarded this year. The prize money was allocated to the Special Fund of this prize section.

The Nobel Peace Prize 1967

No Nobel Prize was awarded this year. The prize money was with 1/3 allocated to the Main Fund and with 2/3 to the Special Fund of this prize section.

The Nobel Peace Prize 1968

René Cassin

The Nobel Peace Prize 1969

International Labour Organization (I.L.O.)

The Nobel Peace Prize 1970

Norman E. Borlaug

The Nobel Peace Prize 1971

Willy Brandt

The Nobel Peace Prize 1972

No Nobel Prize was awarded this year. The prize money for 1972 was allocated to the Main Fund.

The Nobel Peace Prize 1973

Henry A. Kissinger
Le Duc Tho

The Nobel Peace Prize 1974

Seán MacBride
Eisaku Sato

The Nobel Peace Prize 1975

Andrei Dmitrievich Sakharov

The Nobel Peace Prize 1976

Betty Williams
Mairead Corrigan

The Nobel Peace Prize 1977

Amnesty International

The Nobel Peace Prize 1978

Mohamed Anwar al-Sadat
Menachem Begin

The Nobel Peace Prize 1979

Mother Teresa

The Nobel Peace Prize 1980

Adolfo Pérez Esquivel

The Nobel Peace Prize 1981

Office of the United Nations High Commissioner for Refugees (UNHCR)

The Nobel Peace Prize 1982

Alva Myrdal
Alfonso García Robles

The Nobel Peace Prize 1983

Lech Walesa

The Nobel Peace Prize 1984

Desmond Mpilo Tutu

The Nobel Peace Prize 1985

International Physicians for the Prevention of Nuclear War

The Nobel Peace Prize 1986

Elie Wiesel

The Nobel Peace Prize 1987

Oscar Arias Sánchez
"for his work for peace in Central America, efforts which led to the accord signed in Guatemala on August 7 this year"

The Nobel Peace Prize 1988

United Nations Peacekeeping Forces

The Nobel Peace Prize 1989

The 14th Dalai Lama (Tenzin Gyatso)

The Nobel Peace Prize 1990

Mikhail Sergeyevich Gorbachev
"for his leading role in the peace process which today characterizes important parts of the international community"

The Nobel Peace Prize 1991

Aung San Suu Kyi
"for her non-violent struggle for democracy and human rights"

The Nobel Peace Prize 1992

Rigoberta Menchú Tum
"in recognition of her work for social justice and ethno-cultural reconciliation based on respect for the rights of indigenous peoples"

The Nobel Peace Prize 1993

*Nelson Mandela **and** Frederik Willem de Klerk*
"for their work for the peaceful termination of the apartheid regime, and for laying the foundations for a new democratic South Africa"

The Nobel Peace Prize 1994

*Yasser Arafat, Shimon Peres **and** Yitzhak Rabin*
"for their efforts to create peace in the Middle East"

The Nobel Peace Prize 1995

*Joseph Rotblat **and** Pugwash Conferences on Science and World Affairs*
"for their efforts to diminish the part played by nuclear arms in international politics and, in the longer run, to eliminate such arms"

The Nobel Peace Prize 1996

*Carlos Filipe Ximenes Belo **and** José Ramos-Horta*
"for their work towards a just and peaceful solution to the conflict in East Timor"

The Nobel Peace Prize 1997

International Campaign to Ban Landmines (ICBL) **and** *Jody Williams*
"for their work for the banning and clearing of anti-personnel mines"

The Nobel Peace Prize 1998

John Hume **and** *David Trimble*
"for their efforts to find a peaceful solution to the conflict in Northern Ireland"

The Nobel Peace Prize 1999

Médecins Sans Frontières
"in recognition of the organization's pioneering humanitarian work on several continents"

The Nobel Peace Prize 2000

Kim Dae-jung
"for his work for democracy and human rights in South Korea and in East Asia in general, and for peace and reconciliation with North Korea in particular"

The Nobel Peace Prize 2001

United Nations (U.N.) **and** *Kofi Annan*
"for their work for a better organized and more peaceful world"

The Nobel Peace Prize 2002

Jimmy Carter
"for his decades of untiring effort to find peaceful solutions to international conflicts, to advance democracy and human rights, and to promote economic and social development"

The Nobel Peace Prize 2003

Shirin Ebadi
"for her efforts for democracy and human rights. She has focused especially on the struggle for the rights of women and children"

The Nobel Peace Prize 2004

Wangari Muta Maathai
"for her contribution to sustainable development, democracy and peace"

The Nobel Peace Prize 2005

International Atomic Energy Agency (IAEA) **and** *Mohamed ElBaradei*
"for their efforts to prevent nuclear energy from being used for military purposes and to ensure that nuclear energy for peaceful purposes is used in the safest possible way"

The Nobel Peace Prize 2006

Muhammad Yunus **and** *Grameen Bank*
"for their efforts to create economic and social development from below"

The Nobel Peace Prize 2007

Intergovernmental Panel on Climate Change (IPCC) **and** *Albert Arnold (Al) Gore Jr.*
"for their efforts to build up and disseminate greater knowledge about man-made climate change, and to lay the foundations for the measures that are needed to counteract such change"

The Nobel Peace Prize 2008

Martti Ahtisaari
"for his important efforts, on several continents and over more than three decades, to resolve international conflicts"

The Nobel Peace Prize 2009

Barack H. Obama
"for his extraordinary efforts to strengthen international diplomacy and cooperation between peoples"

The Nobel Peace Prize 2010

Liu Xiaobo
"for his long and non-violent struggle for fundamental human rights in China"

The Nobel Peace Prize 2011

Ellen Johnson Sirleaf, Leymah Gbowee **and** *Tawakkol Karman*
"for their non-violent struggle for the safety of women and for women's rights to full participation in peace-building work"

The Nobel Peace Prize 2012

European Union (EU)
"for over six decades contributed to the advancement of peace and reconciliation, democracy and human rights in Europe"

The Nobel Peace Prize 2013

Organisation for the Prohibition of Chemical Weapons (OPCW)
"for its extensive efforts to eliminate chemical weapons"

The Nobel Peace Prize 2014

Kailash Satyarthi **and** *Malala Yousafzai*
"for their struggle against the suppression of children and young people and for the right of all children to education"

The Nobel Peace Prize 2015

National Dialogue Quartet
"for its decisive contribution to the building of a pluralistic democracy in Tunisia in the wake of the Jasmine Revolution of 2011"

The Nobel Peace Prize 2016

Juan Manuel Santos
"for his resolute efforts to bring the country's more than 50-year-long civil war to an end"

Index